THE MINISTER'S

CONSULTATION CLINIC

Pastoral Psychology

In Action

THE MINISTER'S CONSULTATION CLINIC

Pastoral Psychology in Action

Edited by
SIMON DONIGER, Ph.D.

*A selection of questions
submitted by ministers to the
magazine* PASTORAL PSYCHOLOGY,
*and answered by a board of
psychiatrists, psychologists,
social scientists and clergymen*

CHANNEL PRESS, INC., GREAT NECK, NEW YORK

BV
4012
.P34

253.5

Manufactured in the United States of America
by The Haddon Craftsmen, Inc., Scranton, Pa.

CONTENTS

A detailed table of contents will be
found at the beginning of each section.

Introduction

With the exception of this brief introductory chapter, this book is composed entirely of actual questions and answers received by PASTORAL PSYCHOLOGY, a professional journal for ministers, religiously-oriented psychiatrists, psychologists, and lay counselors. Both the questions and answers were written for publication in "The Consultation Clinic," a special department developed by the journal to give practical aid to readers with many of the baffling problems which come to them in the process of their professional work.

The people who ask the questions are primarily ministers, with a heavy sprinkling of other members of the "helping" professions —psychiatrists, psychologists, social-workers, lay counselors and, on occasion, laymen working in the field of church administration. The "answerers" are a panel of men and women who are truly the outstanding people in their professions—theologians, parish ministers, psychiatrists, psychologists, and social scientists; a group of authorities whose wisdom and insight into human behavior stems from rich experience, scholarship, and a profound sense of humility as well as a deep religious fellowship and sympathy with the ills of man.

"The Consultation Clinic" has proven itself as probably the most important contribution which PASTORAL PSYCHOLOGY has made to its readership. Its usefulness became obvious from the very first issue of publication. The journal has been literally flooded with questions from its readers; and testimonials attesting to the help which the discussion and answering of these questions has given them arrive almost as frequently.

The idea of publishing a collection from "The Consultation Clinic" in book form is essentially our readers' idea. It was they who urged that this monthly feature be collected and made available in organized and permanent form. Such requests, along with our feeling that it would be of value to share these materials with a wider body of readers than the one confined to the readership of the journal, is responsible for this book.

Now—what is it that these people ask? What kind of questions do they raise? With what type of problems do they want help? Speaking generally, they seem to want specific answers to specific situations which arise in their "ministry" to people. They want no abstract discussion of abstractions, no theorizing. They want answers to life situations that can be translated into immediate action. Being the wise "ministers" they are, however, they know that all action must have some basis in theory if it is to have a suitable foundation; and so it is natural that some of the very first inquiries which we received were questions which on the one hand might be termed theoretical, but on the other obviously represented a profound, important and practical problem to our readers.

Looming largest among these early questions was the relationship of theology—of the pastoral ministry and of the religious life generally—to the relatively new body of knowledge which goes under the various names of dynamic psychiatry, psychology, psychotherapy, psychoanalysis, and pastoral psychology. Stated directly, or sometimes by implication, these "askers" want to know the actual meaning of this new knowledge to the day-to-day work of the minister. To his preaching; to his individual work with parishioners who come to him for guidance and advice; to his work with groups of children, young people, and adults; to his visiting with the sick; to his evangelism; to his church administration; to his parish relationships; and to his community participation and social outreach. They wonder whether this new knowledge is something which can be merely borrowed and applied to the minister's activities in much the same way that a traveling salesman might apply "psychology" to the selling of his wares; or whether it is something much deeper and more profound—something into which he must grow, something which must become an integral part of his personality and of his work. They wonder whether such mere borrowing would not tend to make of them "amateur psychiatrists"; and, they ask, is not this dangerous? Furthermore, what happens to their specific function as ministers of the Gospel?

They seem to be deeply aware of the warning expressed by Dr. Paul Tillich in an address to the graduating class of Union Theological Seminary, when he said: "You must be aware of these other ways of healing, but you must not substitute them for what you stand for—ministers of the message of forgiveness, and of a new reality . . . (that) bodily and mental individual and social illnesses are consequences of the estrangements of man's spirit from the divine spirit, and that no sickness can be healed without the reunion of the human with the divine spirit."

"Well," our readers seem to say in their questions, "if Dr. Tillich is right in his statement that emotional illness is based on the problems of the relationship of man's spirit to the divine, then surely no mere borrowing of psychiatric or psychological knowledge is the answer to man's problems." It becomes clear that the relationship between theology and the minister's work on the one hand, and psychology and psychiatry on the other, cannot be a one-way street, but must be a mutual sharing and giving—a mutual learning.

Those who have sent questions to "The Consultation Clinic" want furthermore to know about the *conflicts* between religion and the secular sciences, particularly psychiatry and psychology. What about their irreligiousness? They are aware of Sigmund Freud's definition of religion as a "vestige of a childhood neurosis," and wonder how they can accept a psychology rooted in so irreligious an approach. They wonder about the materialism of modern science, about its lack of values and its amorality, about its emphasis on sex and expression and fulfillment of instinctual need; about its stress on "adjustment." They wonder whether this so-called knowledge is really so very new, for they find that many of the basic principles proclaimed as "new" by modern psychology and psychiatry are expressed and propounded clearly, vividly, and repeatedly in the ancient wisdom of religion in the Judaean-Christian tradition. They point to such religious formulations as: "The Kingdom of God is within you," or the Psalmist's "When I declared not my sin my body wasted away," or Jesus' "Wouldst thou be whole?" and "Neither do I condemn thee." They recall such statements as "Physician, heal thyself," or "Ye shall know the truth and the truth shall make you free." They recognize that these concepts have a psychological wisdom which long preceded the so-called "discoveries" of modern psychology; indeed, these concepts are identical with the new psychology's stress on the inner life of man as a major emphasis in healing . . . with its belief in the unity of mind and body, the very keystone of psychosomatic medicine . . . with its insistence on the importance of the counselor having insight into his own personality . . . with its cognizance of the importance of facing reality and the truth.

Yet, while concerned with these seeming conflicts between religion and psychiatry, these "questioners" are nevertheless profoundly aware of the potential contribution which this new knowledge can make to their work; and they are intensely concerned about finding ways in which these seeming conflicts can be resolved, and this new knowledge harnessed creatively and redemptively in the performance of their professional work. They are aware of the great need which exists today for the pooling of *all* potential resources—the utmost sharpening of effort and skill to help man find himself in this alienated world. They have been told by their colleague-physicians that more than fifty percent of the patients who come to them—presumably about physical illness—are suffering from problems which are basically psychic or spiritual. They know that according to current statistics one in every twenty children will someday require the services of a correctional agency, and that one in every ten will need help in the process of his growth toward maturity. They know of the constantly growing toll of alcoholism, suicide, divorce, juvenile delinquency, and crime. They are particularly conscious of the great mass of so-called "normal" people—people for whom they feel a particular responsibility—who are struggling with a sense of alienation, loneliness, emptiness, and frustration; in the words of the hymn, "of the needless pain they bear." They see the recent mass return of people to religion and the Church as a symbol of their search for a place of refuge from the ruthless competition of the marketplace—of their search for a place in

10

the world where they will be accepted for their value as people, as children of God, and not as commodities to be exploited "for what they are worth."

Out of their sympathy and a profound sense of their mission, our ministers are searching for a way to offer these people some hope and comfort, encouragement, reassurance, and fellowship. They, too, are anxious to find ways of making the Church a refuge, so that in the words of the Psalmist, "passing through the valley of weeping they make it a place of springs." But the minister knows that in order to achieve this he must, in the words of John Oman, become "a life understander before he can be a life changer." It is this understanding which he is attempting to achieve through the questions he sends to PASTORAL PSYCHOLOGY. He feels that the old traditional platitudes about religion will no longer do; for while he sees many grow strong through faith in mind and body, he has also seen some made ill and desperate by religious fanaticism—a fanaticism which he today, as a result of his greater knowledge, suspects of being not at all of a divine or religious source, but rather of a neurotic nature. They are suspicious of pseudo-psychological and pseudo-religious slogans which offer as panaceas that "peace of mind" and "peace of soul" which are mere palliatives and escapes from living, rather than aids in facing life truthfully and realistically. These ministers no longer feel at ease with the traditional approach in their preaching—with the exposing of sin, the threat of punishment, "fire and brimstone." They are deeply conscious of the ineffectiveness of this approach through all the centuries that preachers have followed those patterns, and are wondering about the "new reality" of Paul Tillich's message to them to be "ministers of the message of forgiveness." They are aware of the tremendous amount of guilt that is inherent in the universal anxiety from which man is suffering today, and are loath to add to it through the traditional preaching.

These ministers are aware of the recent developments of clinical training for ministers involving intensive clinical work in mental hospitals in preparation for more skilled and professional counseling and pastoral care; they are aware of the new developments in many theological seminaries which now offer such

11

training as part of their regular training for the ministry. Unfortunately, many of them are unable to take advantage of these new opportunities, and they are looking for other ways to fill this need . . . through reading, through discussion and, in part, through questions and answers such as those in this book.

These ministers, in the light of the new findings of psychology, want to know more about the traditional functions of the minister in dispensing authoritative advice and guidance to people who come seeking help. Here, too, they sense the ineffectivness of such guidance in the past; they sense the hostilities and conflicts which ineffective advice may engender with their parishioners and in their communities; and they are searching for a new way of helping, one which instead of directing people authoritatively will enable people to discover their own inner strength and become *self-directing*. A glimpse at the new psychology has brought them a new awareness about the roots of personality as a result of inter-familial relationships; has made them aware of the sources of hostility, of the unconscious motivation for much of human behavior. They are beginning to see the cause-and-effect relationship between "badness" and "goodness" in children; they see the effect of love or its deprivation on the creative and spiritual life of their people, and they have thus become vitally interested in the psychology of childhood and its meaning to their work in religious education, in the organization of youth groups, and in other related work with children and adults. They are challenged by the new psychology's concept that only people who have respect and love for themselves, who accept themselves, are people who can love and accept others; and that much of the cruelty, hostility, and intolerance exhibited by people stems basically from their inability to accept themselves as persons.

And so they ask questions about "permissiveness" and wonder how they can harmonize their role as evaluators and yet use the principle of "permissiveness." They wonder about the emphasis in modern psychology on the elimination of frustration and tension, and question how values and strength of character can be brought about without these. They wonder about the new methods of discipline and their implications of "license" rather than freedom; they are intrigued by an approach which offers a maximum amount of freedom and self-direction even though they may be concerned about its possible after-effects.

They have a new curiosity about the relative relation of heredity and environment. What are the things among the ills of mankind that are unalterable, and which among them can be changed? Which are caused by a destructive environment and which come from the inner basic conflicts of man? And they rightly question why emphasis cannot be put more strongly on preventive work rather than waiting until we reach a crisis, both in terms of the individual as well as society.

More specifically, they want to know how this new knowledge can be usefully harnessed and made redemptive, not only in the minister's traditional role as preacher, but in his leadership of worship, in his pastoral prayers, in his individual counseling, in his group work, in his administrative relationship with the members of his board and his committees, and with the various personality problems which arise in the process of that administration. The minister wants to know the part which his own personality plays in some of the problems which arise in these relationships and their inevitable conflicts, for he senses that some of this conflict may be due to vestiges of childhood in his own personality, to the "dated emotions," as Seward Hiltner so aptly puts it, in his own life.

These are some of the general things with which our "questioners" are concerned. Mainly, however, they ask about concrete and specific problems which affect their work. They want, for instance, to know how a psychiatrist who is a member of a church can be used most effectively in the church program. They want to know how best to choose volunteers to help them carry on their pastoral duties—and how to recognize and then either cope with or help the many disturbed or neurotic people in their parishes. They ask how the rural pastor, far away from the facilities which are available to the minister in the city, can avail himself of this new psychological and psychiatric knowledge so that he can improve his work.

Aware of the importance of conserving their spiritual resources, they ask about the relationship of the pastor's work and his privacy—how can he give of himself to his work, and yet not let it interfere with the wholesomeness and creativeness of his personality. Having become more conscious of the delicacy of their pastoral work, they ask questions about their duties to law enforcement and becoming involved in society's punitive measures. They wonder how this traditional relationship of the minister to his community might affect the possibly more important task of helping individual people in their trouble.

And now, having become vitally concerned with the individual and his problems, they want to know a great deal more about individual counseling: how to set up an effective counseling program; how to "make time for counseling" in addition to their many other pastoral and ministerial duties; how the minister can recognize a deep neurotic who needs referral to specialists, and how he is to choose from among these many specialists the ones really equipped to help best. They want to know the methods of referring, in order to build up a real partnership between themselves and the other "helping" professions. They are interested in knowing about psychological tests in diagnosis and in treatment, and the extent to which such may be used by the ministers. They want to know whether there is a place for counseling by them even with neurotics, and what the danger spots are in such counseling so that they may recognize them and avoid them.

And, finally, they want help *specifically* with specific problems which their parishioners bring them—problems of abnormal grief, an area of special concern to the minister; neurotic problems of isolation and alienation of people who refuse to participate or associate with their fellow men; counseling with the alcoholic. They ask for help in areas of sex expression among children as well as adults. They ask for aid in work with people suffering from various sexual deviations, particularly the homosexual. They want to know more about the application of psychological knowledge in their marital guidance and counseling; about the special role and responsibility of the minister in fatal illness, in suicide, in work with the aged, and a host of similar specific situations.

These are representative of the questions which they ask in earnestness and humility—not in a desire to become substitute and amateur psychiatrists, but in order to find ways of integrating the new knowledge of psychology and psychiatry into their specific traditional function so that, in the words of Isaiah, they may "prepare the way of the Lord," as well as "prepare the way of the people."

Occasionally we get a feeling from questions sent to the journal that this interest is also prompted by new demands which the community has been making of the Christian minister; demands which are received both from direct contact with parishioners as well as indirectly, from studies conducted by central church bodies on "what the community expects from the modern minister." These studies invariably reveal that the relative importance of the traditional function of the minister as a preacher is steadily and rapidly declining; that his role as pastor, as a curer of souls, is assuming greater and greater importance in the life of his parishioners. Thus, the minister is being "pushed" in his search for new understanding both by his inner need and his inner sense of mission, as well as by external compulsions and demands of his society, his community, and his parish.

Another development which has made it easier for the traditional and frequently conservative minister to become interested in the new psychology is the resurgence of interest on the part of psychiatry itself in spiritual values. Only recently, a committee of the Group for the Advancement of Psychiatry released the following statement: "Psychiatry as a branch of medicine has been so closely related to religion that at times the two were almost inseparable. As science developed, however, medicine and religion assumed distinctive roles in society, but they continue to share the common aim of human betterment. This also holds true for that method of psychiatry known as psychoanalysis . . . We recognize the important role religion can play in bringing about an improved emotional and moral state."

Approaching the relationship of religion and science from a still more critical point of view, Dr. John A. P. Millet, Chief Psychiatrist of the Rehabilitation Center of the American Rehabilitation Committee, and an outstanding American practitioner, said in a personal letter to the editor of PASTORAL PSYCHOLOGY recently: "Science which is only interested in mechanistic solutions leaves its exponents bewildered and frustrated . . .

INTRODUCTION

Religion can provide the conviction that the goals of our patients' efforts to get well are worth the struggle . . . The common ground on which science and religion must meet is the ground of promoting a more complete understanding of the causes of unrest and conflict in the lives of human beings."

This new self-criticism on the part of the scientist in human behavior, merged with the intense need on the part of the minister for the help and services of the new sciences, bodes well for a real partnership in human relations.

The questions and answers in this book do not, of course, presume to give a comprehensive picture of the minister's work and his problems. Instead, they are representative of some of the more important problems among the many which arise. It would take several parallel volumes to cover all phases of the pertinent material; and indeed we are hopeful that future volumes of THE MINISTER'S CONSULTATION CLINIC will serve to make this series a thorough outline of the minister's activities and potential activities in this fuller service.

Nevertheless, it can be hoped that this volume will at least serve as a working tool for those active in the field of pastoral psychology, and as a guidebook for those who have not yet added this phase of the ministry to their program. That hope, as a matter of fact, has dictated the order and structure of this book. Its intent is to *explain* by example just what pastoral psychology is and can mean in a ministry; having done so, it seeks to *investigate* the possible areas of conflict between the basic ideas of psychology and of theology and to reconcile them when necessary; then it proceeds to *extend* this merging of the two ideas by demonstrating how they function jointly in such ministerial activities as preaching and evangelism; finally, it *unites* this entire knowledge in studies of such typical counseling problems as alcoholism and suicide.

Section One, then, demonstrates—through case histories and questions and answers about them—many of the basic facts of psychiatry and psychology as used by a counseling minister. How does one launch a counseling program? What are the dangers? How does one distinguish a neurotic from a well-adjusted person —or from a psychotic? Just what do these labels really mean?

16

What are the evidences, the symptoms, the warning signs of a neurosis or psychosis? What about the cases "too tough to handle" in a pastor's study? To whom should they be referred? And how?

Now that the day-to-day activities and the case-to-case procedures have been outlined, the material goes on to a discussion of the fundamental relationship between theology, psychiatry and psychology. Section Two begins, as a matter of fact, with a challenge to that relationship—the kind of thoughtful challenge which many ministers have made in this day of changing theories. The replies received from other ministers and psychiatrists, we believe, point a way to unique cooperation for the service of man and God.

Section Three is thus able to delve into the relationship between this newer knowledge of human behavior and its application to specific functions of the minister: his preaching, his efforts to strengthen the parish, his community work, his evangelism, and so on.

Section Four deals with specific counseling situations in which the total resources of both psychology and religion must be employed—typical cases, yet enormously significant and delicate. It copes with bereavement, alcoholism, and problems of sex; it discusses the alcoholic, the homosexual, and the aged. It discusses grief work and other phases of fatal illness.

Each Section is preceded by a table of contents which describes each question in it, and lists the expert advisers who have responded to it. In several instances we were asked not to use the names of the people who sent in the questions. For the sake of uniformity we have left all the questions unsigned except when the question itself is a part of the answer.

Finally, the Editor wants to express his gratitude to the people who have made this book possible—first, to the people who have asked the questions, to whom we are grateful for their intellectual curiosity and their sense of mission and commitment. And second (and particularly) to the group of outstanding men and women who have so unselfishly given of their time and services in answering.

SIMON DONIGER.

Pastoral Psychology
In Action

of Pastoral Care, Duke University Divinity School, Durham, North Carolina.

How to Refer

The most effective ways to refer people who are in need of such services to specialists, with actual illustrations of letters of referral suggested by outstanding workers in the field. *Discussed by:* Dr. Leland E. Hinsie, Professor of Psychiatry, College of Physicians and Surgeons, Columbia University, New York City; the Reverend Rollin J. Fairbanks; and Dr. Walter Stokes, Psychiatrist-Marriage Counselor, Washington, D. C.

To Whom to Refer

How a minister can get to know the various specialists in his community—psychologists, psychiatrists, social workers, and so on—along with a discussion of the criteria and qualifications involved in referring to specialists. *Discussed by:* Dr. Rollo May, Consulting Psychologist, New York City; the late Reverend David E. Roberts, formerly Professor of Philosophy of Religion, Union Theological Seminary, New York City; the Reverend Seward Hiltner, Associate Professor of Pastoral Theology, Federated Theological Faculty, University of Chicago; and Louise Long, Editor, "Newsletter," Association of Mental Hospital Chaplains, Modesto, California.

Counseling with Neurotics

How the minister can distinguish between people who require referral to specialists; how symptoms can enable the minister to recognize the need for referral. *Discussed by:* Dr. Karl A. Menninger, Chaplain Charles V. Gerkin, and Chaplain Robert A. Preston of The Menninger Foundation, Topeka, Kansas; the Reverend Carroll A. Wise, Garrett Biblical Institute,

Evanston, Illinois; and Dr. Smiley Blanton, Psychiatric Clinic, Marble Collegiate Church, New York City.

How to Set Up a Church Counseling Program

A minister asks:

I will greatly appreciate any help you can give by answering the following questions:

(1) What steps should be taken to inaugurate an effective counseling program?

(2) What methods should be used to get people to consult you?

(3) How much time should the pastor give to counseling?

(4) Should one keep stated hours?

(5) What records should be kept on counselees?

(6) What books on counseling would be especially helpful to a pastor?

I will also appreciate any other helpful information not covered in the above questions.

A counseling minister replies:

To begin with I should explain that my experience is still rather limited, since I only recently joined the staff of this large suburban church, part-time, as the fourth minister on the staff. (Editor's Note: This letter was written in January, 1955.) This service was instituted here without any great hullabaloo. My arrival was announced to the congregation with the title "Counseling Minister," and subsequently we published a small brochure describing the counseling service, and placed it in strategic places in the church. But I shall try to speak to your correspondent's questions in more general terms than my particular experience here implies.

First of all, I would prefer to speak of a "counseling *service*" rather than a "counseling program," because it seems to me that counseling is more a service that the church can render rather than a program it puts forward. Just how such a service is developed depends in large measure, of course, upon the size of the church.

That is to say, it makes a difference whether this is to be an added dimension of service by a single pastor, or the specialized function of one member of a staff of several persons. In any case, the person who is to be the counselor should have some training and preparation, of the kind frequently discussed in PASTORAL PSYCHOLOGY (e.g., seminars, clinical training, and so on).

(1) "What steps should be taken in inaugurating such a program?" The first thing for the pastor to do is prepare himself to be a good counselor. If it is a large church, and a staff person whose primary function is counseling is to be added, it may be appropriate to publish a small brochure explaining the Counseling Service to the congregation. If it is a smaller church, and the pastor simply wishes to add counseling to his program, he may run a brief announcement in the church bulletin to the effect that he is "available for consultation at such-and-such hours." When one man performs all the functions of a pastorate, his counseling work will often be closely related to all of his other contacts with his flock. In many cases, pastoral counseling will take place during home calls or in ways less formal than by appointment in the pastor's study.

(2) "What methods should be used to get people to consult you?" There are plenty of people around who have problems. All that is needed is for them to feel that an understanding person is available, one with whom they can talk freely and in confidence about their problems. Whether or not the pastor is that sort of person communicates itself to people without further advertisement. They know that the pastor is available for consultation, at least at certain hours. If they feel he is the kind of person they can talk to, they will come *when they are ready to talk*. This is the way it must be, for if they do not feel some kind of rapport, nothing much can be accomplished. Nor can anything be accomplished until the person is ready to talk about his problem. There may be rare exceptions to this rule for the *pastoral* counselor, in cases where a pastor feels morally bound to raise a problem with a parishioner who, for one reason or another, has not yet come to the pastor with it. Even in larger churches, where there may be one or more persons on the staff

24

in the special capacity of counselors, there is ordinarily no device necessary "to get people to consult."

(3) "How much time should a pastor give to counseling?" This depends on how much else the pastor has to do, and how fast he works. Every man must "hit his stride" with a proper balance between the various aspects of his job. Even with the single aspect of counseling there is a great deal of variation as to how much different men can take (or "give") in the counseling relationship. But two things should be noted: the modern Protestant church has been in an era of great organizational "busyness" and "program planning," to such an extent that the needs of individuals have often been overlooked; and second, the New Testament offers abundant evidence that Jesus spent a great deal of time and effort with individuals and with small groups. If this latter can in any sense be construed as pastoral counseling, then it is instructive for us in budgeting our time as ministers of the Gospel. In my judgment, twelve to fifteen hours a week of counseling is as much as the average minister (with all of the usual pastoral duties to perform) can handle.

(4) "Is it advisable to have stated hours?" I think it is *necessary* to have stated hours, particularly if counseling is to be but one aspect of a total ministry. The average minister literally cannot afford to have himself interrupted just any time, or he would never be able to get all the other things done he has to do. However, having said this, there is a certain sense in which the pastor is a counselor *all* of the time. That is, counseling may be done in any place and at any time when the pastor comes into contact with his people. Whether such incidental contacts may be called "counseling" or not depends upon the situation and how the pastor interprets it. But, generally speaking, if the pastor finds people turning to him for counseling, he will be well advised to set up certain hours during the week for this, so that too great inroads will not be made on the time that should be spent in study, calling, and so on.

(5) "What records should be kept on counselees?" This depends partly on the concept of the counseling program. If there is any possibility that such records might ever be used for re-

search (e.g., if the pastor should write a book), it is obvious that detailed records should be kept. If, however, these records are strictly for the pastor's use in studying his own counseling efforts, they can be as brief as possible. I do think it is extremely helpful for any pastor to keep some kind of records on his counseling; if nothing else, it relieves him of having to carry so much material around in his busy mind. For ordinary purposes, I think a sheet of paper (or a large index card) on which the pastor can list the counselee's name, address, telephone number, occupation, age, family status, and the nature of the problem is sufficient. He can then add a brief note after each additional contact with the counselee, reporting the progress of the relationship. Obviously, any such records must be kept strictly confidential; when a pastor leaves a church they should either be taken with him or destroyed.

(6) "What books on pastoral counseling would be especially helpful?" The best book on pastoral counseling I know is Seward Hiltner's book, *Pastoral Counseling*. This is the most comprehensive book on the subject, and it is most cognizant of the main trends of thought in modern dynamic psychology. The recent book, *You Can Be Healed,* by Clifton and Clinton Kew (of the Marble Collegiate Church Clinic), is more psychology than it is theology. Beyond these, a pastor might profitably read recent books on counseling and dynamic psychology, such as Carl Rogers' *Client-Centered Therapy*. Pastors who engage in counseling have the responsibility for helping to relate the insights of modern dynamic psychology to Christian theology.

JOHN W. STETTNER,
Counseling Minister,
First Presbyterian Church,
Evanston, Illinois.

Another minister replies:

Two of the keys to an effective counseling program are careful sermon preparation and systematic pastoral visitation.

The sermon is helpful in several ways. People respect a pastor whose sermons show adequate preparation. They have the security of knowing their pastor to be sincere and thorough in his work. He gains enough status to be "worth talking to." Second, the sermon presents the pastor's philosophy of life. People will know beforehand what general reaction they can expect from the preacher when he is confronted with their problems. Third, the sermon prepares the way for counseling through the pastor's application of Scripture to life. The pastor's awareness of his parishioner's doubts, fears, and temptations, expressed through such phrases as "all of us know at times this fear and foreboding" (Luke 21), will encourage them to regard him as a sympathetic listener. Finally, the sermon gives specific instructions about life situations, such as the process of grief in a sermon on death. When parishioners face crises, they may call their pastor and say, "I remember that you talked the other Sunday about this very sort of thing."

Systematic pastoral visitation is another key to an effective pastoral counseling program. It shows the pastor whether he is personally ready to undertake a counseling program. If the pastor can systematically visit the membership on stated afternoons and evenings; if he is willing to arrange his schedule so that up to one hour can be spent with each family; and if he finds that people talk to him freely and easily about themselves, then he is ready for a "counseling program."

I put these words in quotes because such a designation is now artificial. Home visitation will include much counseling; office counseling will therefore be a simple geographical transfer for the convenience of the pastor, or to give some member of a crowded household the privacy he desires. In some instances, of course, office counseling intensifies the meaning of the pastor's relationship to his parishioner. The parishioner is impelled by some sense of need when he makes an office appointment; and in the office he is surrounded by reminders of the dignity of the place. There is a Bible . . . weighty theological tomes . . . the pastor's desk (which may add or detract) . . . perhaps even the sound of the organ being played in the sanctuary.

If the pastor has stated hours for visitation, it is easy to keep stated hours for office counseling. It is often convenient to announce those hours in a pastoral letter when first coming to a church.

27

If the people say that the pastor's sermons "give us something to think about," and if they use his visits as an opportunity to talk about their personal concerns, then the pastor can indeed expect them to say as they leave the sanctuary, "I'd like to see you in private sometime this week, pastor."

Records of office counseling should be as complete as those kept after an evangelistic home visit, a call on a new convert, or any other significant conversation with a member of the congregation. The pastor will obviously have a complete record of office counseling if he records his interviews electronically.

SAMUEL SOUTHARD,
Fort Mitchell Baptist Church,
Covington, Kentucky.

Finding Time for Counseling

A minister writes:

In a church like mine, with over twelve hundred members, how is one to find the time to carry on a counseling program? If the minister is conscientious in working with the few, he must neglect the many, and the expectations in the average Protestant church are that the minister shall "visit" with everybody whether there is a crisis or not.

A teacher of pastoral counseling replies:

A counseling program in a large parish must be controlled lest it monopolize the pastor's time and alienate him from the majority of his parishioners. After all, he is called to be their *minister* and not simply to conduct a clinic at their church. To guard against devoting too much time to counseling, the clergyman might try the following methods:

First, make appointments rather than simply seeing people when they appear without warning. The very act of securing a specific appointment is reassuring and therapeutic. It symbolizes that help is on the way, and that one is no longer alone with his burden.

Second, adhere strictly to the time allotted. Tenacious parishioners will often "buy" extra time by saving dramatic material for the end of the interview.

Third, space the conferences at least two weeks apart. There is nothing sacrosanct about the "once-a-week" counseling procedure. After all, the real growth and progress take place *between* appointments!

Fourth, try scheduling only half-hour appointments. Twice as many people can be seen, and they will "get down to business" sooner when the time is limited. The drain on the counselor's strength will, of course, be great.

Fifth, experiment with group therapy to provide assistance of a general nature for several people at a time. Seminars (of the discussion type but with significant contributions from the pastor) can be offered on "Dating," "Preparing for Marriage," "Post-Nuptial Adjustments," "Religion and Health," "The Search for Faith," "Overcoming Our Fears," and so on.

Sixth, avoid becoming bogged down with chronic neurotics who will drain off valuable time. They usually prefer their "crutches" to the discomfort of learning to "walk" again. Do not be rude or unkind, but firm and humble.

Seventh, preach *pastoral* sermons at least once a month, striving for self-understanding, for healing from within rather than treatment from without. Stress the importance of building (or *re*-building) adequate relationships.

Eighth, pray regularly for those in difficulty. Pastoral counselors often become so involved with the burdens of others that their own devotional lives suffer.

Ninth, if one's religious tradition provides for or permits a sacramental ministry, do not restrict it to Sunday or public services. Holy Communion provides for lateral relationships as well as a vertical one.

ROLLIN J. FAIRBANKS,
Professor of Practical Theology,
Episcopal Theological School,
Cambridge, Massachusetts.

A minister with an extensive counseling program writes:

You raise a very real question.

The first two or three years you cannot do anything extensive in counseling. It will take time. I would suggest that you start with pre-marital counseling if you can find time for that, and you *must* find time for it.

In the second place you can deal with the more critical situations that come to you. Do what you can with them and make referrals to psychiatrists who are available to you, or to physicians.

Gradually as you discover and train laymen to do various jobs in the church, you will have more time to counsel. For example, in our church we have seventy-six deacons who do parish calling. Our board of women calls on the older ladies. We have a special committee that does calling on the custodial cases and shut-ins. Men of the church pretty much handle the financial end of the work. In these last sixteen years we have trained about eighty people who do various types of counseling. In the meantime we have discovered the physicians and psychiatrists with whom we can work and to whom we can make referrals.

I would propose a program something like this: First, I would make my efforts contribute as fundamentally as possible toward helping people face and deal with their problems. Second, I would begin to try to educate my board and the members to the jobs which should be done by the members if they are to grow, and the parish is to become a beloved community. Third, I'd get acquainted with physicians who have counseling insight, representatives of social agencies, and psychiatrists. This way you can build up teamwork which will result in a sharing of the load and the doing of a better job. Fourth, I'd start in with pre-marital counseling. Fifth, I'd gradually educate my people to call for conferences; and I would set aside definite times in my schedule when I would be available for counseling. Sixth, I would organize nurture groups of men and women and young people, in which opportunity is provided for them not only to grow in the life of the spirit, but for them to enter into each other's concerns and provide help for each other.

But you will have to stay in your church a while if you are going to accomplish this. I doubt if you can do much in less than five years. If you stay ten years you can do more. If you stay fifteen, you can do much more.

ROY A. BURKHART,
First Community Church,
Columbus, Ohio.

A pioneer in pastoral care replies:

Our ministers in local churches are constantly challenging those of us who work in the field of pastoral care, research, and teaching to give them more practical help in their task of helping people. This to my way of thinking is a legitimate challenge.

THE MINISTER'S CONSULTATION CLINIC

Faced with the *impossible* task of directing an organization whose budget often runs to considerable sums; with overseeing an educational program; with serving as a public relations officer; with directing a group of people in worship two or three times a week; and with preparing and delivering at least two sermons a week—the incredibly-pressured minister is now asked to serve more effectively as a physician of the soul!

We are told by medical writers that a third of the nation's total population is sick in one way or another. Most of this illness is now believed to fall clearly within the area of spiritual-emotional difficulties. As we have carried the investigation of pastoral care further, the impression that stands out most clearly is the need for time. Pastoral time with a given individual who is suffering, who is struggling to find his way through the confusion and uncertainty in which he is caught. Modern man struggles for a sense of personhood, as have his predecessors before him. But having lost his sense of destiny and a feeling of significance, he seems more confused than his forefathers. Whether this is actually true or not is probably beside the point: he is confused enough.

For several months I have been conducting a series of lectures, together with the Reverend Leon Couch, pastor of a local Methodist church, upon the subject of alcohol. This has brought us into close contact with many alcoholics. Recently an alcoholic said, "If the church is to help us, the minister must come partway to meet us." Another said, "Two years ago I didn't have the guts to look a minister in the eye, I was so low." Most conscientious ministers are shocked at the thought that anyone would consider them unapproachable, or that a "lost soul" (and if anyone is lost it is the person whose life is dominated by alcohol) would not feel free to approach them. And yet that is true of most alcoholics.

"How can I find time to do all those things you described?" our ministers say. And we admit the question is at the heart of the problem. The minister already knows far more than he is able to use; why load him down with still further work? The answer is that if the church is to make a difference in the lives of people, it must personalize its ministry. That is, it must be able to impress upon its people the fact that it is concerned about them as persons. This is the field of pastoral care. But the minister serving from two hundred to four thousand persons with multiple tasks is increasingly baffled by the enormous task he is facing.

A physically ill person needs to be seen every week, a dying person every day, a shut-in every two weeks, an older person at least that often. Every person should be called upon twice a year whether he has special spiritual needs or not, while six to twelve hours of listening time is needed by grief-suffering persons. Two to four hours are needed for pre-marital counseling with each couple the minister marries; while if he is to work effectively with persons suffering from marital difficulties, from twelve to twenty hours and often far more are needed; and now the final blow: if one is to be helpful with an alcoholic, from one to two hundred hours are needed.

The answer, like most answers to the problems of the church, is this: select and train laymen who will assist the pastor. We have long used laymen in pastoral care. The Methodists have recruited a million new members in the last two or three years through the use of laymen in evangelism. The strength of the evangelism of the Southern Baptist Church lies in the zeal of the laymen. In the south, the Southern Baptist will ask you to attend his church before he asks you what your job is, and will brag about his church before he brags about his kids. The use of laymen in various pastoral care tasks is not a new idea, *but the training of laymen and sending them out to call in major areas of the pastoral care field is new*. I have spent a great deal of thought on the contents of such a training program, and have outlined it in my guidebook, *You Came Unto Me, a Guidebook in Pastoral Calling for Ministers and Laymen*.

In addition to the guidebook, I have prepared what I call *clinical teaching material* which is based upon six calls, three of which have been made by ministers and three by laymen. Each of these calls is not only evaluated, but teaching instruction is given which may be used in the instruction of laymen. My suggestion is that a copy of the guidebook be secured for the laymen who are to do pastoral calling, and that the group be gotten together for a general discussion of the project. This should be followed up with three lessons of the clinical teaching material in which the group discovers just how to develop a call and some of the difficulties involved. Then the group may start their calling, probably beginning with calls upon shut-ins and older people, as the dynamics in these situations are not so strong as they are in some of the others.

In later sessions other lessons of the clinical teaching material may be presented. This is a device for keeping the interest strong, and it is a gradual way to open up the field with its possibilities of helpfulness. The clinical material is based upon one call with a shut-in, one with an elderly parishioner, one before an operation, one of an evangelistic nature, one of bereavement, and one "routine."

It is my thought that as the group develops, the members of the group should be permitted to choose their own areas of interest. One will prefer to do evangelistic calls, while another will get interested in the field of counseling with alcoholics, and still another will become interested in shut-in persons. Theoretically and ideally a given caller should make different types of calls, for this will enrich his own work and help him maintain his enthusiasm. As the group's interest develops, and you recognize that some who start will drop out, while others will be added, a library of books may be collected for the use of the people upon whom they are calling as well as for their own study. A bibliography of such books appears in the guidebook and we are constantly adding to this list.

RUSSELL L. DICKS,
Professor of Pastoral Care,
Duke University Divinity School,
Durham, North Carolina.

How to Refer

A minister writes:

Since many ministers work as members of a community team, there are often instances when we are called on to write letters of referral. Sometimes it is difficult for a minister to decide what to put into a letter of referral, say, to a psychologist.

Would it be possible for some ministers, psychologists, psychiatrists, and medical doctors to express what they would consider proper material for a letter of referral? Perhaps a general outline could be given.

A psychiatrist replies:

This is my idea of a letter of referral. It should contain only *the facts* of the case, with professional judgments left out. State in simple terms *what* you observed, not the meaning you give to it; state *what* the patient tells you, not your interpretation of it.

Too often we make the mistake of telling the clinic what we think, when it is far more important to tell the clinic what is on the patient's mind.

Too often, also, because we are entranced by words and concepts, we err in showing how astute and clever we are. In the meantime the troubles of the client are obscured by our erudition.

What are the simple facts? Here is a sample letter of referral:

Dr. John Doe, Chief
Mental Hygiene Clinic
50 Broad Street

Dear Doctor Doe:

I am referring Mrs. Richard Roe to you in the belief that her condition may be alleviated or cured by your facilities.

35

When we first saw her in April, 1951, she told us of her great sadness. She looked extremely downcast and she cried bitterly as she related her troubles to us.

In March, 1951, her youngest "child" (as she put it), married and moved to another city. She said she dreaded the day when the children would no longer be around the house.

Mrs. Roe is 46 years old. She herself thinks that she is in the change of life, but she adds that her chief preoccupation is her distress at being left alone. Her husband died in 1947. She grieved over the occasion, but was greatly consoled by the youngest child. She says today that she does not know what she would have done, if she had not had the boy with her.

She suffers from insomnia, headache, dizziness, and loss of appetite.

She has always been kindly disposed to religion. Indeed, as she herself puts it, religion has always been a source of great sustenance to her. It is so today, though we feel that now there may be medical or mental hygiene complications for which she needs the kind of attention that only your field can render.

We are grateful for the opportunity to refer Mrs. Roe for your consideration. We hope that our combined efforts may restore her to soundness of mind and body.

> LELAND E. HINSIE, M.D.,
> Professor of Psychiatry,
> College of Physicians and Surgeons,
> Columbia University.

A pastoral counselor replies:

Letters of referral can be quite brief. Brevity serves two purposes: it enables the parishioner to tell his own story or his own "side" of the story to the new counselor; and it avoids the possibility of the pastor's telling more than is necessary and relevant, including *his* diagnosis of the situation.

There are two general types of referrals, as well as a combination of both. A parishioner may be referred for *evaluation purposes only*. For instance, does this woman's emotional disturbance have a physical basis which can be treated medically? Are this man's needs so severe as to warrant more skilled help than a clergyman is qualified to provide?

The second type of referral seeks to transfer the parishioner to another counselor *for treatment*. For instance, can you accept Mrs. Robbins as a patient? Will your agency undertake such counseling as this husband appears to need?

There is also a combination of these two kinds of referral in which an evaluation is sought and "if in your judgment this man requires psychiatric care, will you either accept him as a patient or refer him to a competent therapist or clinic?"

A letter of referral should indicate the general *area* of need. If a parishioner is being referred to a psychologist for an evaluation based on some of the projective-type of tests, the pastor might explain, "I am particularly desirous of ascertaining whether this woman has sufficient personality resources to enable her to accept a separation from her husband due to his impending military assignment abroad."

A referral to a psychiatrist might be prompted and explained in this fashion: "I have had six interviews with Mrs. Smith with little apparent progress. Her hostility, if anything, has increased. Just what role am I playing in this counseling relationship? Should it be permitted to continue? If so, how can it be made more helpful?"

Any referral should include the person's *full* name, address, and telephone number. If such a person's financial situation is very limited, it is only fair to mention this because the physician may already have more than his share of charity patients.

ROLLIN J. FAIRBANKS,
Professor of Practical Theology,
Episcopal Theological School,
Cambridge, Massachusetts.

A psychiatrist-marriage counselor answers:

In connection with referrals by ministers to specialists in the psychological fields I should like, from a background of much personal experience, to suggest that in arranging the consultation the minister should be conservative about building up in his parishioner an overly optimistic view about what the consultant can accomplish and how simply and quickly he can do it. Often patients have been referred to me with a pat assurance that I could "fix them up in no time" and I have had considerable difficulty correcting this misapprehension before therapy could be approached.

The plain truth is that most cases which justify referral present deep-rooted personality problems which, in their very nature, make successful therapy a tedious and often expensive process, with no possibility of miraculous short-cuts. It should be clearly visualized that with most personality disorders the therapeutic results are likely to be unspectacular, although of solid value. The more highly successful therapeutic achievements are offset by other cases in which results are indifferent or nil, for reasons often beyond control of the therapist. So it is much wiser if the referring minister will give the consultant a cautious build-up and be equally conservative about the results that are forecast.

Wherever possible the minister should try to have a personal acquaintance with his consultants. They are usually glad to get acquainted and to take the time necessary to reach mutual understanding about the details of referral, including cost, duration of treatment, and prognosis.

As to the kind of information the consultant would like to have from the referring minister, I believe that the most important things are these:

(1) A summary of the problem as the minister sees it.

(2) A brief description of what has been done by the minister to help the person who is referred.

(3) A statement by the minister of his observations on the general family and social adjustment of the person being referred. This can be of very great value to the consultant.

WALTER STOKES, M.D.,
Washington, D. C.

To Whom to Refer

A minister asks:

What can you say to the pastor who wants to be able to refer people for more intensive counseling than he is himself capable of, but is confused by the variety of psychologists, psychiatrists, and other counselors?

A psychologist with ministerial training replies:

This is a difficult problem, partially because the field is still so unstructured that particular academic degrees are not necessarily a proof of competence in various forms of therapy, and partially because therapy is chiefly an art and therefore dependent upon qualitative personal factors. Some minor principles can be offered. If the person wishes help specifically on a psychosomatic symptom (e.g., ulcers) or if the problems have psychotic aspects, psychiatric help is clearly indicated. If the problems are emotional, but deep-seated and with a long history, psychoanalytic help is probably indicated. However, these minor principles do not help much because it may be difficult for the pastor to know what the person's problem really is.

This brings me to the main recommendation I would make: that the pastor refer *through* someone—counselor, psychologist, or psychiatrist—in whose professional integrity he has confidence. In my experience, the personal factors (such as integrity and character of the therapist) are apt to be more crucial than the particular school to which the therapist belongs. Then, if the person referred needs a different kind of treatment from that which the minister's assisting, consulting therapist can give, the therapist can be expected to make further referral himself.

ROLLO MAY, Ph.D.,
Consulting Psychologist,
New York City.

39

A minister replies:

I must say that I have sympathy with the minister when he says that he is confused by the variety of psychiatrists, psychologists, and other counselors representing different schools. One possible form of collaboration between a pastor and a psychotherapist involves referring more serious cases to the latter, and letting him make the final decision as to whether long-range therapy is indicated; and if so, who should undertake it. When the minister succeeds in establishing such a relationship with a psychiatrist or psychotherapist whom he can trust thoroughly, this arrangement works rather well.

Another possibility involves building up a personal list of counselors in whom one has confidence. This may be difficult to do. Even if the minister knows several psychiatrists personally, it may be extremely hard for him to estimate their professional competence. Moreover, even assuming that some of the patients let the pastor know "how things are going" in their therapy, the reports of such patients are not to be taken at face value. A patient can easily overestimate or underestimate the professional skill of his own therapist.

Because it takes a great deal of time, and perhaps special opportunity, for a minister to build up a list of counselors in whom he has personal confidence, it occurs to me that Christian ministers with special experience in the field of counseling might well make their knowledge accessible to fellow clergymen for referral purposes. In large communities there might be a bureau with a list available of competent counselors on whom the parish clergyman might call for assistance. The bureau would take the responsibility for keeping this list up to date and dependable.

Among these various alternatives, the best one seems to me to be the one in which the minister establishes a close working relationship with one or two psychiatrists. These professionals can help the minister avoid two types of error. First, the tendency to refer too many cases to therapists: that is, to pass off to the psychiatrist comparatively trivial problems or the normal difficulties of normal people, problems the minister himself should be able to assuage on his own. Second, they guard against an error at the other end of the spectrum—the tendency for the minister to be too ambitious, to try to handle cases which are beyond his depth—possibly without realizing that they are beyond his depth.

It is impossible to escape the fact that the minister will, in any case, be exposed to contradictory advice. Some psychiatrists look favorably upon lay analysis; that is, therapy carried on by non-medical people; others are violently against it. On such problems the minister can form his own opinions only through extensive study and experience.

DAVID E. ROBERTS,
Late Professor of Philosophy of Religion,
Union Theological Seminary,
New York City.

Another minister replies:

In the long run, there is no answer to this question which does not include the pastor's getting to know these people personally in his own vicinity, and making up his own mind about them. But a few general comments can be made which he may find helpful.

First, any kind of psychotherapy always involves something more than science, but it needs to be grounded on a solid scientific foundation. Both sides of this statement are important. If there is no evidence that a counselor has studied seriously what science can teach him, this is clearly a mark against him. On the other hand, mere knowledge is not enough. Psychotherapy is an interpersonal relationship of a special kind; and many believe that the kind of person a therapist is will prove as significant as the kind of knowledge he has. Here the cardinal question would seem to be: Is he a genuinely understanding human being?

Second, although it is true that there are schools and groups of psychotherapists, the amount of basic similarity in approach of all those with good training and extensive experience is very great. Like some church denominations, an outsider may see more similarity than the groups see themselves. There are persons of

41

talent, experience, insight, and warmth in several different groups who would approach a patient or client with the same basic skill and understanding.

Third, there is no degree or diploma which in itself will testify to the person's therapeutic skill; but along with other evidence, these things are important. A psychiatrist must have an M.D. But to be trained in psychiatry, he needs work beyond the M.D. And to be trained in intensive psychotherapy or psychoanalysis, he must have had some of this applied to his own life, and have done it himself under supervision. This is a requisite for acceptance by the American Board of Psychiatry and Neurology.

A psychologist even with a Ph.D. may or may not have training and experience in counseling or psychotherapy. That can easily be discovered by seeing whether he has had a personal therapeutic experience, and has done counseling for some time under supervision—over and above his academic work for his degree.

Fourth, we may be legitimately reassured that no competent counselor or psychotherapist will have a negative attitude toward anything in the religion of his patient which is constructive in character. This is true regardless of the therapist's personal views toward religion. There has been a fundamental change on this point during the past few years. If a therapist now cannot take this attitude toward his client's religion, he is considered to that extent incompetent by his colleagues. If in doubt, we can ask a therapist directly about his attitude toward the religion of his patients. If he tells us that he respects whatever is constructive about it, and believes in helping the patient disentangle that from whatever has become neurotic about it, he is giving the right answer. The pastor cannot expect the psychotherapist to be an evangelist.

There are, and will be, increasing steps by the therapeutic groups for licensing systems of various kinds, designed to protect the public from the incompetent. In the formal sense, the identification of the competent is bound to become simpler in the years ahead. And yet such procedures can never touch more than the externals of competence, helpful though they may be. So long as psychotherapy is a humanistic and not solely a scientific procedure, the real competence of the therapist can never be assessed solely by his degrees, his training, or even his theories. For this we can only say: Know your man.

SEWARD HILTNER,
Associate Professor of Pastoral Theology,
Federated Theological Faculty,
The University of Chicago.

A chaplain replies:

The problem of referral is a difficult one and one which requires some knowledge not only of the training but of the personality of the psychiatrist to whom the referral is made. As a rule some member of the State Mental Hospital staff nearest you can recommend psychiatrists who have passed their National Boards, but such a recommendation is valuable only if one knows something of the personality of the man himself. A knowledge of successes or failures with other patients might also be a guide for the minister. Unfortunate experiences with any member of a profession are too often apt to color the outlook on everyone else in that profession. Undoubtedly there are both good and poor psychiatrists, just as there are both good and poor ministers, so that it is always well, on moving into a community, to discover the resources for mental health in that community.

The Council of Social Agencies is usually a good source of information as to available psychiatrists. Of course, any local Mental Hygiene Clinic and frequently a good M.D. can recommend the best psychiatrists in the community. Having surveyed the field in general, it is well for a minister when he moves into a community to become personally acquainted with the psychiatrists and psychoanalysts in his own and nearby communities. In this way he does not have to depend on hearsay, but can formulate his own judgments as to whether or not the psychiatrist's personality will be what is needed by the specific patient. The latter is of course impossible unless the minister himself has had training. Every minister should have a certain amount of understanding of mental illness and at least a cursory knowledge of the accepted ways of treating various types of mental illness.

LOUISE LONG,
Editor, "Newsletter,"
Association of Mental Hospital Chaplains,
Modesto, California.

All four members of our panel in discussing resources for referral and treatment of people with emotional difficulties, are referring to individual psychiatrists or psychologists. One other important resource should be added to these, and that is the mental hygiene clinic, operating either as a separate entity under community auspices, or as part of the hospital setup. In a very real sense, the mental hygiene clinic which operates as a team, consisting of psychiatrist, psychologist, and psychiatric case-worker, is often less confusing to the minister who is unacquainted with the quality of resources in his community.

The minister can feel more at ease in his use of the mental hygiene clinic both because the mental hygiene clinic represents a synthesis, frequently of what is best in all the three professional disciplines involved, and also because a community presumably has already spent a good deal of time in evaluating the qualifications of the personnel involved in the team. It is true, of course, that there are still too few such mental hygiene clinics to really meet the need. Their numbers, however, are definitely growing, particularly since the passage of the Federal Mental Health Act.

—Editor.

Counseling with Neurotics

A minister asks:

How does one distinguish between those people who should be referred by a minister to a psychiatrist, and those who do not require psychiatric attention? What symptoms reveal that it is either advisable or imperative for a person to consult a psychiatrist?

A psychiatrist and two chaplains reply:

The answer to this question depends a good deal upon a number of factors, such as the minister's training, his personality, and his role as a minister. He should consult with a psychiatrist or refer to a psychiatrist when some of the following situations arise:

(1) When the religious problem presented by the individual is beginning to reveal a long-standing underlying personality problem to which religious solutions have already proven ineffective.

(2) Sudden deterioration in behavior of a middle-aged person, indicating organic changes (paresis, arteriosclerosis, involution, and so on.)

(3) Severe guilt feelings without a sufficient reality basis.

(4) Bizarre behavior or ideas (this should go without saying, but some clergy will allow even obvious trouble to go without referral.)

(5) Monotonously repeated standardized efforts of a person to adjust to all new situations in the same way, disregarding the unique demands of each.

(6) Homosexual behavior.

(7) Marital conflicts in which the mutual hostility is irrational.

We would like to summarize as follows:

(1) A rule of thumb: whether to refer depends on the *per-*

sistence of the maladjustment, the *intensity* of feeling expressed, the *irrational* elements, and the *degree of deviation* from accepted modes of behavior. Sometimes only one of these factors, sometimes all three, must be considered.

(2) Referral does not mean desertion. The minister should continue pastoral care for the person whom he refers, and he should work with the members of the family as much as possible.

KARL A. MENNINGER, M.D.,
CHAPLAIN CHARLES V. GERKIN,
CHAPLAIN ROBERT A. PRESTON,
The Menninger Foundation,
Topeka, Kansas.

A minister replies:

We shall indicate some of the things a minister needs to know and how he can learn them. But at the same time we must emphasize that this question is impossible to answer in a few brief paragraphs; and that its importance demands continuing and considerable study by all who counsel.

First, as the question implies, the minister must know symptoms and their meaning. To elaborate on this would be to write a book. Instead, here are some books already written: Menninger, *The Human Mind;* Hinsie, *Understandable Psychiatry;* Cameron, *The Psychology of Behavior Disorders.* But reading a book may leave a minister with a sense of loss; can he really recognize a person with these symptoms when he sees one? Sometimes it is easy, and sometimes even the experts disagree. A period of clinical training is the best approach to an answer to this part of the question.

Second, the minister must know the psychiatric resources in his community, both public and private, and what kind of persons they will and will not accept for treatment. It is frustrating to tell a person that he needs treatment when none is available for him. The minister should get acquainted with the psychiatrists in his community and learn what kind of persons they want to have sent to them.

Third, there are certain obvious things that can be said. The person who has undergone a sudden change of personality which hampers his personal relationships should be referred. The person with bizarre religious ideas, the person in a severe or even mild depression, the individual with ideas of grandeur or persecution—these should be referred, usually to a mental hospital.

Fourth, the pastor should be aware of all psychiatric resources for children in his community. For the untrained pastor, contact with these clinics is the best way to discover the kind of child they prefer to treat and how they wish referrals to be made.

Fifth, the manner in which the referral is made is important. There are many considerations here: whether the person should be referred directly, or whether the pastor should work through the family; what should be done before the referral is made in order to make it effective; what relationship should be established before the referral is made; just how it should be made. Much understanding is required for effective referrals. The minister should continually study the referrals he does make in order to learn how to do it more effectively.

Sixth, if a person is a member of the parish, the minister should maintain pastoral contact with him after the referral. He may still be of help to the person as a pastor, though he should do no counseling without the knowledge and consent of the psychiatrist. He must understand what the psychiatrist is trying to do, and see that his contacts do not run counter to those of the psychiatrist. At times this presents real difficulties, yet cooperation should be the rule. The welfare of the patient is the major consideration.

CARROLL A. WISE,
Garrett Biblical Institute,
Evanston, Illinois.

Another psychiatrist answers:

There are classifiable groups of people who should be sent on to a psychiatrist by a minister. In many cases, both the pastor and therapist can work together to help such people. There are three types:

(1) Psychopathic

This type of person is characterized by inability to learn from experience; he has almost complete lack of conscience and accompanying sense of guilt. These people are often very charming.

47

Nevertheless they lie, they steal, they forge, and they are almost impervious to any type of treatment. Because of their charm and their superficial normality, the minister is often led astray in the treatment. I remember one case of a minister who attempted to befriend a psychopathic boy who had been caught stealing. He took the boy into his own home and treated him like a son. About a month later the boy decamped with all the money in the house, including the silver and some watches. Very often these people appeal to the minister as having been unloved, mishandled, and persecuted.

(2) Psychotic (or, in the vernacular, insane)

Only twenty percent of the people who are "insane" have anything physiologically wrong with their brains. The other eighty percent are "insane" because of emotional conflict—perhaps on a basis of nervous instability not discernible by any tests we now have. The first group in this series is:

The manic depressive. This type is characterized by elation, overactivity, flight of ideas, inability to keep attention on one thing. They usually make foolish investments, spend all the money their families can get, and buy with reckless abandon. This state of elation and overactivity can switch within a few hours to a state of depression, in which the person is sad, inactive, and self-accusatory. Such cases are to be watched very carefully, because a person with even a slight depression may commit suicide. Therefore, when the minister interviews a person who is really depressed and begins to talk about being sinful, unhappy, selfish, etc., no time should be lost in consulting a psychiatrist.

The schizophrenic or dementia praecox cases, of which there are two types:

Paranoid type—in which the person feels persecuted. It is sometimes very difficult to determine whether the person is actually being mistreated or whether he is misinterpreting things. Ministers often make the great mistake of assuming, when the paranoid tells a sad tale, that he is really being persecuted. Of course, sometimes there are elements of mistreatment in such cases and often a great deal can be done for them by the minister working with the psychiatrist.

Persons with hallucinations and delusions. These are usually so obvious that the minister has no great difficulty in recognizing that they are mentally sick and need the help of a psychiatrist.

(3) Cases of neurosis

These are people who have serious emotional conflicts, but are still able to keep in touch with reality.

Hysteria—generally two types.

The person has some physical symptom caused directly by emotional conflict: such as paralysis of the hands (sometimes due to a sense of guilt over masturbation); hysterical blindness; deafness. Such cases can often be cured by suggestion, but the symptoms usually return or "pop out" elsewhere unless a person is given more fundamental treatment.

False accusations—in which the person often accuses the doctor or minister of making sexual advances.

Anxiety neurosis. Such people suffer from a great deal of anxiety which they usually transfer over onto their work, their families, illness, the world situation, etc. Although these are real situations and really can be the cause of anxiety, the amount of anxiety felt by these people is out of proportion. Such people usually have some unconscious conflicts which need to be removed by the psychiatrist before they can have a healthy, normal life.

Obsessive and compulsive neurosis. The obsessive person has some thought which recurs again and again and again—usually unpleasant. For example, one woman kept thinking "damn God." She had been told that she had committed the unforgivable sin and was about to commit suicide.

The compulsive individual is one who must carry out repetitious acts, such as locking doors over and over again, turning off faucets, putting on clothing a certain way, saying the same prayer in the same position over and over.

These, in general, are the types of psychopathic, psychotic, and neurotic cases with which the minister may have to deal, and which should be referred by him to psychiatrists.

SMILEY BLANTON, M.D.,
Psychiatric Clinic,
Marble Collegiate Church,
New York City.

Recognizing the Neurotic—and Living with Him

A minister asks:

I've heard people with whom I must come in contact in my ministry described as neurotics (and I can believe it!). I would like to know two things—how to recognize a neurotic, first. How they react, and how they are different from other people. And second—how one can live with a neurotic and be happy.

A psychiatrist answers:

Let us begin by stating some of the reasons why it is not easy to distinguish neurotics. Neurotic people are, of course, still people—and like other people require essentially the same satisfaction of needs, are subject to essentially the same restrictions of society and convention, and are (potentially, at least) as capable of managing the complex compromises of successful adjustment as other people.

Certainly in comparison with severely mentally ill persons, whom we call psychotic, the neurotic's personality equipment is less damaged. By legal standards he is sane; and by the moral standards of most people he is considered "responsible." The quality of difference is hard to put one's finger on because the neurotic does seem so much like all of us. And recognition is further obscured by the fact that we are often forced to admit that we are *all* just a tiny bit "neurotic."

Neurosis is widespread, and it varies amazingly in its manifestations. Each of us has some unresolved attitude as a hangover of our childhood which can be called our "neurotic potential." It may bother us little, if at all; on the other hand, a neurosis can lead to even more marked disability than some cases of actual psychosis.

The essential difference between "neurotic" and "normal" people lies in the proportion of feelings and attitudes which are

50

beyond voluntary control. The severe neurotic is one whose behavior is in the main inflexible and misunderstandable even to
himself.

But how can we recognize a neurotic person, in the sense of
those who would be considered clinically ill? Of course some
knowledge of the specific characteristics of the various neurotic
illnesses as outlined by the experts is helpful in making a decision
about any particular situation. But here are some general guide-
posts.

Probably one of the most ubiquitous characteristics is that the
neurotic feels somehow that his symptom is silly, or unnecessary,
or causes him trouble. (However, this is not entirely true because
the core of the neurotic problem is by definition beyond the
awareness of the individual.) It might be better to say that the
neurotic usually realizes that something is amiss, *even if* he
doesn't know or understand exactly what or why. It is rather
like a person's recognizing that he has a fever without knowing
the cause. Another guidepost is the general feeling of loss of
self-esteem of the neurotic. This again is something *felt,* but not
understood.

To the outsider, irrational (but not bizarre or peculiar) behavior and ideas are a sign of neurosis. Over-reacting to relatively
insignificant incidents; petty, yet vehemently maintained prejudices or grudges; over-concern for details or a "special system"
for doing things; the need for undue reassurance from others
about doing well; undue sensitivity to criticism; touchiness in
contacts with people; excessive apologies; an unusual amount
of inconsistency in dealing with people and jobs—all of these are
objective signs of neurosis.

The first thing to be recognized about living happily and helpfully with a neurotic (that is, after considering how much one's
own problems affect the person with whom one lives) is that a
neurotic cannot help himself all alone. Much is said along the
lines of "It's all up to you" or "No one can help you but yourself." But that is only part of it. True, the neurotic must be
willing to be helped and must do a great share of the work. Yet,
just as his problem originally developed in relationship with
other people—people important to him—it must be *readjusted*

51

in relationship with other people. And again, these must be important people.

Fundamentally, the greatest contribution to living happily with a neurotic person is the encouragement and support one gives him in seeking and gaining professional help. If this is not possible (and most decidedly even when it is possible) the second most helpful thing is recognition of the *nature* of a neurosis. It is vital to realize that a neurotic is not willfully behaving as he does. *Any* illness, even pneumonia, has some secondary, coincidental advantages: these may well be overemphasized, but they are not primary. The neurotic may not seem to want to "change his ways" just as a crippled person is loath to relearn walking; but in the case of the neurotic, he may never have known how to walk well at all. A neurotic is not stupid, nor is a neurosis just for the very intelligent. A neurotic is immature only insofar as his particular symptom or symptoms are concerned.

To assist the neurotic in finding an appropriate job, to deemphasize his difficulties, to avoid challenging him about his symptoms—all these help. To be tolerant of his fears and shortcomings is useful, provided that one is neither condescending nor complacent.

A neurotic in the long run will appreciate a triple-barreled attitude on the part of others which says: "I understand that you have a problem; I may not know its exact meaning for you, but I am sure you would feel better were you in control of it, rather than the other way around." A neurosis has its roots deep within the personality and takes nourishment away from precious self-esteem, self-confidence, certainty, and trust. It hides itself with equal skill from outsiders and from the person himself. To be neurotic is rather like being a prisoner in a tower without knowing who one's captors are; and at the same time, being incapable of crying out for help in understandable words. The neurotic sometimes cannot thank you for your help and understanding. But he will appreciate it.

TARLTON MORROW, JR., M.D.,
School of Medicine,
University of Pittsburgh.

Another psychiatrist answers:

Answering these two questions in a manner which can be expected to satisfy the correspondent is no easy task. It would seem that he has one neurotic person in mind—possibly a member of his immediate family. In addition, it appears that one or more of his parishioners (or vestrymen or elders) are people with whom he finds it rather difficult to deal. To put it in another way—they are people whom he finds it difficult to adjust to without such uncomfortable feelings cropping up as impatience, boredom, irritation, intolerance or contempt.

On the other hand, he may be harassed by what seems to him to be a great number of people making unreasonable challenges to his patience and understanding. Here indeed would be a particular threat to his role as a minister, for he is expected at all times to be an example of the Christian virtues of patience, tolerance and comfort.

This correspondent seems to have a stereotyped picture of what a neurotic person is; he thinks there are special ways in which the neurotic manifests undesirable characteristics. And he believes these characteristics are not observable in those who are not neurotic. He seems to use the word "neurotic" in an invidious sense, as though neurotic people were inferior to other human beings—less desirable, and either to be pitied or avoided at all costs.

The truth of the matter is quite different. There are many neurotic people who are much easier to live with than some normal people. And there are as many differences in the personality make-up, the attitudes, and the behavior of individuals afflicted with a neurosis as there are among those who are not so afflicted, or who at least seem not to be so afflicted. It is encouraging that this correspondent seeks clarification of the problem; for it would be distressing indeed were he to develop an artificial distinction in his mind between "neurotic" and non-neurotic human beings.

Many attempts have been made to define neurosis and the neurotic personality in terms which would be acceptable and

53

understandable to any reasonably intelligent person. But these attempts are not always convincing, since all so-called "normal" people have some tinge of neurosis in their make-up, while all so-called neurotic people have an essential normality. In addition to that "normality"—and for a variety of reasons—they may show such evidences of distress as exaggerated fears, fluctuations of mood, uncomfortable self-consciousness, or a variety of bodily disturbances which signalize the presence of unresolved anxieties. While these symptoms may make their lives uncomfortable, and may even impede their adaptive efforts, the symptoms are usually subject to partial or complete removal once their causes are determined and steps can be taken to eliminate them.

JOHN A. P. MILLET, M.D.,
Chief Psychiatrist,
American Rehabilitation Committee.

confidence through experience in his own ability to be of help then he can safely go all the way to help even the extremely neurotic person. But he can also give the minister of time that are [...]

The Limits of Counseling with Neurotics

A minister writes:

How far can a minister safely carry a counseling situation with a person he suspects of being extremely neurotic? In other words, what are some of the signs which should indicate to him that the case is beyond his ability to handle?

A minister-counselor replies:

How far a minister can safely counsel an extremely neurotic person depends upon how much training and experience the minister has had in therapeutic counseling. The chief signs the minister should look for are his own feelings of uncertainty and insecurity regarding the individual's process of counseling. When the minister is uneasy or under stress because of the seriousness of the disturbance unfolding before him, he has the best possible indication that he may no longer be helpful to the person he is counseling.

Part of the confidence which we have learned to place in the person undergoing therapy has been based upon the immense capacity of such persons to move ahead toward a more realistic life-orientation, once given an accepting and understanding situation. But another part of that confidence in the person is derived from the fact that the client has the capacity to explore those aspects of himself which may be threatening and fearful at a rate which he can safely handle.

In order that this capacity to explore fearful, hysterical or bizarre aspects of himself may operate at a safe rate within the person, a safe counseling situation is needed. If the minister is frightened and fearful of his own ability to help, this will be detected by the counselee; and it is probably true that he will then not be of help. Where the minister has gained a feeling of

55

confidence through experience in his own ability to be of help, then he can safely go all the way to help even the extremely neurotic, provided that he also can give the months of time that are needed.

RUSSELL BECKER,
Assistant Professor of Psychology,
The College of Wooster,
Wooster, Ohio.

A psychiatrist replies:

If the minister "suspects" the person of being extremely neurotic, then that in itself is probably an indication of need for psychiatric help.

The signs which indicate that a case is beyond the minister's ability will vary with the experience and the knowledge of the minister. One must hope that the minister will have sufficient knowledge of personality maladjustment and its symptoms so that he can recognize them and advise the best management.

The initial evaluation should determine the *degree of incapacity* of the individual in relation to his job, his family and his other life activities. If he is severely incapacitated, he most certainly needs the best of professional help.

Even though not completely incapacitated, an individual may show signs indicative of severe maladjustment; and in the majority of instances, such individuals should have the benefit of psychiatric help. Whenever a person has serious conversion symptoms (i.e., when his emotions are affecting his bodily organs—stomach, heart, lungs and other organs), he should have medical care. There are many other types of neurotic symptoms which the minister should recognize as symptoms which usually spell a need for psychiatric treatment—excessive compulsiveness, suspiciousness, obsessional and ruminative thinking, phobias, unwarranted degrees of anxiety, persistent displacement of emotional feelings, pathological depression, chronic feelings of insecurity in relation to other people or responsibilities, and prolonged feelings of unworthiness without constructive efforts at overcoming these feelings. Each of these indicates a degree of mental conflict, a state of instability, and a sickness situation; each indicates that the minister must refer his parishioner to a psychiatrist.

WILLIAM C. MENNINGER, M.D.,
The Menninger Foundation,
Topeka, Kansas.

"Slightly Neurotic" People

A minister asks:

What can be done to help slightly neurotic people—people who do not feel enough need to ask for help, and yet seem to be heading for a fall? I'm thinking of people who drive themselves too hard, for example, and may become sick; people who are suddenly less able to get along with their fellows and their families, and so on. At times you will see trouble brewing before your eyes; or you will hear about it from the worried friends or relatives of such people; yet the individual himself does not come to you for help.

A professor of religion answers:

This question is asked by almost everyone who likes people and observes them carefully. The number of people one sees and knows who seem to be "riding for a fall" is legion. It should go without saying (but it doesn't!) that the direct approach to such people seldom succeeds. In two cases that have come to my attention recently, well-intentioned men tried it and failed. They seemed to assume they could walk right up to the individuals in question, and then—in a friendly way, of course—tell them it was obvious that something was wrong. "Why not," they asked, "see a doctor before things get worse? Or get it off your chest by talking it out with me?"

The direct approach questions the individual's ability to handle his problems himself; it arouses anxiety that is difficult for him to control. In a few instances it may break down his defenses and lead him to speak of his difficulties; but it is far more likely to increase his resistance to being helped, for the time being, at least.

The helper must act *indirectly* if he wants to be more certain of helping. There are things he can do even if the individual

58

never turns to him. The first and most obvious thing is to make himself available. He can display not an inquisitive but a friendly interest in the individual. He can plan to encounter him from time to time, meeting him socially or working with him on some project in an organization to which both belong. These contacts should yield an increase of understanding of the individual and his problems. For even if they are not referred to, aspects of one's problems are bound to be revealed in some of his acts and attitudes.

The helper will do well to record both his general observations and significant parts of each conversation soon after each contact. In this way he has the beginnings of a case record which can be studied at leisure. It should be mentioned here that progress in preventive pastoral work waits upon the development of accurate records which describe not only a variety of cases but show how the helpers acted in response to them.

If, after these various encounters, the person who needs help has gained confidence in the pastor—if he is relatively sure of his friendly interest—he is likely to "get it off his chest" at last. And then the pastor may proceed according to established counseling principles. If the individual does not take the helper into his confidence, the helper has nevertheless added to his general understanding of the individual with every contact.

A second part of the helper's activity can be in the area of private investigation. He should know the home situation, the nature of the work in which the individual is engaged, his medical history, and his "philosophy of life." A good deal about this last can be gleaned from conversation with him. The rest of the information can usually be gained quite naturally from members of the family and close friends, who are usually the ones who have brought the individual's problem to the helper's attention. In any event, the helper should avoid the role of an FBI agent. He must be content to gather his information quietly, above all never drawing the attention of those who are not already concerned about the individual to him.

This growing record of personal observation, significant conversation, and general information should help clarify the individual's problems in the pastor's mind. Of course, it must always be remembered that nothing short of the individual's self-revelation can lend anything like certainty in these matters, unless the problems are organic and obvious. Most important is the fact that this accumulating fund of knowledge about the individual may suggest ways in which he can be helped *indirectly*.

For one thing, the helper can share with the individual's intimates whatever insights he thinks he may have about the case, checking his insights against theirs. For another thing it should be possible for the helper and these intimates to determine which factors seem to ease and which exacerbate the individual's problems. Thus one may at least show the individual's family how to be more objective in their dealings with him . . . how to make life a good deal more tolerable for him . . . how to provide a more understanding and encouraging environment.

Finally, it should be recognized that for all the helper's interest and activity, the individual may indeed have to "ride until he falls." It is not necessary to regard this as disastrous, though it will certainly be disruptive. Anton Boisen has taught us that even the severest crises are not necessarily evil in their issue. A psychological crisis can at least be the occasion for the individual to face up to problems from which he can no longer escape. The outbreak of repressed acts and attitudes can make possible a more adequate adjustment to life. The possibility of learning through suffering is a cardinal doctrine of high religion. Sometimes, when we have done all we can, we must believe in this. Meanwhile, the helper will be more likely to see the fall coming, and better able to help it become a creative event in the individual's life, if he has remained close to him and kept his eyes open.

ROBERT H. BONTHIUS,
Professor of Religion,
The College of Wooster,
Wooster, Ohio.

A physician replies:

It is difficult if not impossible to help psychoneurotic patients who will not help themselves. In our clinic about fifty percent of the patients in whom symptoms such as indigestion, fatigue, headache, pain in various parts of the body, and sleeplessness are found to be due to an emotional disturbance, refuse psychotherapy. They insist there must be an undiscovered physical cause. For a patient to admit that the trouble lies in his inner life requires more humility than many patients possess. Some of these, however, will admit they are nervously tense, and may be induced to read Fink's *Release from Nervous Tension*. Many have gained the necessary insight from Rhoades' *The Self You Have to Live With*. I recommend this book highly. The fact that it has been reprinted fifteen times indicates its helpfulness.

J. H. PRATT, M.D.,
New England Center Hospital,
Boston, Massachusetts.

61

Danger Spots in Counseling

A minister asks:

I have just read the blank verse poem entitled "Twentieth Century," by W. Burnet Easten, Jr., in the July, 1951, issue of *Theology Today*. In this poetic case study, a counselor-friend leads a woman to see her own moral and spiritual bankruptcy, but is not able to lead her into a saving faith. She ends up in a sanitarium. The question the counselor-friend then asks himself is:

> "My God . . . So soon . . . I hit much nearer to the mark than I supposed . . . Could I have brought it on? . . . Perhaps . . . An awful thought! . . . And yet, I'm sure it would have happened anyway."

The question of any conscientious pastor is *"Would* it have happened anyway?"

The pastor feels the heavy responsibility of leading people to "see themselves," so that they can be led from spiritual bankruptcy to spiritual health. What actually are the chances that an unwise or mistaken approach on the counselor's part can result in mental derangement which might otherwise not have occurred?

A minister replies:

In a given counseling situation, when a parishioner cracks up emotionally, the religious counselor may well ask: "Could I have brought it on?" It is an inescapable question. And it must be faced honestly and realistically.

If the pastoral counselor has little knowledge of personality, and if he ignores the essential procedures of counseling, he may indeed be responsible. The degree of his responsibility will be determined by the degree of his inadequacy.

Wherein is the religious counselor a contributing factor? How can he harm the emotionally sick individual? First, when he is more concerned to get the parishioner to acknowledge guilt and moral failure than he is to share with him the healing resources of understanding and the reinforcing power of a positive religious faith. Second, when analysis of the person's difficulties seems more important than integration. In such an approach to an emotionally-harassed person, the result may well be "paralysis by analysis."

The fact that there is a real peril in the religious counselor's dealing with a neurotic personality must be readily admitted. But the surgeon faces risk and accepts it. So does the psychiatrist, whether he admits it or not. It is inherent in any situation where the factors are complex and hidden.

It is my conviction, tested in pastoral experience, that the pastor has a definite responsibility toward an emotionally sick parishioner, no matter how minor the case may seem to be. It is assumed, of course, that he will cooperate with both the psychiatrist and the physician. But the pastor has resources to offer an individual torn by the conflict of guilt which no other counselor has. It is the resource of Divine forgiveness. Even if the patient is too sick to grasp this concept or to relate himself to it, nevertheless the pastor's presence, his friendly interest, and his use of prayer, have a very real therapeutic value.

LLOYD ELLIS FOSTER,
Old First Church,
Newark, New Jersey.

A psychiatrist replies:

It is indeed a heavy responsibility to assist people in understanding themselves, their associates, and the world in which they live. It is always a dangerous undertaking. Those who administer insight must first know the individual well and, second, must be able to estimate carefully how much insight a person can stand at a given time. In general, the pastor should be sure there is sufficient supporting spiritual strength to make it possible for the individual to employ insight constructively.

It is questionable whether an unwise or mistaken approach on the counselor's part can result in mental derangement which might otherwise not have occurred, except in the case of people who are already close to the borderline of mental illness. Too much or too sudden insight can precipitate an already mentally-deranged person into suicide or other tragic action. *Therefore, the counselor must watch for these signs:* eccentricity, sudden change in personality, fundamental instability, or recent marked instability. In such instances, it is advised that the counselor have the advice of an understanding physician. It can be said here that there are many outstanding general practitioners who are just as able to advise the pastor as are some psychiatrists.

Dr. William B. Terhune,
Psychiatrist,
New Canaan, Connecticut.

A professor of pastoral psychology and counseling replies:

The spiritual bankruptcy which characterizes such a large segment of our secularized society presents a formidable problem to any thoughtful pastor, and cannot be by-passed if the minister is to be true to his calling. The questions asked by this minister, however, imply a direct and critical approach—one carrying with it not only a condemnation of the situation but of the person involved as well.

Condemnation of existing unhealthy and un-Christian situations is a necessary part of the minister's work, but to condemn the sinner along with the sin is to fail to meet people at the point of their need. Condemnation is in fact a dangerous threat to personality stability when dealing with those who have the kind of over-strict and immature consciences which create and support feelings of excessive guilt over failure to meet self-imposed demands.

And for the more nearly normal person, condemnation simply doesn't lead to the desired results; it is deflected as being inappropriate. Awareness of spiritual bankruptcy is not developed by criticism; awareness of need for constructive action comes only when something better is demonstrated; and when it is demonstrated in such a way that the person of his own accord wants to experience this new sort of life. The same is true for people who are already aware of the emptiness of their lives, and are sick because a sense of futility has overcome them. The need here is certainly not for condemnation, which only blocks constructive growth; the need is rather for an appreciative acceptance of the person as he is, an understanding of why he acts as he does, and a demonstration in actual group living of a better way of life, one that is indeed worth living.

I would take issue, too, with the thought that people can be led toward a goal chosen for them by the pastor. I do not believe that people can be led very far in spiritual growth in any direction, least of all toward a goal chosen by someone else. The real need is for the creation of an intimate interacting fellowship; one in which a person can experience the kind of interpersonal relationships which make the inadequacies of his customary mode of life apparent. Instead of being told that life as he is living it is spiritually empty, he discovers for himself in a living situation that there is a more satisfying way to live.

Indications of mental illness (and these are far more common than excessive feelings of guilt) are found wherever withdrawals from interpersonal association are noted, whether such withdrawals appear caused by solitary timidity or by behavior which drives others away. And here, again, the need is not for condemnation, but for acceptance in an intimate fellowship in which one can learn by experience that defenses which lead to isolation are no longer necessary, and that one has a worthwhile contribution to make in his own right.

ROBERT C. LESLIE,
Associate Professor of Pastoral Psychology and Counseling,
Pacific School of Religion, Berkeley, California.

"Probing" and "Introspection"

A minister asks:

From time to time I read an article in some popular magazine warning about the harm which may come out of the "probing" by a psychiatrist, psychologist, or psychotherapist working with adults or children. Most of these articles do not condemn psychiatry and psychology "if kept in their places." I get the impression that they feel it is a last resort only, like certain kinds of surgery—and not to be considered until all other possibilities have been exhausted. Often the writers of these articles speak with authority, in the sense that they or some member of their family have apparently been harmed by what they think of as too much probing and introspection.

This troubles me. For it seems to me that psychotherapy and counseling, while they can be helpful in extreme instances, are really important only if they can help people before things become too difficult. My own experience has been reassuring. But there are so many of these articles that the matter continues to trouble me. Could you have this question discussed, perhaps getting some comments from other ministers as well as from some psychiatrists or psychologists?

A minister replies:

Popular interest in psychoanalysis and psychotherapy has had a double-barreled reaction. Not only has it served to demonstrate the healing which can be obtained through such treatment, but it has also increased the suspicion which the layman has of those who deal with the intangibles of the psyche. Many of the articles to which the questioner refers are undoubtedly a result of such suspicion.

First let us understand that there is a difference between "probing" and "introspection." From the standpoint of a philosophy of counseling which recognizes and respects the personality and individuality of the client, intensive probing would be damaging. It would in many cases be a violation of the feelings of the individual, ignoring his right to make the ultimate decision as to what will or what will not be dealt with in the counseling interview. Not only will such probing build up a hostility and defensiveness against the counselor, but it will further weaken the already unhealthy personality structure. While such probing might expedite the procedure so far as time is concerned, the end result will be vastly inferior to a technique which strengthens rather than weakens the personhood of the client.

Introspection implies the possibility of a different approach. It can be achieved through a non-coercive therapy which allows the individual to set his own tempo and pipe his own tune. While the allegations of the popular articles cited might be applied to introspection which came out of a highly interpretative form of therapy, it is doubtful that they would remain true of that form of counseling which does not force the individual to see what he is not prepared to see until he is indeed ready and willing to look upon himself.

We must recognize that it is possible to deepen the severity of a person's problems by forcing introspection. We are all familiar with the way in which a perfectly healthy person can be made to feel quite ill by constant suggestion as to how poorly he looks: how pallid, how tense, how wan! Unless the counselor or therapist has a genuine loving concern, an *agape*-motivated desire to be of therapeutic help, a similar reaction may take place. A person could be driven insane by forcing him to be introspective; but if his introspection is voluntarily productive, restoration of health is possible. Hence there is no necessity for the pastoral counselor, who is truly motivated by loving concern, to hesitate to counsel those whose problems are not yet acute.

Most ministers will find that the majority of their counseling opportunities will be with parishioners whose problems have not become too difficult. Acute problems will be referred to competent psychiatrists and psychotherapists. The ability and degree of training of the minister will set the limits on the types of counseling he will feel able to handle. However, he need not be deterred from working with people whose problems are not severe for fear of harming them. If he allows them to determine the amount of introspection they are willing to do by reflection of their feelings rather than by interpretation, if he refrains from encroaching probing, the danger of harmful reaction to his counseling is relatively small.

PAUL E. IRION,
Long Grove Evangelical and Reformed Church,
Prairie View, Illinois.

Another minister replies:

Psychiatric treatment does not invariably include psychoanalysis; and the process of analysis is not a process of questions and answers, and not a matter of "probing." It is more accurately a skillfully-induced self-revelation on the part of the patient; after the typical resistance is overcome, the psychoanalyst appraises or interprets what the patient voluntarily tells him.

I am not a psychiatrist, but simply a well-informed pastor of long experience. In this long experience, there has never been any need to "probe." When a client decides to "unburden" to a clergyman, it is usually an "all out," sincere and honest attempt to tell everything. At least I have found it so; and I do not refer a client to a psychiatrist unless such reference is indicated. Such referrals have been but a small percentage of those counseled by me.

If, though, I find myself out of my depth, I *do* refer the client. We pastors cannot handle mental *disease* any more than we can handle other diseases unless qualified by previous medical preparation and an M.D. degree. On the other hand, a number of psychiatrists have referred patients to me when the diagnosis has been a moral or "spiritual" disturbance.

I have great confidence in psychiatrists; I have yet to find one who has failed to play fair with either me or any patient referred by me. Whatever our profession, we must stay within our own field: and mental disease, whatever its etiology, requires specialized and expert handling by some branch of medicine. Pastoral therapeutics require previous technical training as well.

"Probing" is not one of our techniques. It is not even necessary—an occasional, psychological nudge or hint usually proves sufficient. "Letting sleeping dogs lie" is a more frequent technique than we laymen realize; and stirring muddy waters is not quite the same thing as filtering it.

Finally: quackery is invariably dangerous. But a "good pastor" who knows and loves his flock can often prevent the development of serious neurotic end results. He must know his techniques and his limitations, and he must proceed with love and care.

RAIMUNDO deOVIES,
Dean Emeritus,
Cathedral of St. Philip,
Atlanta, Georgia.

A psychiatrist replies:

Several important factors must be kept in mind in finding the answer to this question. In the first place, one should never forget the strong element of curiosity which exists in most of us; thus, the very act of maintaining an inquiring state of mind can be both an asset and a liability. I assume that curiosity about the human body and how it functions, along with the maintenance of an objective point of view regarding these phenomena, are essential elements in the make-up of a good physician. Certainly one could scarcely expect to help people without being very curious as to why they are ill and what can be done to relieve them of their distress. This curiosity, however, can easily become a professional liability in the psychiatrist or the psychologist if it is unwisely used. No other profession permits so much direct questioning as psychiatry; none affords such unlimited opportunity to be curious about personal aspects of the lives of people —aspects which may or may not be any of the psychiatrist's business. I make it a practice never to ask a personal question of a patient until I first ask myself "Is this question clinically necessary for my understanding of this individual?"

The second point to keep in mind is that we are dealing with people who have a right to select the material they present to us. Patients will usually talk about surface subjects which are bothering them; they will then extend their conversation into more pertinent areas when they feel it is safe to do so. Therapeutic readiness, of course, is directly related to both the amount of confidence they have in their physician and their faith in his ability to help them. In "probing" one can violate an individual's fundamental right to the privacy of his own thoughts. Instead of being an actual therapeutic tool helping the patient to an increased understanding, it can really become the obstacle which nullifies your skills.

There is a wide gap between the body of knowledge which we call psychiatry and psychology, and the information a person has about himself and his functioning. The normality of certain well-known mechanisms can be accepted without question in professional fields, and at the same time be totally rejected by the laity. The reason for this is that all of us spend a lifetime building up defenses of one kind or another to protect ourselves from injury. We have a biological need to satisfy instinctive drives and at the same time reduce tensions and anxieties—so that our behavior will be socially acceptable, so that it will conform to the standards we have set for ourselves and the pattern which society expects us to follow. These defenses are extremely useful and protective in nature. The patient may even defend himself against your probing question by telling you something which is not true *in order that he may further protect himself*. I believe, therefore, that there is danger in "probing"; that instead of facilitating the therapeutic process it actually becomes an impediment.

I have deliberately refrained from commenting on any possible advantages which might accrue from the process of "probing" —and there must be some. Even though I am unable to think of them at this writing, it is almost inconceivable that any point of view in psychiatry or psychology should be as one-sided as the one I have advanced. Some persons appear to be greatly relieved when they know you still accept them in spite of their faults. One can, however, prepare the way for a confidential disclosure of shortcomings without "probing."

I might comment on the desirability of some capacity on the part of the individual to be introspective. I believe it is a therapeutic asset, provided it is not carried to the extreme. This is a controversial point and rightly so, but for many reasons I prefer the introvert to the extrovert.

MILTON E. KIRKPATRICK, M.D.,
Director,
Greater Kansas City Mental Health Foundation,
Kansas City, Missouri.

Psychological Tests

What is the role of psychological tests in pastoral counseling? What tests can a minister use which will help him in his counseling, and what are the pitfalls which he must avoid?

A minister and a psychologist reply:

Only properly qualified personnel should administer and interpret psychological tests. A minister who is not sufficiently schooled in psychological testing may do more harm than good if he attempts to work with tests independently.

It is felt, however, that in certain instances a minister may use tests as a technique in getting the "client" to "talk out" his problems. For example, he may use certain personality inventory or pencil and paper tests even though they have been found to be of little use in the evaluation of personality. He may use them as an aid in pointing out possible areas of conflict during the counseling session; as a basis for discussion in the interviews; as a means of impressing the patient, and convincing him that something positive is being done.

In addition, the minister may use certain projective tests, if he has been taught to administer them correctly, and if he has them interpreted by a qualified clinical psychologist. Tests which he may use in this manner, after proper supervision, are:

"Draw a Person Test," wherein the patient draws figures and associates about them; "Sentence Completion Test"; "Thematic Apperception Test," where the patient tells stories about semi-structured pictures; "Multiple Choice Rorschach Test," a shortened form of the "ink blot" test, together with the patient's associations.

The writers have been using these tests in this way: the minister administering them when he felt the need, and the psychologist interpreting them for his use in counseling.

CLIFTON E. KEW, Ph.D., Head Psychologist,
CLINTON J. KEW, Consulting Minister,
Psychiatric Clinic,
Marble Collegiate Church,
New York City.

A minister replies:

The minister who is interested in measuring growth will work with his staff, whether volunteer or professional, in developing some kind of measurement methods able to demonstrate results achieved.

There are various ways in which growth can be measured. It can be indicated by tests of knowledge—tests which show the amount and content learned. There are ways to measure changes in attitude. There are ways to test the prevailing or "presenting" attitudes of a group; and the value of this is that the same kind of measurement can be used again at a later date to discover what changes have been achieved.

There are certain prepared tests which the minister can use with real results. In our church, for example, we use the Bernreuter Personality Inventory with our ninth graders. This is designed to measure success as a personality. Neurotic tendencies, self-sufficiency, introversion and extroversion, dominance and submission, sociability, confidence—the norms for both men and women have been established for high school, college, and adult ages.

We use this same Personality Inventory with young couples seeking marriage counseling. This gives us a picture of how their personalities and their responses to behavior compare. If there is any definite indication of serious deviation, we then often use the Minnesota Multiphasic Personality Inventory. This is a diagnostic test constructed entirely on the basis of clinical criteria. It is a much more complicated instrument than the Bernreuter, but its use can be learned by a minister if he takes time to study it.

Another instrument that can be used is Personality Inventory for Children, by Fred Brown. This is a diagnostic tool helpful in planning therapy. It is designed to discriminate between normal children and those with psychoneurotic problems.

The Rogers Test of Personality Adjustment is designed to measure a child's adjustment toward his fellows, his family, and himself. Clinically-trained users will find that responses to the test provide valuable leads for further contact with the child. The test may be given individually or in groups.

It seems to me that the most important place for testing is in the realm of personality, where we can help all boys and girls and young people obtain objective pictures of the ways they behave. A minister does not need a vast amount of technical training to learn to use these instruments. It is important, of course, that he always couples his use of them with plenty of good common sense. If he has the opportunity to take added training in their use it will, of course, improve his skill.

Roy A. Burkhart,
First Community Church,
Columbus, Ohio.

A chaplain answers:

Psychological testing is the field of the clinical psychologist. Pastoral care is the field of the minister. However, the resourcefulness of the pastor is greatly increased at many points by a knowledge of psychological testing. His art of referral is strengthened. He will understand the province of the clinical psychologist and the problems his techniques can approach. He will be more able to assist families to understand testing. He thus becomes an alert extension of professional guidance centers. His own skill of observation is sharpened and his counseling benefited. For example, a knowledge of projective testing will open new viewpoints toward imaginative expressions, and he will find their contents full of psychological meaning. An understanding of administrative and interpretive techniques in objective testing will increase the value of such expressive cues as emotional blocking, personal language, and characteristic behavior. Testing knowledge is helpful when counselees raise problems touching on testing. Resourcefulness is deepened for assisting potential ministerial candidates.

The resourcefulness of the pastor in his group work would be deepened also by a knowledge of measurement methods. Here direct administration of tests would bring reliable and standardized instruments to bear upon attitudes, interests, participation and isolation, and the polling of opinions within his church groups. Such group survey projects could plot growth and attitude change periodically; and the counseling returns which would come from such projects would have some testing points of reference.

Testing should be done only by the minister with training. Without such training, the use of tests in counseling could be hazardous. The parishioner who is burdened with anxiety comes to his pastor with the expectancy that it is pastoral "care" which he will get, and by it find relief. The pastor who would shift this expected role by the introduction of testing would bring new tensions into the picture, for testing arouses tension. This tension is likely to be increased during the period of interpreting test results.

JOHN A. WHITESEL,
Chaplain,
Syracuse State Hospital,
Syracuse, New York.

A social scientist replies:

It is probably not wise for the minister who has had no training in this area to use psychological tests; these usually require considerable training and experience for their administration and especially for their interpretation.

Ministers are often faced with perplexing human problems presented by a church member whose personality is usually the key to the situation. Psychological tests, when handled by a competent person, can reveal much that is helpful. But when used and interpreted by someone lacking clinical training, such tests may be very misleading and even injurious.

Various standardized personality tests or inventories are easier to administer and to interpret (according to the instructions for scoring) but these tests usually provide only diagnostic classifications, indicating that the individual being tested has the characteristics of, or responds like, large groups of other individuals called neurotic, etc.

It would appear wiser for the minister not to attempt to be an "amateur" psychologist or psychiatrist, but to rely upon what he can elicit by interviewing the member and encouraging him or her to talk freely. The methods of non-directive counseling would seem to be the most fruitful or desirable for the untrained minister. He can and should call upon more specialized help if he finds the member has difficulties beyond his ability to handle, or exhibits conduct and feeling which suggest serious maladjustment.

LAWRENCE K. FRANK,
New York City.

SECTION TWO

Pastoral Psychology—
Basic Principles

tinguish between "necessary" and "unnecessary," fruitful and destructive frustration. *Discussed by:* Lawrence K. Frank, Social Scientist, New York City; Dr. O. Hobart Mowrer, Professor of Psychology, University of Illinois, Urbana, Illinois; Dr. Erich Fromm, Psychoanalyst and member of the faculty of the William Alanson White Institute of Psychiatry, New York City; and the late David E. Roberts, who held the post of Professor of Philosophy of Religion, Union Theological Seminary, New York City.

Limits of Permissiveness 99

Tension and the Spiritual Life 104

uting toward changes in society which would obviate such crises in the first place. *Discussed by:* Dr. Karl A. Menninger, The Menninger Foundation, Topeka, Kansas; Dr. Gotthard Booth, Associate of the Seminar on Religion and Health, Columbia University, New York City; Dr. Charles Morris, Professor of Philosophy, University of Chicago, Chicago, Illinois; Lawrence K. Frank, Social Scientist, New York City; and Dr. Rollo May, Consulting Psychologist, New York City.

The Interrelationship of Theology and Counseling

**A minister sends a challenging question—
in essay form—on theology and counseling:**

The pastor has much to learn from the experience of the counselor. Counseling has achieved an intimate knowledge of the "suffering individual." Few pastors will maintain that they have successfully brought the insights of their religious faith to bear on the problems of their parishioners in any such fashion. Doctrine has been abstract. Dogma, originally intended to preserve and explain a vital experience, has retreated into the realm of intellectual assent, often far-removed from the milieu in which the modern individual lives. The pastor is dismayed and appalled at the seething mass of passion and fear which is revealed when psychology lifts the veil on the man in the pew. The counseling movement is bringing the pastor face to face with living people, and is providing him with techniques and insights which offer help.

Nevertheless, it is important to inquire whether the learning that may go on between religion and counseling is quite so much a one-way street as some writers seem to suggest. The full potential inherent in this conversation between pastor and counselor will not be realized until more stress is laid upon the fact that religion has legitimate lessons which counseling must learn. Ways must be discovered for proceeding upon a more basic premise than the one that pastors are concerned to learn what counseling has to offer. The whole movement of counseling will not be as fruitful as it ought to be until counseling is prepared to enter into a relationship which is not merely that of teacher and pupil, but one of mutual searching and revision of theory and practice in the light of common experience, and for the benefit of those with whom it works.

81

There are signs that counseling is not unaware that it must question itself. The article by Carl Rogers, "Divergent Trends in Methods of Improving Adjustment," in the December, 1950, issue of PASTORAL PSYCHOLOGY reveals this uneasiness which is emerging within the ranks of counselors, and which needs to be faced clearly, and pushed through to a solution.

The issue around which this self-questioning has arisen is: what is the nature of the *counselee*? As Rogers indicates, the dominant trend in counseling has been to regard the counselee as a mechanism to be adjusted to an obtainable standard of mental health. "There has been a proliferation of objective and projective techniques which probe into further and further recesses of the personality. . . . The basic trend in all of clinical psychology and psychiatry is toward the development of complex and objective forms of evaluation. . . ."

Rogers does not despise what this trend has added to our knowledge of people, and religion must not. It is precisely in its intimate, first hand acquaintance with the individual that this whole movement has made its great contribution. Nevertheless, Rogers professes himself to be deeply disturbed by this "major trend," especially in its broader implications. It leads, he thinks, to a basic loss of confidence by the person in himself. Traditionally, the injunction, "Know thyself," has been taken as the key to a happy, useful, and creative life. But this is precisely the injunction which this "major trend" in counseling has declared to be an impossibility. The counselee cannot know himself. He is other than he thinks he is. His efforts to see himself clearly are foredoomed to failure. While it has not yet achieved any prominence in counseling circles, Rogers fears, rightly, that the end result of such an evaluation of the counselee must be "a philosophy of social control by the few. . . . The management of the lives of the many by the self-selected few would appear to be the natural consequence."

This dilemma is not limited to the field of counseling. It is the dilemma of virtually every element in our culture. All of those forces in the Renaissance and more particularly in the

Romantic movement, from which Freud gained at least some of his inspiration, began with the ideal of liberating the individual from the chains in which he was bound. But their end has not been the free individual. They have succeeded only in losing the individual altogether. Instead of creating the "free individual," they have actually created the "mass man," without resources for defending himself, swept by totalitarian forces over which he can neither assert control nor desire to assert control. He wants only to "escape from freedom." Clinically, counseling deals with the individual, in a painstaking and time-consuming process that is the despair of the average pastor, as well as of the counselor who works in a public mental institution. Practically, however, counseling has lost the individual with whom it started to work. It deals, not with a "person," but with an "object."

It is to the credit of counseling that it has recognized this dilemma, and that Rogers can hail a "minor trend" in the field as attempting to face the problem realistically. The solution, he believes, is for the professional worker to think, "not *about* or *for* the individual, but *with* him." This process will not impose arbitrary standards upon the counselee. It will rather free him to be what he is capable of being. This, says Rogers, must be the goal of counseling. What he seeks is "a thorough-going and detailed implementation of a philosophy of respect for the individual as a person with the right to, and capacity for, self-understanding, self-evaluation, and self-determination."

Nevertheless, it is possible that a forthright Christian faith may provide the only setting in which what Rogers desires may be achieved, and that what is really required is "a thorough-going and detailed implementation" of Christian theology. On the one hand, Christianity would seem closer to the "major trend" in counseling than to this "minor trend." It, too, is inclined to believe that the deepest wisdom for the individual is not to be found in the injunction, "know thyself." With the "major trend" in counseling, Christianity doubts the ability of the individual to arrive at true self-knowledge through his own unaided efforts. This Christianity knows as the problem of sin that "corruption of Adam, whereby man is very far gone from original righteousness, and of his own nature inclined to evil,

83

and that continually," so that "he cannot turn and prepare himself, by his own natural strength and works, to faith and calling upon God," and has "no power to do good works."

Thus, Christianity seems to be in a position to defend and maintain the legitimate insights and knowledge of human nature which have come from this "major trend" in the field of counseling. On the other hand, Christianity does not stand in the danger in which Rogers rightly feels this "major trend" is involved, and which what he calls the "minor trend" seeks to avoid. For Christianity, the individual does not derive his value, or status as a person, from what he is in himself, but from the evaluation which God has placed upon him, and from His concern for the individual which sends Him seeking into the far corners of the earth, and causes Him to make even "the descent into hell" of which the ancient creed speaks.

II

Christianity likewise has a contribution to make at the point at which counseling considers the nature of the adjustment which it seeks to make in the life of the unhappy counselee.

This problem appears continually in counseling literature; but it, too, appears in sharp form in Rogers' article. There he declares that the counselor must always decide "whether certain areas of conflict should be resolved or left untouched." "When an individual has undergone the degree and kind of therapy which is best for his type of personality as objectively measured and determined, and has moved as far as is judged wise in the direction of those values and goals which the professional group regards as constituting sound mental hygiene, then the maximal amount of mental health is thought to have been achieved by this individual," he writes. A similar point of view is succinctly stated in Ina May Greer's review (December, 1950, issue of PASTORAL PSYCHOLOGY of Lowrey's *Psychiatry for Social Workers*.) It seems to her, she writes, that one of the most impressive contributions of the book is the author's "just emphasis upon the facts that each individual has his own limitations beyond which he cannot hope to go, that no matter how sick he is, he has his own assets, and that those of us who attempt to help him are not licensed to upset an existing equilibrium, wry and unhappy though it be, unless we are certain that we can offer, or help him find, a better and a more productive one."

It must be pointed out that this is the point of view of that "major trend" which Rogers is calling into question. He himself prefers to operate on the assumption that "there is no such concept as 'normative health.'" This probably will allow him to avoid the difficulty that the "major trend" may lend itself to a premature classification of individuals into personality types which is as repugnant to the spirit of democracy as was the medieval classification into "orders" capable of differing levels of spiritual attainment.

By adopting no concept of "normative health" other than that which is suitable to the individual, however, Rogers does not succeed in removing a further difficulty which must not be overlooked. Both "major trend" and "minor trend" seem to be lost in an intolerable relativism. What, precisely, is the limit of achievement open to this individual? When has he obtained the optimum adjustment of which he is capable? Is it better to employ brief therapy, and allow the individual to live happily with his neurosis? Or to use the lengthy and elaborate techniques of the deep therapy required for a total reconstruction of the entire personality? In brief, what is the final reality to which the individual must make adjustment? Is it himself; and shall we say that if the homosexual is living happily in his little homosexual community, this is the most for which we have the right to hope for him? Is it his society; and shall we say that if the individual is living without tension in a totalitarian state, this is the most for which we have the right to hope for him? Or will this tendency lead, as Huxley once feared, to that type of society in which one man reads Shakespeare for the entire culture, while the rest live in a thrilling, "sensate," antiseptic state of euphoria?

If Rogers is right in pressing home his point against the "major trend," then we are also right in pressing home this other point against the relativism implicit in both the "major trend" and the "minor trend."

It is the contention of Christianity that the final reality to which man must "adjust" is God. It may not be the obligation of the practicing clinician to press this home upon the suffering individual. He may feel it better to leave the individual with a mild neurosis, rather than confront him, for example, with what Christianity takes to be the truth that "God hath made of one all nations of men for to dwell on the face of the earth," and to insist that he is not "healthy" until he has come to terms with it. There are probably few counselors who would look upon racial prejudice as a "desirable neurosis" in which the patient might be safely left. Nevertheless, it would seem unsatisfactory, from the point of view of Christianity, to be content solely with "those values and goals which the professional group regards as constituting sound mental hygiene." How are these goals and values to be determined? Are they merely the consensus of the society as constituted at the moment? If "the righteous are sold for silver, and the needy for a pair of shoes," is Amos a prophet, or a neurotic who must be adjusted? If this particular society, and its consensus regarding goals and values, is perverse and not in accord with the goals and values of "true humanity," how are these "true values" to be determined?

The "major trend" of counseling would seem to be lost in a cultural relativism; the "minor trend," in an individual relativism. Christianity can be content with neither. It must not lose sight of this concrete, suffering individual whom counseling has rediscovered for it. But it must not lose sight, either, of its God whose nature is demand.

III

This leads inevitably to a third area in which Christianity questions counseling; the nature of the *counselor*. There seems to be no general agreement on this matter within the field of counseling itself. At one extreme, the counselor is pictured as little more than a mirror, accurately reflecting to the counselee the state of his own psychic life. At the other, the counselor is pictured—as Rogers suggests in his description of the "major trend"—as the active agent by whom the one seeking help is passively molded. Clustered in the middle are the vast majority of theories which suggest, with varying emphases, that trouble has arisen for the individual, as Sherrill put it in his book, *Guilt and Redemption,* "out of dynamic but malignant human relationships, and [may] be relieved by entering another dynamic but controlled relationship with a suitable person who is the therapist."

Generally, counseling has recognized the fundamental soundness of this description of the healing process and has gone to great lengths to make certain that the therapist is, in fact, a "suitable person." It is common practice for the analyst himself to experience analysis before he is considered competent to engage in healing. This is for a deeper reason than that he should have this experience in common with his counselee. Both Freud and Jung, as well as counselors and analysts ever since, have laid great emphasis upon the strain to which the counselor is subjected in the counseling process. He must understand himself at the deepest level of his being if he is not to be overwhelmed as a person by what the counselee puts upon him, and asks of him. Sherrill, indeed, goes so far as to suggest that the counselor must be pure, objective, or "agape" love. This is not to be understood as an "Olympian" detachment, but as an active love which can walk through the deepest kind of hell with the suffering individual, and remain unscathed by the experience, though not unaffected by it.

It surely need not be pointed out that understanding, and self-understanding in particular, will be a tremendous asset for the one from whom so much is required. Further, there are undoubtedly techniques by which an approach to this necessary status may be achieved.

Nevertheless, it must be asked whether the human personality is indeed capable of what counseling seems to ask of him. It has been the conviction of Christianity that, in this universe, God Himself is the source of agape love, and that the deepest security of the soul can be achieved only by entering into a dynamic relationship with His love. The God who is Demand is, at the same time, the God through whom the demand is satisfied. This is held to be the chief contribution of the "work" of Christ. In Him the relationship between the God of "wrath" and the God of "love" has been made plain. Thus, religion is often accused of heightening feelings of guilt, through its requirement that the individual must finally "adjust" himself to a God before whom no man living may claim to be righteous. Religion, however, is not only the source of increased tension in the life of the individual. It has profound resources for the relief of tension as well. The "evangelical experience of God" is that resource. Before Him, the soul may sing with Charles Wesley: "Make me a captive, Lord, and then I shall be free."

It is probably correct to say that religion in our own day has not been as successful in relating the individual to the love of God, as it has to His wrath. In general, emphasis on the "evangelical experience of God" has been left in the hands of a fundamentalism which sought to foster the experience apart from the realities of life. The greatest interest in the contribution that counseling has to make to the life of the soul is to be found in that form of religion loosely known as "liberal." Insofar as this has served to bring the experience of God into contact again with the realities of life, it is all to the good. But the rise of the "new theology" must serve as a warning that it is at least possible to lose the power of the Gospel in the attempt to bring religion into vital relationship with the life of modern man. Words and pigeonholes, however, are of little help or significance. What is of supreme importance is the discovery that in the evangelical experience of God the individual enters into a healing relationship with an agape love which is not achieved by man within history, however far his understanding and tech-niques may take him along the road toward it.

IV

Christianity must not turn its back upon the counseling movement. It has rediscovered for faith the concrete, suffering individual, whereas theology had produced a bloodless, vitiated abstraction. Counseling also provides an elaborate, detailed knowledge of the individual; and a variety of techniques for dealing with him. Nevertheless, in its joy that it has been brought again into contact with the person who, in the context of all his relationships, is its chief concern, religion must not be led to surrender what should properly be its own field of activity, nor to neglect its own distinctive insights and contribution.

Whether the counseling movement can be converted to Christianity is another matter. Now it is enough to say that through his relationships with the counseling movement, the pastor should be led to examine afresh the insights and resources of his own theology. He will find old dogmas brought to life, and old doctrines made vital, within a setting which will not confront him with the dilemmas and necessities which counseling seems to be increasingly facing, with little prospect of resolving them within the terms it has laid down for itself.

ROBERT ROY WRIGHT,
Editorial Board,
Abingdon Press,
Nashville, Tennessee.

A professor of pastoral theology and counseling replies:

First, it is an extremely healthy sign that the question is raised. It undoubtedly expresses the feelings of many wise and sincere ministers. I might say that these same questions are raised by most alert students in the first quarter of a basic course in counseling. Few find the answers in that quarter. The growth that Mr. Wright suggests in his last paragraph brings them out later with deeper insights. I am sure that many pastors must go through somewhat the same experience as students in a class, only they do not have the same opportunity for discussion and expression of their views.

Mr. Wright has correctly sensed the parallels between what Dr. Rogers calls "major" and "minor" trends in counseling and phenomena in religion. But he wants to hold on to the "major" trend in religion. One question comes: "Is not the evangelical Christian experience much closer to the 'minor' trend in counseling that he indicates in his article? And can this religious experience be produced by fitting a personality into a pattern presented by a theological 'major' trend?" Or to put it differently, is it true that "the letter killeth, but the spirit giveth life?"

Mr. Wright also seems to have a need to assert the ultimate authority of Christianity against what he calls the cultural relativism of counseling. As a counselor, I would ask, "What is less 'relative' than the realities of human life as experienced in the therapeutic relationship?" For a person to experience the reality which is himself in relation to another self in a relationship of understanding and acceptance, is transforming, and partakes of qualities which are far from relative. But they are expressed in dynamic rather than static terms, therefore the concepts of absolute and relative are meaningless. Here we are dealing with the image of God in man, the image from which there is no escape except through illness. We are dealing with something too profound and real to permit the counselor to make "absolute" pronouncements.

In his third point Mr. Wright expresses some doubts about the capacity of a human being, any human being, to fulfill the role of a counselor. Not perfectly, to be sure. But some persons seem to be able to give enough love and understanding to others that healing occurs. Not all of these persons are formally ordained into the Christian ministry, and not all who serve in the ministry are capable of giving the kind of love which is healing. But man, if he is not too sick, is capable of responding to love with love. This is the daily testimony of the counseling room. Through love persons find freedom to love. It does place a heavy demand on the counselor, be he secular or religious (so-called). One reason why there is so little creative change in so much of our religion is that this requirement is not met. Where, and to the extent that it *is* met, the grace of God is mediated through personality, and healing occurs.

CARROLL A. WISE,
Professor of Pastoral
Psychology and Counseling,
Garrett Biblical Institute.

Frustration as a Preparation for Life

A minister asks:

I want to raise a question for some of your editorial advisers. I ask it in a spirit of honest inquiry, not as the captious complaint of an old fogey but as the expression of a sincere desire to learn.

To begin with, let me report in somewhat condensed form a story which recently came to me. It seems that a little boy was completely upsetting a Sunday School by making himself aggressively and noisily disagreeable. A social worker who was visiting the school made some inquiries; she found that the day was the boy's sixth birthday. It was the custom of the school for a child to signalize his birthday by placing an appropriate number of pennies in the offering box while the rest of the children sang a song. But this boy did not have six pennies and so he felt frustrated and therefore tried to make everyone else as uncomfortable and unhappy as he was. The social worker went to the home, provided the boy's mother with six pennies which were given to him the next Sunday, and he took them to Sunday School and acted like a little gentleman not only then but thereafter.

Well, as a minister, my first reaction would be to seek to modify the Sunday School program so that pennies would no longer be required for recognition.

My next thought is that the little boy had gotten results by means of misbehaving; it worked. A child's mind is logical even if immature. If he gets results, he infers that the method is good. Therefore, the next time he wants to be recognized or reassured, why not raise some more Cain?

But the real question is this: how old should a person be before he can learn to handle frustration in a wholesome, socially acceptable way? And, how best can we teach him to do this?

Life, as I have lived it and observed it, is attended by many frustrations. We do not always get what we want. We do not even always get what is best for us. We are often disappointed and we are sometimes pretty emphatically defeated. The people I consider the most wholesome, the best integrated, the finest personalities, are those who have learned how to deal with failure or defeat. They have not been uniformly successful; they have known what it is to be unaccepted and unwanted; and at times they have been genuinely discouraged and depressed. But somehow they didn't stay licked. And when I think of them I question the wisdom of any policy (educational, psychological, or religious) whose chief emphasis is to try to keep people from feeling frustrated.

So I ask the experts to think about this and give us some helpful guidance. How can we prepare people to face life as it is with all its uncertainties and obstacles? How can we teach them not to blame their parents, or their teachers, or their employers, or the government, or the social order—even though some of these may be guilty—but to work out for themselves a wholesome and constructive adjustment to an imperfect world? Here, I think, lies one of the greatest opportunities for the allied forces of psychology and religion.

A specialist in childhood replies:

This question illustrates the change in our traditional evaluations of child behavior that comes with the mental health viewpoint.

The questioner assumes that the little boy's misbehavior was deliberate and intentional, and hence the social worker's provision of pennies appears to be rewarding his misbehavior—making disorderly action pay. But the mental health interpretation is that the little boy felt isolated, unhappy, and disturbed, and his misbehavior was a symptomatic expression of the feelings from which he was suffering.

Given the six pennies he was able to belong, to meet the requirements of the group, to feel accepted, and able to meet life situations adequately.

The real question is then posed—how old should a person be

before he can learn to handle frustration in a wholesome, socially acceptable way? And, how best to teach him to do this?

Children who have not been unnecessarily denied or frustrated *as children* gain confidence in the world, learn to trust people, and retain their courage and thereby develop competence for living as adults. When a child meets with a situation he cannot manage he may exhibit various forms of behavior that look as if he were trying to be "bad" or troublesome, but which usually are the only way he can carry the load of disappointment, of anxiety, or of guilt he feels.

The child is strengthened to meet the inevitable frustrations of later living by being given warm, cherishing care, indulgence if you please, so that as a child he won't be prematurely exposed to too heavy burdens. The adults who are the troublesome, disorderly irresponsibles are usually those who in childhood were denied what as children they legitimately should have had—who were not permitted to be children, to feel as a child, but were sternly disciplined and deprived to teach them a lesson, or were expected to exhibit a stoical acceptance of whatever happened.

This is the traditional policy of "catch them young and treat them rough," and is supposed to be good for the character. But with more understanding of child growth and personality development, it seems more desirable to provide a warm, cherishing child rearing, helping the child to face life courageously, with confidence in himself and faith in human beings, so that he will be able increasingly to meet the demands and limitations of living as they are encountered in adult life.

LAWRENCE K. FRANK,
Social Scientist,
New York City.

A psychologist replies:

Success or failure in meeting "defeat" is mainly determined by the attitude of a person *toward himself*. If, in the face of adversity, we keep our self-respect, we will learn from our experiences, but they will not crush us. If, on the other hand, we have a low opinion of ourselves and are guilt-ridden, even minor misfortunes can be the occasion for the release of such powerful self-criticism, anxiety, anger, or depression that we may "go to pieces" completely. The crux of the problem in the training of children does not, therefore, lie either in artificially protecting them from or exposing them to "frustration." The more basic task is to help the child move steadily in the direction of personal consistency, integrity, and mature selfhood. If we succeed in this undertaking, the child, with but a minimum of specific guidance from us, will assimilate his "defeats" and be strengthened rather than weakened thereby.

Rosenzweig and others have noted that the "frustration tolerance" of mentally healthy personalities is high, and that for neurotic and psychotic individuals it is low. Two schools of thought have understandably arisen regarding the question as to how to help children grow up with *high* frustration tolerance. One school—represented, perhaps, by the social worker in the example—has held that many of us, children and adults alike, have more frustration than is good for us and that mental hygiene should be directed toward softening our experiences. The other position—suggested by the author of the question—holds that frustration is unavoidable and that the sooner we learn to deal with it, the better.

One resolution of the dilemma posed by these two points of view would take the form of a compromise: True, children must learn to meet and manage misfortunes; but it is the responsibility of parents and other adults to see to it that the frustrations and conflicts children encounter are within the range of their competence at any given stage of development. There is far more to the problem than mere correct "dosage" of frustration at any given age level. Psychological resiliency, regardless of age, is mainly determined by the individual's self-regarding attitudes (or, in psychoanalytic terminology, by the nature of the relationship prevailing between ego and superego).

But in thus resolving a dilemma, we have begged the question. Granted that honest and justifiable self-esteem (ego-superego harmony) is the best fortifier against the ravages of frustration, how, then, do we help children grow in this quality? The answer is almost as broad and as deep as life itself; and no epigram, however incisive, can encompass more than a fragment of the total

94

truth. But there is one consideration which is particularly relevant here.

The social worker's position gains its principal justification not so much from the fact that she *removed* the frustration underlying the boy's aggressive behavior, as from the fact that she took the trouble to *understand his problems.* For an intelligent inquiry into the *causes* of disturbed or disturbing conduct there can be no adequate substitute. At the same time there are circumstances when understanding, like love, is not enough. Discipline has its place in the rearing of children, no less than reason and reasonableness; and every good parent knows this intuitively, however confused he or she may be by modern psychiatric or psychological theories.

One of the great lessons which modern psychotherapy has taught us is that human behavior can often be modified, almost miraculously, merely by helping people become *aware* of their wishes and motives. There has been a very natural tendency to generalize this finding and to assume that mere awareness-of-self is the answer to *all* problems of change, of growth, of education. But such generalization is unwarranted. Psychotherapy, while uniquely potent in the neuroses, is relatively ineffective in treating antisocial personalities, and it likewise fails to provide a comprehensive model for child-training. There are occasions when children must become *aware of others,* as well as of themselves; and to this end understanding must sometimes be supplemented by force. The fact that the psychotherapist is not ordinarily in a position to exert much force with his patients, and properly limits himself to interpretations which are designed to help patients gain insight into their difficulties, should not be taken as indicating that psychotherapy provides a model for *all* educational operations. Psychotherapy is a specialized form of education, but the whole should not be patterned after a part.

Nor should we feel that the force which must sometimes be displayed by parents and others is necessary only in a purely negative sense. As we now know from the study of identification, children gain much of their own "strength of character" from their parents; and they do this only if parents consistently display both reason *and* responsibility, understanding *and* authority

95

in their relationship with their children. Reason without force is as destructive in its own way as is force without reason. Here, as in many other life circumstances, moderation and balance are our best mottoes.

O. HOBART MOWRER, Ph.D.,
Professor of Psychology,
University of Illinois.

A psychoanalyst replies:

I do not think that children should be brought up with the sense of renunciation as far as basic human claims are concerned. The boy was naturally deeply hurt and I feel that the only way of handling it is to change the procedure and to tell the boy that his reaction is basically all right, except that it should be expressed in a more adequate and mature way.

The idea that by giving in to him he is taught always to try to get his way seems to miss the essential point, namely, the difference between those demands which are, as it were, part of the inalienable rights of man and those other demands which are egocentric demands. It seems to me that the boy's reaction very clearly falls under the first category.

ERICH FROMM, Ph.D.,
Member of the Faculty,
William Alanson White Institute of Psychiatry.

A minister-teacher replies:

The capacity of an individual for dealing with frustration depends upon the degree of his inner stability and upon the weight his total organism attaches to a particular frustration. Hence, frustrations which one person can successfully cope with may be highly injurious to another; and an obstacle which seems trivial to an observer could, for emotional reasons, be especially intolerable to the individual concerned.

In general, the way to help children handle inescapable restrictions is to reduce *emotional* frustrations to a minimum. Even severe physical and mental limitations can be incorporated into a framework for creative activity if the individual is not blocked emotionally. There is an important distinction between helping

96

a child adapt to group patterns and imposing upon him the pressures of adult will-to-power. Often what makes a genuinely necessary restriction maddening to a child is that it is accompanied by domineering and angry attitudes. Reasonable restrictions which are maintained matter-of-factly and with accompanying affection tend to enhance security, not frustration.

If the basic cause of general frustration (such as lack of adequate affection or security) can be removed, then a reaction of "raising Cain" will not be endlessly repeated. An attempt to put a stop to disorder by getting the child to stifle his resentment is likely to be futile or harmful or both. Except for the momentary purpose of protecting the rights and interests of others, the "presenting symptom" (raising Cain) should not be dealt with by coercion or by censure. And the only permanent way to remove it is to get at the cause.

A reaction on the part of a child which is not "socially acceptable" in *some* connotations of the latter term may nevertheless be more favorable than unfavorable so far as mental health is concerned. For it may show that the child is alive and kicking, instead of withdrawing or capitulating, in the face of quite difficult circumstances.

It is impossible to generalize about the limitations people should learn to accept. For a victim of cerebral palsy or poliomyelitis, where is the line between a realistic adjustment (which avoids fruitless bitterness) and a continual search for maximum accomplishment (which avoids an unnecessarily severe degree of invalidism)?

So far as mental health is concerned, people can "get sick" in either direction; i.e., from inability to cope with unavoidable limitations, *or* from being hemmed in by emotional and other restrictions which they cannot break through. Any person may encounter circumstances to which he cannot adjust; every man has his breaking point. Short of that fact, the healthiest people are those who have learned to discriminate, on the basis of self-knowledge, between unalterable and alterable limitations. Acceptance of the former and refusal to accept the latter are both signs of emotional maturity.

Psychology and religion can best help people make this sort of discrimination by releasing their (God-given) creative capacities. So far as religion is concerned, the problem is closely connected with the whole matter of unselfishness and sacrifice. Genuine unselfishness and creative sacrifice are possible only insofar as an individual has inner riches to bestow. He may be "poor" financially, or intellectually, or physically, but he is not cramped and blocked where the life of feeling is concerned. On the other hand, much that goes by the name of "unselfishness" is actually accompanied by forms of masochism and of a disguised will-to-power which *do* go hand in hand with frustration.

The author of the question seems to me to have confused two different things, both of which are relative to the individual. First, there are those disappointments and failures which can be used constructively by a person in learning his own limitations, and in learning the rights (and the cruelties) of others. Second, there are those "feelings of frustration" which are a sign of destructive inner conflict, which may be remediable, and which certainly should not be allowed to remain if they can be removed. Harm results when the latter are confused with the former, and counseling is sometimes the only means whereby a person can discover which is which—e.g., by actually outgrowing forms of self-sabotage that previously appeared to be classifiable under "life's inevitable disappointments and failures."

I know of no form of psychology which claims that *all* frustration can be avoided or removed. The main difference psychoanalysis makes, so far as this problem is concerned, is between meeting residual frustrations with a relatively full access to one's capacities for feeling and insight, as contrasted with having to meet them with a personality which, because of emotional blockages, cannot use its own resources freely and flexibly.

DAVID E. ROBERTS,
Late Professor of Philosophy of Religion,
Union Theological Seminary,
New York City.

Limits of Permissiveness

A minister asks:

In the pages of your excellent magazine we are reminded again and again that the pastor is not to condemn his flock, that he is to be "permissive" in his relationship to them; that for the sake of their mental health he is not to be obviously shocked by their actions. In general, I agree with this instruction given by nearly every one of your authors. I realize that if a person feels that his pastor will condemn him, he is not likely to come to him for help.

The question that I want to raise in this regard is this: How far are we to carry this non-judging attitude? Are we to be so permissive in our pastoral relationships that we refuse in any way to rebuke acts and attitudes that are evil?

A situation has arisen in a nearby community which I think illustrates the problem very well. I have these facts from a highly respected Christian leader in that town. A young professional man, a leader in church and youth work in the community, came home to his pregnant wife one evening and flatly announced that he was through with her; he packed his bags and walked out. He forced her to get a divorce, and immediately married another young woman of the town. That woman gave birth to a baby within just a few months after the marriage. While there is no proof that the young man is the father of the child, the conclusion is almost inescapable that during his first marriage he had had adulterous relationships with this second woman, resulting in her pregnancy.

It seems to me that there are two gross sins involved here. The first is the sin of adultery. The other, which to me is equally bad, is the sin of irresponsibility to his first wife. To leave a woman when she is pregnant is a downright immoral act.

The fact is, however, that despite these two sins, the young man, as far as anyone can find out, is not in the least penitent

99

about his conduct. And the church has not rebuked him at all. He still ushers at the morning service of the church. He still leads the Boy Scout troop. Apparently his pastor has felt no desire to admonish or rebuke him for his conduct, either privately or publicly; indeed, he almost seems to be condoning the conduct by keeping him in his place of leadership in the church.

What is the pastor's duty here? Of course, he has a responsibility to the young man who has done these sinful acts, but does he not also have a responsibility for the discipline of the church? Should not church membership, and especially leadership, require a certain standard of moral and ethical conduct, or at least a broken and contrite heart and a desire to do better? What do we do as pastors with those impenitent sinners who are in the church? St. Paul flatly told the Corinthians to remove from their church a man who was practicing gross immorality and was arrogant about it. (I Cor. 5:2) Are we to do the same? Or are we to utterly refuse to judge our people?

I would greatly appreciate some help on this point.

A professor of theology replies:

The question is very well put and enables us to sharpen our understanding of "permissiveness."

The kind of attitude which the minister and the congregation have taken toward the young man in question is not "permissiveness." It is, unfortunately, an attitude which too many people identify as permissiveness. Many a poorly-trained counselor thinks of permissiveness as "letting the counselee do or think anything he wants to do or think." That is a very different idea from the true conception of permissiveness, which is "establishing an atmosphere in which the counselee will become honest about his thoughts, emotions, feelings and drives." The former situation is properly identified as relaxation of discipline. The latter situation requires consummate skill on the part of the counselor, and results only from the maintenance on his part of a firm professional discipline.

It should also be kept definitely in mind that permissiveness is a term which has reference and applicability only to the technique of counseling—a very special instance of human relations.

Unfortunately, many people want to generalize permissiveness and apply it to all sorts of situations, notably in the home, in the schoolroom, in the church, and even in society at large. The term permissiveness is a technical term, adopted to identify an atmosphere that can occur and needs to occur in a counseling situation. It is *not* an atmosphere that can occur in a home, a school, or a church because these are not counseling situations.

When the attempt is made to adapt the concept of permissiveness to a total church, what actually develops is a situation which, on close observation, proves to be dilapidated discipline. The writer of the above question senses this fact very clearly. When the concept of permissiveness is forced to do duty as a guide for parental behavior, it winds up by producing in the parent an attitude of loose concern and a tendency to abandonment of guidance of his children. Child psychology is making abundantly clear that such attitudes are destructive and not creative of personality. It is certainly obvious that permissiveness cannot be adopted as the fundamental concept for larger units of society. I should not care to continue to live in the city of Chicago if our police force and courts interpreted their functions in terms of permissiveness.

Certainly every minister needs to acquire the skill of establishing in a counseling situation that atmosphere which leads the counselee to honesty about his thoughts and emotions. Establishing that atmosphere is something very different from relaxing judgment. A counselor does not become permissive by being non-judgmental. It just isn't that easy. On the contrary, by going through the stern discipline of establishing permissiveness, the counselor—*for purposes of counseling*—becomes (in the counselee's eyes) non-judgmental. Actually the counselor is making judgments throughout every moment of an interview, but therapy requires that the counselee be unaware of this process. It is not the counselor who is non-judgmental, but the relationship between counselor and counselee which is non-judgmental.

The case we are studying raises not only the question of the types of social situation in which permissiveness is a relevant conception, but also the question of the extent to which a minister can be a counselor. In the case under review the minister

101

obviously has a duty to his congregation as a whole. He ought to restore discipline, both in the sense of identifying for his congregation and its members the expected level of behavior, and in the sense of establishing processes whereby in love a sinner is sought out and helped. It may be that in this instance the minister needs first to recover his function as the ceremonial leader of a moral community. For the time being someone else may have to counsel the young man, though his minister has the responsibility for seeing that the counseling gets under way.

Finally, I trust that on the pages of PASTORAL PSYCHOLOGY it has never been said that a pastor is not to condemn his flock. I know that over and over again it has been said that condemnation *of a person* has absolutely no place in pastoral counseling —and with that I agree. But I would not care to belong to the flock whose leader was not willing to condemn—albeit I do appreciate those ministers who are always able to do it by saying "I will show you a far better way," and then make good on their promise, so that a better way continually condemns my lesser ways.

W. B. BLAKEMORE,
Dean, Disciples Divinity House,
University of Chicago.

A psychiatrist replies:

It is not the place of psychiatry to admonish or even advise the clergy as to the proper conduct in the discharge of their duties, whether administrative, pastoral, or, above all, sacerdotal. Your correspondent, however, is evidently in conflict over the propriety of a colleague's conduct in permitting a self-confessed adulterer to continue in his position as an usher at church services.

If there are no canons governing the disposition of such cases, it would seem appropriate for the minister, if he felt uncertain as to the proper course of action, to discuss the problem with his superior, or, in the absence of hierarchical authority, to refer the matter to the vestry or to the elders of the church.

Since the individual in question was apparently unashamed of his conduct, his continuing desire to function in a position of conspicuous leadership would seem to represent either a posture of defiance or else of denial that any act had been committed contrary to the laws of his religion or the ethics of his society. In the former case, there would seem to be no appropriate solution other than to ask for his resignation. In the latter, he might well be in a state of mental confusion of some consequence, if not, indeed, the victim of a psychosis. In any case, it would seem a charitable and appropriate pastoral act to discuss the situation with him fully, and to explore the possibility of his seeking psychiatric help.

Dr. John A. P. Millet, M.D.
Chief Psychiatrist,
American Rehabilitation Committee,

Tension and the Spiritual Life

A minister asks:

Any idealistic pattern of life must involve stress and inner tensions. Is the new psychology an endeavor to free the individual (or the "patient" or "client," if you prefer these terms) from such inner tensions by making and keeping life "non-directive"— in other words, not subject to the stresses and strains of imposed external authority?

Religion, as I understand it, sets a well-defined and somewhat rigid pattern. The Christian religion, for instance, is inescapably centered in the life and teaching of Jesus Christ, involving self-denial and surrender to a higher will.

Such a life pattern may be compared to a bothersome toothache; but if to cure the toothache we must get rid of our teeth, then what? What other values will go out with them?

A psychologist replies:

This minister's analogy of the aching tooth being equated with tension in psychological life—and the loss of the tooth as the alternative to the aching tooth, suggesting a tensionless but obviously unsatisfactory state of affairs—may be taken as the framework for the answer to his question.

In formulating the problem in this way the writer assumes that the only treatment of an aching tooth is its removal, and that the dentist would be satisfied to leave the mouth toothless, a condition which would naturally prevent the proper intake of food and would thus induce a state detrimental to the health of the total organism! Were the removal of psychological tensions to result in a *psychological* organism's being incapacitated in this way, it is certainly doubtful that the procedure would find advocates.

However, it is possible to see the situation quite differently. When a tooth aches, it means that something is wrong. It calls attention to the fact that part of the body is sick. The kinds of tensions which the "new psychology" attempts to eliminate are those which detract from the general constructive progress of the individual as a whole because they drain off psychological energy.

In dentistry a bad tooth is filled, treated, or if necessary, removed, in order that it may cease to prevent proper mastication by its undue sensitivity. Thus, those unnecessary psychological tensions which have their origin in unsolved problems in the individual's past, are eradicated in order that he may move forward unimpeded toward his self-chosen goals.

It is doubtful that any life can be non-directive, but the values which the new psychology aims to make the individual free to cherish and work for (and these may include the choice, for example, of following a religious life) are values which are chosen positively by the healthy individual rather than being selected as a result of internal pressures which he himself does not understand.

The new psychology would urge prompt treatment of the tooth; that is, prompt eradicating of those psychological tensions which do not bear on the main purposes and issues of life, in order that the individual may move forward freely, and with all available energy, toward those goals which he himself has chosen as most worthy of self-dedication.

MOLLY HARROWER, Ph.D.,
Psychologist,
New York City.

A professor of religious education replies:

I wish it were possible for me to engage in conversation with the person who has asked this question, for I am not sure that I understand just what it is that he is asking. Since I cannot do that, I must attempt to clarify the nature of his question and to sort out the issues which are involved as I see them. In so doing I may be missing the point of his question.

The term "new psychology" has generally been used to refer to the approach to psychology which came into being shortly after the turn of this century. This approach was "dynamic," or more concerned with the function of the whole person than with

105

the structure of the "mind"; more with the "why" of human behavior than with the "how." Its approach was clinical rather than experimental, and it often went beyond description to therapy, and to philosophical speculation. It has included a number of "schools," so that it is hardly precise to speak of the "new psychology" in regard to a position on any single question. Psychologists are quite human. They are fallible. They are subject to biases. They often disagree among themselves. This is the first difficulty with the question. Perhaps, therefore, it would be best if I were to present my own thinking on the subject of "tension" and "conflict."

"Tension" is a term borrowed from physics to denote the state which exists when an organism is in some sort of disequilibrium. For example, hunger is a state of tension. A chemical imbalance exists in the organism due to the fact that the cells have exhausted the essential nutrients needed for the generation of energy. Unless a balance is restored, the organism will perish. A hungry person is restless (tense), tends to be preoccupied with thoughts of food, and is in a state of general discomfort. So he has a drive-to-get-food which is born of a combination of his discomfort and his experience of how food may be had; that is, his muscular system begins to be activated in specific ways. For instance, he may feel an urge to get up out of his chair, put on his hat, and go down to the restaurant.

"Conflict" is a term which refers to a *clash* between needs, or ends, or values. For example, the hungry man needs food. He also needs to be accepted by his fellow men, and he fears punishment if he breaks a law. It may be that the only food available belongs to someone else who will not share it. Shall he look further or shall he steal it? That is a "conflict."

The psychologist recognizes the inevitability of both tension and conflict. He sees that "problems"—which are occasioned by the necessity of resolving "tensions" and working through "conflicts"—are the spurs to the development of personality and character. Life itself proceeds on an alternation between tension and relaxation. In fact, pleasure comes not so much from satiation as from the act of becoming satiated. No hunger—no fun in eating. No doubt—no faith. It may not be too much of an over-

106

simplification to say that civilization, including religion, has arisen as a result of man's need to work through his conflicts, to find release from his tensions, and to deal with his anxieties in the face of life's challenge.

The psychologist is aware, too, that need which is too long unsatisfied may result in death; that conflict which is overwhelming may result in complete paralysis of human activity; and that situations which are too ambiguous may result in the breakdown of personality. It is a truism that we all have our breaking points. Martyrdom is merciful compared with brain-washing.

The psychologist also knows that some tension and some conflict is "neurotic"; that it springs from situations incorrectly perceived and from needs which are spurious. One may think he is hungry when actually he is lonesome or bored.

Therefore the counselor who is guided by the concepts of the new psychology would be concerned to help a person *clarify* the nature of his tensions and conflicts. He would seek to free him from neurotic tensions and conflicts. He would try to support him in, and, in some cases, to protect him from overwhelming situations. He would help him to discover adequate ways of dealing with them. Last of all, he would help a person live creatively with conflict. I, for one, do not belong to the "cult of non-conflict."

I do not know how any counselor could actually free a client (an individual, a patient) from tensions altogether, although he might be successful in freeing him from neurotic and non-creative tensions. The psychotherapist has not yet found a way to help the confirmed psychopath or the psychotic who has completely broken and given up. On the other hand, I doubt that any psychiatrist through counseling alone could make a tensionless psychopath or psychotic out of a healthy person.

The other issue raised by this question has to do with the nature of religion, particularly Christianity, itself. Does Christianity set a definite and rigid life pattern? There have been many who contended that it does. However, this is the legalistic or Pharisaical approach to religion, which puts the keeping of the law above all else, and which is more concerned with the letter than the spirit of the commandment. Jesus set forth principles

107

and held up values, but I cannot see that He prescribed a rigid life pattern. Furthermore, values and ideals can be as neurotic as the means for their attainment—which is to say, unrealistic and defensive in nature. It is true that commitment to particular ends cannot be separated from means, but rigidity in means may become the very thing which will defeat the ends to which one is committed. In other words, our commitment is first to ends and not to means. Rigid moralistic patterns may be a kind of Maginot Line of defense, highly vulnerable to mobile attacks, against the temptation to "sin." What is needed is a "defense in depth," which means that man has room for maneuverability away from his secure base.

Much space could be given to a discussion of whether or not Christianity demands self-denial and surrender in the sense which seems to be intended here. This would lead us into a discussion of the nature of the "self." Perhaps the best we can do here is to refer the inquirer to Bonthius' *Christian Paths to Self Acceptance* and to Roberts' *Psychotherapy and A Christian View of Man.*

PAUL B. MAVES,
Drew University Theological School,
Madison, New Jersey.

Another minister replies:

Tension is comparable to friction: it is good or bad depending on the situation. The lack of friction under the wheels of an automobile, and the excess of it in the bearings, causes the automobile to spin its wheels and burn out its bearings. As a result it is ruined and gets nowhere.

The same is true of a person who gets his tensions in the wrong places. He "spins his wheels and burns out his motor" but gets nowhere, only injuring himself. When his tensions are properly adjusted, however, he moves smoothly toward his objective.

The "new psychology" which I accept does not seek to eliminate all tension, but rather to adjust it to its rightful uses. It would be impossible to eliminate tension and maintain any semblance of a social order. Even animals are subject to some types of tension, and one would probably have to go to the lowest form of life to find it absent altogether.

I do not believe that the writer meant to imply that "self-denial

108

and surrender to a higher will" is the ultimate goal of the Christian religion. Isn't there a purpose for this? And isn't it this purpose that puts the friction under the wheels and causes the person to move rather than just to spin his wheels? Without this "dynamic" from within, a legalistic conception of Christianity could quite well cause unresolved tensions by the high standards it sets. But with this dynamic, although it causes tensions, they are of the type that helps the person move toward his goal rather than spin his wheels in one place.

Tension is good. We cannot live without it. But we cannot live *with* it if we get it in the wrong places.

Lt. Col. Wayne Hunter,
Chaplain,
United States Army.

A minister who is a pioneer in pastoral counseling replies:

Of course human living involves tensions. It will do so as long as choices have to be made. If one chooses the goals represented by the Christian faith, that choice will indeed require self-denial and surrender to a higher will, and tensions are involved in such a choice. But who wants to live the life of a vegetable, without tensions?

Non-directive counseling, however, as I understand it (although personally I cannot go all the way with the non-directive counselors), does not mean "keeping life non-directive" and so freeing the client from tensions. Human life is end-seeking, and must move in some direction in seeking its chosen ends. Non-directive counseling leans heavily upon the conviction that if, in a counseling situation, the counselee is freed from any feeling of external compulsion, the forces seeking wholeness and health will assert themselves. He will make a free choice of his own goals, unimpeded by inner neurotic compulsions. That is to say, the counseling may be non-directive, but the movement of life will not be. The Christian counselor will certainly hope that the goals chosen will be such as characterize Christian living.

Charles T. Holman,
First Baptist Church,
Albion, New York.

109

Sudden Conversion Versus Counseling

A minister writes:

One of the things that is plaguing the church at the present is the question of what has happened to the old religious concept of conversion. The concept has been seriously challenged by the new psychological theories that imply that personality change is the result of slow "growth," whether such growth is attained with or without counseling assistance.

For example, in an article in the November, 1954, issue of PASTORAL PSYCHOLOGY, Seward Hiltner reported the questions and answers in a counseling situation between "Pastor Hay" and "Jim," an adolescent who came to the counselor for guidance concerning his interest in the ministry. The immediate point in question was the "call" Jim had received; and the discussion sought to determine whether it was sudden or the result of a gradual process of growth. Let me quote from Dr. Hiltner's report of this conversation:

JIM: How did *you* know when you had the call of Christ?

HAY: It may be hard to explain fully, Jim. There wasn't any sudden flash or direct call. It was more of a growing realization of a need both within myself and in society. I saw a need for Christian witness and I had a slowly growing gnawing until I would try to do something about it. Is that what you had in mind, Jim?

JIM: Yeah, I think so. My sister, she's a Baptist, she asked me how I knew that Christ was calling me. I couldn't quite explain it to her. Well *(he trails off)*.

HAY: Well, let's see, Jim. Maybe together we can work on it. Would you say it was a quick flash or a slow growth?

JIM: It was a slow growth—and yet I'm not sure.

HAY: In other words, you have a two-way feeling as to whether

110

Christ should call in a moment, or over a period of time. Kind of split inside yourself and can't quite explain the feeling deep inside you?

JIM: Yeah, that's it all right. I feel it down here, but I can't quite explain it. *(Here Jim became silent, and was plainly wrestling with himself. This lasted for about five minutes. Then Jim plainly relaxed, but still said nothing.)*

HAY: You're working too hard, Jim.

JIM *(with a laugh):* You said it.

* * *

HAY: How did you come to decide on this church vocation business, Jim?

JIM: Four years ago in the Blank Camp, I decided I'd like to do something for God. I thought about it for a while. Then last summer I felt it again, and it has stayed with me. I really want to be a preacher. Something happened.

HAY: You might say you had a religious experience?

JIM: Yeah. It's hard to explain *(here Jim gestures several times toward his abdomen, struggles for words, and then finally stops struggling).*

HAY: Something welling up from the inside?

JIM: That's it. It's just hard to explain. *(There followed another silence of several minutes, with Jim struggling.)*

* * *

I know nothing of the science of psychiatry, but I know this is a problem for us parish ministers that needs to be set straight, and I think it might warrant a discussion. It sure needs clarification!

Jim could not give a clear answer to the conflict that he was facing, since his sister presented one side, and his minister the other, and it is not something that he can deal with from the *inside.* How is an immature high school student to deal with a matter that has a large amount of paradox in it? To interpret his five minutes of silence as a struggle is not fair. It is rather the embarrassment of inability which he did not want to show to his minister friend.

It seems to me that there is a matter of psychological condi-

111

tioning in which the "conversionists" are wiser than the "counseling" ministers.

A minister replies:

Let us focus on the problem of "instantaneous conversion" versus "growth" first. Several facts in the case of Pastor Hay and Jim indicate "growth" in the direction of the ministry as a vocation: (1) four years before in camp, a feeling that he would "like to do something for God," (2) a renewal of that feeling three years later in camp, (3) the conversations with Pastor Hay and other contacts with him. We might add that his perplexity to explain things to his sister would indicate a strong religious influence on her part.

Even with all these things pointing toward the growth idea, we have to deal with the fact that sixteen-year-old Jim had a feeling of suddenness about it all. This was something he was unable to explain. In fact he was not quite satisfied to call it either "quick flash or slow growth." He said it was both. Could it have been both?

It appears that many seeds were planted along the way, and now in Pastor Hay you have the right personal climate for them all to germinate simultaneously. This may explain some of the suddenness. Jim is overwhelmed by something that has been rather submerged up to this point.

Pastor Hay did not take sides in an issue of suddenness versus slow growth. He gave Jim ample opportunity to express himself any way he liked. (He did, however, state that his own decision came through a gestation process.)

This whole thing is like the decaying of teeth or the graying of hair. My dentist says it takes a cavity many months to develop. There is no shock until it comes to my consciousness that my tooth is in fact coming apart.

The consciousness is jolted by something that has gradually thrust itself into perception. It is like the case of Hamlet who strongly felt, as the result of many rumblings of the unconscious, that his uncle had murdered his father. But he just hadn't yet pushed the right button that gave him the *total* of all these things. The ghost of the father told him the fact and he replied,

"O my prophetic soul!" It was as if to say, "I'm just now learning what I knew all along."

Pastor Hay becomes a rather good example of what Mr. Hiltner sets out to illustrate—how we "give ourselves" in pastoral care.

I do not believe that Pastor Hay or any other counselor can avoid the paradoxes of existence; nor can he shield the teen-ager from them. It is doubtful whether he should try. It is at this point that young people need personal support in the shape of thoughtful pastoral care. Care which, in fact, will serve as their supply line while they go out and do battle with the paradoxes.

Yes, the paradox is there. It is a stone of stumbling. The pastor ought to be a ready source of strength, not to help reduce the paradox, but to give Jim enough fortitude not to let it go until it yields its blessing. There is always the possibility that Jim could take one side of the paradox and deny the other so as to escape tension. Pastor Hay made no attempt to pressure him in either direction. He waited with a "friendly silence."

I felt that the pastor was wise in not intruding into the more private part of the struggle. Obviously Jim had a lot of feelings that were not yet ripe for verbalizing. This is often the paradox from the inside—expressed viscerally.

I cannot quite accept the fact that there are a group of "conversionist" ministers as opposed to a group of "counseling" ministers. No good counselor would rule out either the "quick flash" or the "slow growth." He would be willing to accept and discuss the facts either way.

The paradoxes are best born (and in some sense, perhaps, resolved) in a fellowship. The pastor is the one who does most to manipulate the flow of the fellowship toward arid areas. He is a communications specialist, communicating himself and the fellowship to anyone in particular need standing under the bruising lashes of paradox.

My experience with teen-agers has taught me that they have inestimable resources to deal with paradox. They sometimes may need a spiritual pump-priming from pastor and church, but they do not want this to be a substitute for personal production.

MYRON C. MADDEN,
St. Charles Avenue Baptist Church,
New Orleans, Louisiana.

**Another minister replies with this thoughtful essay
on the psychology of conversion:**

One of the most hopeful elements in human nature is the capacity of people to change for the better. Men and women can rise from one level to another; they can go from a low to a high quality of life.

The reformed drunkard supplies a dramatic example of this. One day he is in the gutter, the slave of alcohol. He has no job, no money; and his wife, after a long struggle to keep the home together, has left him. But then you see this man some time later and he has become straightened out. Alcohol no longer holds him prisoner; he has a job and a little money in the bank; his wife has come back to him; he is an upright, useful citizen; he has become a changed man. And what has happened to him is a symbol of what happens to many. There are thousands who yesterday were weak, fearful, despairing, and self-centered who today are strong, courageous, hopeful, and humane. They have become changed men and women.

Our religion not only affirms the human capacity to change for the better; it summons every one of us to live out his highest capacities. On page after page in the Bible there is the urgent plea for us to change for the better, to rise to newness of life. Jesus Himself puts it this way:

"Except a man be born again, he cannot see the kingdom of God."—John 3:3.

I

To be born again—to undergo a spiritual rebirth which leaves us changed—is known in the language of religion as "conversion." Unfortunately, the word "conversion" has been brought into disrepute by certain evangelists and revivalists who have given it overtones of emotionalism, mass hysteria, and "hitting the sawdust trail." Actually, all the word itself means is "change"; and the converted person is one who has changed his way of life.

Some years ago Professor E. D. Starbuck, of California, made a very careful and comprehensive study of religious conversion,

114

and to gather material for his survey wrote to many people prominent in the religious field asking about their experiences. Some of the replies he received would have delighted the heart of Billy Graham, for they told of an overwhelming experience at a revival meeting, or in a meadow, or in a jail, or even in a saloon, which left the person a completely changed man. But the reply Dr. Starbuck got from Edward Everett Hale was very different from these, and, I think, more typical of the experience of most of us.

Edward Everett Hale wrote that there had never been any dramatic, overwhelming religious crisis in his life. He had been brought up in a Christian home; since childhood he took it as a matter of course that he was to learn as much as he could about the world and was to do what he could to relieve the needs of others; all his life he had known and respected wise and intelligent men who were religious; and in spite of occasional doubts and questionings, his own religious convictions had undergone a gradual deepening and enriching through the years. Then Dr. Hale said this:

> "A child who is early taught that he is God's child, that he may live and move and have his being in God, and that he has, therefore, infinite strength at hand for the conquering of any difficulty, will take life more easily and probably make more of it, than one who [lacks this training]."

Dr. Hale, you see, puts this whole idea of conversion in the proper perspective for us. He thinks of it in terms of a person's growth and development. To him, conversion has to do with a quality of life and with a spiritual awareness that can begin in childhood.

II

So, for a moment, let us follow the example of Edward Everett Hale, and think of conversion in terms of the developing child:

Every baby is born self-centered. The newborn infant is concerned only with his own needs and how to fulfill them, only with his own comforts and how to assure them. It is true, as the saying has it, that "a well baby is a good baby," for the simple reason that the baby who is well-fed and comfortable has nothing else to do but to be good. But suppose that baby gets hungry or uncomfortable at 2:30 in the morning. He doesn't think to himself, "Mother's worked hard all day and needs her rest, so I won't disturb her." On the contrary, he's far too self-centered for that; so he immediately starts crying and carrying on till he has been fed and made comfortable again. As the normal, well-brought-up child grows and develops, however, his horizons become broader; he learns to think of others beside himself. To use the language of religion, he becomes "converted" from his self-centeredness.

Again, the baby is born with his talents and potentialities undeveloped. The child prattling in his playpen may someday become a dedicated scientist, a far-seeing statesman, or a great humanitarian; but at the moment these potentialities are only latent. And the youngster banging with a hammer on his mother's favorite coffee-table may someday become a well-adjusted, outgoing, upright, and honest adult; but for the present those potentialities, too, are only latent. But as the normal, well-brought-up child grows and develops, his potentialities are turned into actualities; he learns to express his abilities and talents. To use the language of religion once more, he becomes "converted" from the inadequacy and ineptitude of infancy.

Once again, the baby is born with a great capacity for wonder and reverence. The utter fascination which a flower, a baby chicken, or even a brightly-colored stone can have for a child, reveals this. Of course the youngster has no idea of a divine Creator, or a supreme Designer, who has made this wonderful world of ours. But as the normal, well-brought-up child grows and develops, his natural capacity for reverence is directed into the knowledge and love of God. In the language of religion, he is "converted" from vague feelings of awe and wonder into a genuine spiritual awakening.

So, in essence, the process of growing-up is a process of conversion. The growing child is converted from self-centeredness, converted from inadequacy, and converted to an awareness of the love and power of God.

116

III

But there are many adults whose development does not follow that pattern. Their growth becomes arrested; or for one reason or another the development of their personalities goes off on a tangent.

For instance, there are grown men and women who have retained the self-centeredness of infancy. Not long ago a psychologist maintained that the "other woman" in most divorces was not some designing female, but the husband's own mother. While he was growing up she catered so much to his whims and desires that he remains self-centered and emotionally immature even after he is married and has children. And that person is never going to find happiness until he is converted from his self-centeredness, until he becomes a changed man.

Again, there are grown-ups who have never learned to express their latent abilities or talents. Perhaps there was not enough money at home so they could go to school and receive special training along the lines of their natural bent. Perhaps they got off on the wrong foot by taking a job unsuitable to them. Perhaps they've never stumbled into the hobby which can give them real satisfaction. At any rate, they go through life as failures, or near-failures, and they never find happiness until they are converted to a way of living in which they express at least some of the higher capacities that are in them.

And then, there are adults who have never developed the capacity for reverence and sense of wonder which were theirs in childhood. They have gone on year after year, taking life at its superficial face-value, remaining unaware that they live and move and have their being in God. And these people never find happiness until they have a religious awakening, until they are converted to an awareness of the spiritual foundations of life.

What is more, adulthood brings its own special problems and trials; and if we are to be happy we have to become "converted" to the wholesome and constructive way of facing them. Recurring financial difficulties were the lot of one family, and they were caused by the wife's buying sprees during which she'd run up

117

enormous charge-account bills in various stores—all for new clothes for herself. When the bills came in, there would be a scene. Her husband would tell her she was wildly extravagant, that she was jeopardizing their credit-rating and financial security; he would cajole, he would rave, he would threaten, with the result that finally the woman would burst into tears, and promise to do better. And for a while she would. But then, about the time the bills were finally paid off, she'd go off on another buying spree—all on clothes for herself—and the process would begin all over again. After every one of these episodes she was filled with guilt and remorse. She knew she had done wrong; she didn't want to hurt her husband's financial standing; she didn't want to be extravagant. But these emotions were all on the surface. Far deeper—and more powerful in determining her conduct—was the knowledge that she was becoming deaf; and with it was the fear that deafness would keep her from being attractive. Her one recourse, she felt, was to dress attractively; the only way she could keep from being depressed about her growing deafness was to get new clothes. Hence these buying sprees. It was only when she became "converted" to an acceptance of her deafness and bought a hearing aid that the buying sprees stopped.

In childhood, you see, conversion is largely a matter of growth in surroundings that are conducive to development. But in adulthood conversion is likely to be more drastic, for it involves a definite change, a transformation in our thoughts and attitudes and forms of behavior. It involves a deliberate stepping from one level of life to another.

IV

Now this conversion in adults may take place suddenly, dramatically, overwhelmingly; or it may come about gradually, slowly, imperceptibly. There is an analogy to this in falling in love. When Benjamin Disraeli married Mrs. Wyndham Lewis, the widow of his close friend, he did not love her; he married her for her money and social position. But in the atmosphere of "lasting tenderness" which she created for him during the thirty-three years of their married life, Disraeli in time became enchanted with her and devoted to her. On the other hand, at about the time that Disraeli was Prime Minister of England, Theodore Roosevelt was a student at Harvard and had met Alice Hathaway Lee, the woman who became his wife. This is what Roosevelt wrote: "I first saw her on October 18, 1878, and loved her as soon as I saw her sweet, fair young face. We spent . . . years of happiness such as rarely comes to man or woman." Disraeli fell in love slowly, gradually; but to Roosevelt the experience was sudden, cataclysmic. And so with conversion: to some it comes as a sharp break with the past; it can be likened to a river which encounters a steep cliff in its course and makes an abrupt turn. To others, conversion is more an enriching and enlarging of the past; it has a parallel in a river that grows deeper and broader as it flows toward the sea.

The essence of conversion, however, has to do not with its speed, but with its depth. In the genuinely converted person, his basic inner drives, his primordial impulses and urges have been changed. Conversion is not so much a matter of *doing* differently, as of *being* different. We can think of this in terms of a man trying to heat his house with an inferior grade of coal. No matter how much he shovels or how hard he works, he can't keep his house warm in cold weather. But then he "converts" to gas, and his house from then on is comfortable. The house is the same; the ducts and radiators are the same; even the furnace is the same. But the source of power is different.

And this is what happens to the converted personality. His appearance is the same; his talents and abilities are the same; even his temperament is the same. But because they are animated by a new power, by new attitudes and loyalties, his total life becomes very different. In the depths of his being he has become a changed man; he is born again.

WILLIAM S. HILL,
St. Peter's Episcopal Church,
Uniontown, Pennsylvania.

Heredity and Environment

A minister asks:

I am seeking a discussion which maintains that environment contributes equally with, if not more than, heredity in neurotic problems. Can you suggest articles on this topic?

To be concrete, let us suppose that a man's male forebears were all unsuccessful in matrimonial ventures—betrayed, in fact, in each instance—and accordingly this "heredity" develops in the man a fixation that marriage would be disastrous for him. What would be the proper treatment in such a case?

A clinical psychologist replies:

Your correspondent's question falls, naturally, into three parts: The matter of references for articles; the evaluation of the psychological outlook of the man with the exaggerated fear of the influence of heredity; and the question of his proper treatment.

Concerning the first, the type of article which is required will differ according to the degree of scientific background of the reader. Most valid writings on this topic are, frankly, somewhat technical. Three may be suggested, all of which may be obtained from university libraries.

1. "The Obsolete Dogmas of Heredity," by Thomas Howells, *The Psychological Review,* Volume 52, 1945, pp. 23-35.

2. The chapter on Heredity, Environment and Maturation in Munn's *Psychology,* Second Edition, published by Houghton, Mifflin Company, 1951.

3. Koffka's book, *The Growth of the Mind,* particularly the chapter on Maturation and Learning. This paragraph from the latter may be an interesting epitome of the problem.

"In any discussion of development, we are confronted with this opposition of inherited and acquired traits. Whether this opposition can be bridged, whether that which is inherited must
120

first have been acquired by our ancestors in the course of racial development, are questions which we shall leave out of our consideration. Yet this opposition is found in the development of every individual, a fact which we can only note in passing without further inquiry . . . We should have this problem clearly in mind at the beginning of our inquiry because in their development, *capacities* are controlled by laws inherent in the organism (heredity) and are very loosely dependent upon the individual's achievements (his opportunities in his environment), whereas the *abilities* of the individual are chiefly determined by his experiences and achievements."

In general, it can be said that those writers who are oriented toward a behavioristic psychology place their main emphasis upon environmental opportunities. Those who are impressed by instinctive action tend to emphasize the individual's inheritance; the Gestalt psychologists have attempted a synthesis of the two points of view.

The outlook of the man discussed by your correspondent is obviously governed by an erroneous and confused notion of what can be inherited. In the first place, he is anticipating that he will inherit specific ways of behaving, specific failures in interpersonal relationships in marriage. However, it is almost universally recognized that the acquired characteristics (that is, the specific patterns of behavior learned by one individual in his lifetime), are not transmitted to offspring. Consequently, no ways of behaving in regard to the marital partner can be inherited. The only thing that could be inherited in this situation would be a certain type of nervous system which, let us say, is particularly subject to certain types of irritation—for example, an extremely aesthetic physique with consequent fatigue and irritability. Given this physiological make-up and inherited nervous structure, the individual might be hypersensitive; and due to his hypersensitivity might have difficulty in interpersonal relationships. But this is a very different thing from assuming that a specific behavior pattern was preordained, for it is in no way inevitable that poor human relationships in marriage must result from hypersensitivity.

There is, however, a more subtle confusion exhibited here, for the writer speaks that "his male forebears were unsuccessful in matrimonial ventures." Is one to assume, therefore, that on the other side of the family, the women were successful? Or, if it is the mother and grandmother who were the betrayers, is it assumed this characteristic will be inherited by the woman with whom the man in the example contemplates marriage? The use of the word "betrayed" is in itself an interesting one, for, on the one hand, he claimed that the men were unsuccessful, and, at the same time, by the fact that they were betrayed, that it was not their fault.

However one analyzes this, one gets the general impression that the individual is seeking to disown responsibility for his own actions by claiming "hereditary" influences which have loaded the dice against him. It is probably this aspect of his personality which would come up for treatment clinically, and the degree of treatment would depend on the extent to which this attitude of shelving blame or responsibility was permanent and ingrained or only the result of a passing misunderstanding.

"Treatment" might vary all the way from simply a clarification of what can actually be inherited, to reading of straightforward scientific articles on the subject. But if this is a more deepseated character disturbance, reading of the articles would do little good; and treatment would consist of an attempt to develop in the individual sufficient strength and maturity so that he would accept the full responsibility for his own actions. In the first instance, "treatment" could obviously be undertaken by any better informed friend. But, obviously, no armchair differential diagnosis can be made at this point since such an orientation to marriage, such a need to disclaim responsibility for one's own actions, might be part of a much more seriously disturbed psychological picture.

MOLLY HARROWER, PH.D.,
Psychologist,
New York City.

A psychiatrist replies:

The days when heredity was considered all-important in determining the maladjustments (neurotic tensions) of an individual seem so far removed in the dim, distant past that it almost seems incredible there should be any difficulty finding articles which give environmental factors their due weight. However, since this seems to be the case, let me recommend two specific writings, both by myself, which I feel sure will be helpful in this question. The first is an article, "The Self Image: A Theory of the Dynamics of Behavior," to be found in the April 1952 issue of the journal *Mental Hygiene*. The second is a book, *Saints, Sinners and Psychiatry,* published in 1950 by J. B. Lippincott Co. I am sure that after reading either one or both of these, the reader might seriously question that heredity plays any role at all!

The specific illustration presented for discussion gives, in my opinion, the very essence of a neurosis, which is not some peculiar pattern of behavior, but rather an unassailable assumption which lies back of behavior and which is the root and foundation of behavior.

Back of every detail of everybody's behavior lies an assumption of some kind. Some of these assumptions are factual and realistic, and some of them are not. The important thing is seemingly not how factual and realistic they are, but how these assumptions jibe or correspond with the assumptions of the culture with which we try to identify ourselves.

The next important thing about assumptions which breed neurotic difficulties is that they are apparently unassailable, i.e., they are attitudes and beliefs that seem so completely natural and self-evident that one just takes them for granted. Even when the assumption is challenged it seems totally senseless if not downright wicked or immoral to question it or depart from it. This is due to its having been "ingrained" in the person at such an early age that no language was available for dealing with it critically; it was based on repeated, uniform experience; or, it was presented by an accepted authority (usually parents or parent substitutes) to a person who was young or who felt young; a dependent person, incapable of finding his own answers. The assumption is a post-natal acquisition and therefore cannot be hereditary.

When a person is burdened by an assumption which is greatly

out of tune with the facts and/or which is out of harmony with the assumptions of those about him who have meaning for him, he will feel troubled and neurotically ill. Assumptions that lead to neurotic illness have two components which are important: First, convictions concerning what is "right" and what is "wrong" in any given situation, which will and do clearly determine the course of behavior to be pursued; and second, what specific reward is supposed to be forthcoming for any given detail of behavior.

The problem to be dealt with in the case illustration presented, as in any neurotic problem, boils down to helping the person to: (1) see what his behavior is; (2) uncover the assumption which determines the behavior; (3) arrive at full knowledge of or insight into the source of the assumption; (4) get courage to experiment with new patterns. Insight is an indispensable part of therapy, but an equally important part is the establishment of new patterns.

Only those who have faced some of their own assumptions should try to do this healing job, for only they can have the necessary compassion for the unassailability and the strength of the assumptions of someone else. This test is also the key to an understanding heart, rather than a judgmental heart. Until we are familiar with spotting our own assumptions and dealing intelligently with them, we will be like a bull in a china shop trying to help another person with his.

The troubles of the neurotic are intensified through the guilt which always is associated with violating assumptions which have their origin in moral values—and this includes most assumptions having connotations concerning interpersonal relations; and the strength of their basic assumptions regarding the maintenance of life itself. Additionally, there is the rage, resentment, and frustrated entitlements which forever pursue the people who are blindly led by their assumptions, since the rewards are seldom up to par. If they were, the person would not be disturbed by neurotic symptoms. The need for freedom from guilt keeps people in their rigid, distorted patterns.

Despite the tremendous importance of environmental factors

in determining neurotic illness, there does appear to be a gross underrating of somatic factors in these illnesses. These somatic factors seem to be based on heredity in a sizable proportion of cases, and in a great many more cases on pre- or post-natal accidents or illnesses which, in my opinion, have not received their due attention from psychiatrists, pediatricians, educators, or parents. The problems created by this type of organic, somatic, neurological deficit, have specific earmarks and need to have much wider recognition, but such a discussion would not seem to be called for in this communication.

The pendulum swings from side to side. At one period heredity is overstressed. In the era we are passing through, environment has been overstressed. Gradually, as we gain more complete knowledge, the pendulum will shift again toward the importance of heredity, but never so far again as it was in the days when books like those about the Jukes and the Kallikaks had weight.

CAMILLA M. ANDERSON, M.D.,
Psychiatrist,
Salt Lake City, Utah.

Another psychiatrist replies:

Practically all writing in modern psychology and psychiatry stresses the fact that environment contributes more to neurotic problems than heredity. To take the example of the man whose male forebears were all unsuccessful in their matrimonial ventures—"betrayed, in fact, in each instance"—and who, accordingly, feels that marriage would be disastrous for him: in my opinion, the experiences of his forebears would have nothing to do with passing on this conclusion by way of his blood stream or his genes. Their experiences have become part of his environment in that he has heard by way of mouth what happened in each instance.

Not only has he heard what happened, but he has undoubtedly heard values put upon what has happened, and opinions. Consequently, as a result of these values and opinions which have been given, along with the information of what happened to his forebears in marriage, he has been led to feel that a similar outcome in marriage might occur to him. This is not a working out of an hereditary pattern in any sense of the word, but merely a working out of environmental attitudes upon personality.

The proper treatment in such a case would be to indicate to the man that his success in marriage depended upon his own capacity for love and understanding of women and having the credibility, both conscious and unconscious, of choosing the woman with whom he could be companionable and adaptable and with whom he could work out a happy family life.

O. SPURGEON ENGLISH, M.D.,
Department of Psychiatry,
Temple University.

Self-Love

A minister writes:

There is an element which seems to show up in most of the schools of psychology as well as in our theologies. That troublesome element was baldly stated by Dr. Wesner Fallaw in "Beyond Egoism" in an issue of PASTORAL PSYCHOLOGY. He states: "Self-love destroys, altruism creates persons anew." This statement sums up a conviction which has pervaded the Christian church since Paul. It is deeply embedded in our whole Western culture, wielding great power over our ethical-religious and psychological attitudes.

This element worries me because for years one of the hardest chores I have had to do has been to help people gain peace of mind, which has so very often been lost because the injunctions of society, often including the church, forbid one to love oneself. "Self-love" not only "destroys"—it is felt to be nasty. Yet people suffer when they feel that the person they cannot help loving is nasty.

Jesus loved Himself. His beatitudes appeal to self-interest. His adoption of the great Commandment recognized self-love as a norm to which He compared the ideal altruism. All eleven of the greater religions likewise use self-love as basic for comparison in their statements of the Golden Rule. How may I love my brethren if they are akin to me and I may not freely love myself?

A professor of psychology of religion replies:

It is very strange to find a Christian who believes that God loves him, yet he cannot love himself. If one is worth that much to God, why is he worthless to himself? Again it is contradictory to feel ethically impelled to love another person, and to omit loving oneself. There is a false disjunction here that claims *either* I love others *or* I love myself, as if one could not love both.

Actually hating oneself is equally as hateful as hating another, and loving oneself is to that extent as loving as loving anyone else.

There is a half-truth manifest in self-denial. It is the urgent imperative of justice and fair play that one should not love himself more than other selves. But to love myself less than others is equally unjust and unfair. *Selfishness is undue regard for self to the disregard of others, and this is what Christian ethics would disapprove.* But selfishness is not to be confused with self-love, as in careless or fuzzy thinking it may be. Self-love is affirmative with no denial of love to others, but rather desiring to "love others as oneself." It is, in this way, the ethical standard and emotional development by which we are able to love others.

What are the psychological roots of this reluctance to love oneself? Self-rejection arises usually from a feeling of being rejected by others. In the process of weaning; learning to stand alone; being put to bed in the dark alone; being pushed out to play and fend for oneself; sent off to school to compete with others; or displaced at home by the birth of younger siblings who take the center of parental attention—one is apt to feel left out, neglected, and unwanted. Parents may heedlessly accentuate morbid feelings of rejection by scolding, punishing, abrupt weaning, rigid toilet training, or absence-treatment on the false assumption that children need firm discipline more than comforting love. Consequently, many children grow up rejecting themselves because they feel rejected by others, and hating themselves for lack of warm affection from others.

Love and hate are emotional relationships, and how one feels toward himself reflects attitudes others show toward him. If one is scolded and punished by parents, it is natural to expect hell and damnation as a "sinner in the hands of an angry God." Conversely, if one rejects or hates himself he will be unable to accept and love other persons human or Divine. If we desire a loving society or persons capable of appreciating others, we will need to practice non-rejective affection in the family first of all. Until persons are shown how to love themselves, they will not be free to express genuine love to others. And unless we can find ourselves growing in supportive and secure relationships of lov-

128

ing one another, peace of mind as well as peace of the world is far removed from lonely, despairing self-rejection.

PAUL E. JOHNSON,
Professor of Psychology of Religion,
Boston University School of Theology.

A psychiatrist answers:

I have been pondering the query which one of your ministers addressed to you. He has a point—and a very strong one.

However, the question as it is frequently put, is set off in an entirely false psychological light.

To consider self-love as *the* thing that interferes with altruism means to take the etymological meaning of the terms only, and too literally at that.

Your correspondent is perfectly right when he points out that Jesus—and, therefore, Christian doctrine—far from rejecting self-love, does even underscore its fundamental value.

Yet there is considerable confusion on the subject between modern psychology and traditional religious thinking. This confusion stems from many sources.

Thus, the term self-love is frequently used as a popularized version of what is known as narcissism. The term carries with it an overtone of opprobrium, and it is also supposed to be something not quite normal. All this is wrong (entirely) from the standpoint of true human psychology. Without self-love, and without fear of death, we would walk under any taxi or streetcar or train, for there would be no fear of death to deter us and no love of our own self which would prompt us to preserve our own life, or avoid suffering. Psychologically, in other words, self-love and fear of death are not only normal but truly necessary; they are psychobiological prerequisites for self-preservation and survival. Both Christian doctrine and the findings of psychology agree on this point. However, they stop here for a moment only and then each one goes its own way. The psychologist knows that *in addition* to the energies which are used to maintain one's own life and self in the broader and deeper sense, there always are energies which are turned toward the outside world, to

129

objects outside the person himself. These produce the normal love for others, for things, animals, and people. The love of other people (outside one's own self) is called altruism. It is when these energies, instead of turning toward others, turn back on one's own self, that a peculiar type of self-love develops—a kind of self-centeredness, self-adulation, self-admiration, as if one is *in love* with one's own self. This is not self-love in the ordinary sense of the word; modern psychology invented a special term for it: *narcissism*. It is erroneous to use the term self-love to mean narcissism.

Narcissism is no more self-love than altruism is exclusively self-sacrifice. The mistake frequently made in this connection is to equate (silently and ever so imperceptibly) altruism with self-sacrifice, a sort of specializing in martyrdom.

It is rather remarkable, and very significant, that altruism in the highest religious sense, and altruism in the sense of being most normal psychologically, mean one and the same thing: love of others, the ability to put one's self in the place of others, which means to do unto others only what one would wish to be done unto one's self—or, as the more frequently used negative form puts it, not to do unto others what one would not want to be done unto one's self.

The point then in the whole discussion is this: self-love ought not to be confused with narcissism, and altruism ought not be confused with masochism, true self-sacrifice with martyrdom, joy of living with sinful self-indulgence.

GREGORY ZILBOORG, M.D.,
Prof. of Clinical Psychiatry,
New York Medical College.

Prevention Versus Treatment

A minister asks:

It seems to me that in much counseling and related work we deal with symptoms and treat results, rather than really coming to grips with basic and underlying causes. Counseling is important; but isn't there some way in which we can at the same time do a little preventive work? Must we allow most cases to become clinical before we notice them?

As I see it, many of our mental ills are a result of our society—hence we need to restructure and re-educate society if we are to get at basic causes. Or is this not so? Instead, is the difficulty within the nature of man himself?

A psychiatrist replies:

This inquiry is really much more complicated than it looks; it involves at least five questions, perhaps more.

Let us take the first sentence. The inquirer observes that in counseling we deal with symptoms rather than coming to grips with underlying causes. The rest of the paragraph seems to imply that he regards this as "bad," or at least not so good. I don't agree with him. It is precisely for this that counseling is valuable, or at least this is one of the things for which counseling is valuable. If a tourist gets off the road and appeals for help, the remedy needed in the counseling is a simple matter of direction. It isn't necessary to go into the underlying causes, which may be that he didn't look at the map, or that he didn't listen to the previous direction giver, or that his speedometer is not registering correctly. The symptom is that he is off the road and needs to be told where the right road is, and that's all. Leave the speedometer adjustment or hearing-aid adjustment to the technical mechanics.

Indeed, it is just this tendency on the part of the clergyman

131

to feel that he has a responsibility for "coming to grips with underlying causes" that alarms some psychiatrists who feel that the interest of the clergy in psychiatry tends to encourage them to get out of their depth in just such explorations.

In the next sentence the inquirer changes his tune, so to speak, and wonders about the possibility of not only some curative but some "preventive" work. I am not sure just what he means there; it is my impression that his daily and weekly ministrations to his parishioners constitute a very important form of preventive work, and good counseling would certainly include some other and more specific types of prevention.

What he means by the next question, I don't know. A case isn't a case until it becomes clinical, strictly speaking, so the answer is "Yes." As for re-educating society, no one objects; indeed we are all in favor of it, but the question is how? The difficulty is indeed within the nature of man.

KARL A. MENNINGER, M.D.,
The Menninger Foundation,
Topeka, Kansas.

Another psychiatrist replies:

Prevention is certainly a purpose which deserves more attention than it generally has been receiving. The minister in particular is in a unique position to help because he has the opportunity of visiting homes and observing the difficulties of his parishioners before they have become "clinical." PASTORAL PSYCHOLOGY tries to serve an increasing need of American ministers to learn more about what such help requires.

The parable of the two sons (Matthew XXI, 28-31) makes the essential point that spontaneous performance is better than deliberate or enforced virtue, although the former may be completely ineffectual. Psychoanalysis has taken us further; it has made us much more aware of the amount of self-deception which exists among people who seem healthy in body and mind. The very excellency of healthy behavior may be the preliminary to a "breakdown," an emergence of infantile attitudes which had been concealed behind the healthy front. Such deceptive health can be discovered by a sensitive observer and enable him to do

132

something directly or indirectly to alleviate the underlying anxiety.

The Council for Clinical Training, for example—and psychological examinations of candidates for the ministry—are intended to sharpen the perceptiveness of the ministers by making them conscious of their own rigidities, as well as of those in their parishioners and colleagues. Through individual counsel and through sermons, the minister has an unequaled opportunity for effective prevention.

The questioner, in line with many humanistic sociologists, seems to jump to the conclusion that the causes of illness could be eliminated by "restructuring and re-educating society" to make it fit "basic human nature." This call for the man-made millennium overlooks the fact that the neurotic, psychotic, and psychosomatic patients have grown up in the same society as their healthy brothers and sisters. The individual maladjustment results from a complex interplay between the individual constitution and many environmental factors: personalities of parents, position in the family, economic conditions, etc. Social values and structures take part in it, but as material modified and edited by the family situation. Only the elimination of individuality as envisaged by Aldous Huxley (*Brave New World*) would approach the conditions of a "healthy society," allowing escape from pain. This world, however, would be a completely static, mechanical world, and even if possible, hardly one to be desired.

The mechanistic era of science has left us all with varying degrees of confusion regarding "means" and "ends." The materialist expects that an ideal state of health could be based on integrated social, economic and health services in which all individual material needs would be taken care of by proper "social engineering," that happiness and health would be identical with psychosomatic mechanics. Actually, if this side alone is considered, unhealth is likely to result as much from enforced subordination under any social program as from present economic deprivations. Psychosomatic medicine is constantly increasing the evidence that although man cannot live without bread, he still can digest it only when certain individual needs are fulfilled which defy "restructuring of society." As Freud once remarked

133

to one of his earliest Christian disciples: "Men always knew that they had a spiritual side; it was up to me to remind them that they have an instinctual side, too." Freud succeeded so well that many of his followers now emphasize the cultural and personal needs of man which transcend the sphere of biological needs and their cultural distortions.

The present impatience with our society originates from the fact that people have at all times relied for psychological security on the cultural order of their society. In old and stable cultures spiritual concepts, socioeconomic structures, and biological selection have achieved social orders in which dilemmas between "religion," "science," and "material needs" do not exist; such results have been the outcome of spontaneous historical growth, not of conscious planning. In contemporary Western culture the component parts have become independent from each other.

No parent can avoid influencing his children by his personal selection of inherited and newly acquired values, many of them equally defensible on rational grounds. In this confusing situation it is only natural to look for a solution by manipulating what seems most practical: the material side of society. This faith, however, is a revival of magic thinking, as constructive as the wearing of charm bracelets. The present transitional period is undeniably a very trying one for people with a sense of responsibility; but it is also a period of creative opportunity for the evolution of a new culture in which humanity may become able to rest for a while. Which form this new culture will have spiritually, economically, and sociologically, nobody can foresee with any certainty. To invent an "ideal solution" and impose it on the people by legislation would be the only way to end the present period of uncertainty. As long as opinions differ as much as they do among various religious, humanistic and materialistic solutions, totalitarianism would be the only way of having a "good society"—at the price of liquidating all those who would react with illness to the new order!

From my experience in psychotherapy I would conclude that such sacrifice of individual freedom and of transcendent faith is not a necessary condition for health. Religious faith can support a life without anxiety. True enough, neither ministers nor psychiatrists help everybody, but can any human solution be perfect in this world? Can we be sure enough of any "truth" to force it upon our fellow men as long as health can be found in our individual souls?

GOTTHARD BOOTH, M.D.,
Associate of the Seminar on Religion and Health,
Columbia University,
New York City.

A professor of philosophy replies:

Since personality is built around a biological base through a process of social interaction, we need to attack problems at both the individual and social poles. Neither is more important than the other, since the two are interdependent. We can, if we wish, "come to grips with basic and underlying issues" in either sphere, and we will, if we are wise, notice and deal with tensions and blockages as early as they can be detected.

The task of counseling is not merely that of fitting individuals into society as it now is, but to liberate individuals to perform the creative task of reconstruction which is equally vital to the health of the individual and to society.

CHARLES MORRIS, Ph.D.,
The University of Chicago.

A social scientist replies:

As this question indicates, we are increasingly recognizing that the individual personality arises in and from our cultural traditions, the beliefs and assumptions about nature and human nature that we use to make life orderly and meaningful. And increasingly we are realizing that so many of the difficulties and conflicts, the antisocial and self-defeating conduct of individuals, are efforts to live with the incongruities and discrepancies, the often irreconcilable conflicts in our traditions.

This becomes clear when we recall how we have for generations taught our children that they are wicked and sinful (or fallen from grace), evil and perverse, making them feel worthless and inadequate, and at the same time have expected them to live up to our high ethical aspirations. By these teachings we

135

not only rob them of confidence in themselves and trust in people, but we give them an image of the self that is directly in conflict with their own aspirations.

If we are to "restructure and re-educate society," as suggested, then we should look critically at our beliefs and assumptions, especially our conceptions of human nature, as contributing to, if not generating, the personality problems we wish to prevent.

LAWRENCE K. FRANK,
New York City.

A psychologist (with ministerial training and experience) answers:

The questioner is correct in his implication that much counseling and psychotherapy deal with symptoms. Sometimes the relieving of symptoms is all that can be done for the person in need. But it is obvious that whenever possible—and it will be to some extent possible in the majority of cases—good counseling and psychotherapy, on their respective levels, should be aimed toward aiding the person make a change in his character pattern. This does not at all necessarily mean a total change. Obviously in most cases the change may be very slight. But whatever change does occur will help him to obviate the occurrence of his particular problem when next it might appear, rather than merely being relieved of his difficulty at the present time. To some slight extent character change is always part and parcel of the experience of real insight into oneself.

It is true, likewise, that the high incidence of emotional difficulties and adaptive problems in our society are related to the fact that our culture is in the process of traumatic change. This correlation of the individual's difficulty of integration with basic cultural change is true generally through history—for particular examples, the first century B.C. in Hellenistic culture, the time of Augustine and the fall of Rome, the last centuries of the Middle Ages, as well as our own period. But the questioner also seems to me to imply an oversimplification of the problem. Certainly we need to work energetically for social change, but there seems little doubt that Western society will not emerge from its present trauma for several decades. In the meantime we simply have to do our best for the increase of emotional clarification, not only for the sake of individual happiness but also as a leaven in the loaf of society. If we try to do too much either in helping people or changing our society, the chances are we shall accomplish less than when our aims are more modest, and we realize that real change—or growth—always takes a long time.

ROLLO MAY,
Consulting Psychologist, New York City.

SECTION THREE

Pastoral Psychology
In The Total Ministry

how may he be effective without endangering his specific role? *Discussed by:* Dr. R. H. Felix, Director, National Institute of Mental Health, U.S. Public Health Service, Washington, D. C.; Chaplain Orval H. Austin, Louisville Council of Churches, Louisville, Kentucky; and Dr. Luther E. Woodard, Coordinator of Mental Health Activities, State of New York, Department of Mental Hygiene, Albany, New York.

141

Divinity School, Durham, North Carolina; and the
Reverend James B. Ashbrook, First Baptist Church,
Granville, Ohio.

Preaching as an Opportunity
in a Rural Church

A consideration of the opportunity which the rural
minister has, through preaching, of opening doors to
the members of his parish, thus leading to the possibility for individual work which would ordinarily be
impossible in a rural setting. *Discussed by:* The Reverend William E. Hulme, Wartburg College, Waverly,
Iowa.

The Relationship of Preaching
to Pastoral Counseling

An inquiry into applying the principles of individual
counseling to the kind of preaching which would enable the minister to "speak to all conditions" of men.
Particularly emphasized is the approach of non-directive counseling and its contribution to the reduction
and elimination of guilt-inducing preaching. *Discussed
by:* The Reverend David A. MacLennan, Brick Presbyterian Church, Rochester, New York; Dr. Halford E.
Luccock, Professor Emeritus of Religion, Yale Divinity
School, New Haven, Connecticut; and the Reverend
Russell Becker, Assistant Professor of Psychology, The
College of Wooster, Wooster, Ohio.

The Pastor and His Privacy

A minister writes:

I have been asked to prepare a report by my Conference Superintendent on "The Place of the Parsonage and Its Role in the Church Life." The report will be used in classes for student ministers and young rural pastors of my denomination.

The age-old problem for young ministers—when there is no pastor's "study" in his church, and when in consequence the parsonage itself becomes a center of both social and religious activities in the community—is this: "How does one keep an open door of welcome in the parsonage, thus truly meeting the needs of the congregation—while at the same time maintaining a life of privacy for oneself and his family?"

Now my problem is this: I cannot find books or articles on the subject. There is little said on the subject in seminaries. And yet I know that there are vast practical and psychological problems involved—problems of ease of relationship, respect, and general attitude . . . along with the problem of freedom to live one's life to some extent at least. Can we have a discussion of all these points in the Consultation Clinic?

A professor of religious education replies:

Once upon a time the writer was asked to lead a seminar in a youth conference on the Christian use of leisure. He began by asking the members of the group what they did with their leisure. The first response was certainly the most horrible experience which can come to a discussion leader—*complete silence!* After what seemed ages, one young person spoke up: "We don't have any leisure!" The others agreed.

This response may or may not have been correct so far as these young people were concerned, but it is certainly the response which many an harassed pastor would give. This is especially

143

true of those pastors who serve in smaller communities, and those who live in parsonages next door to the church. Many are the pastors and pastors' wives, too, who have no place to go for privacy during their waking hours because the good people of the church seem to think that the parsonage and its equipment is theirs to use with the freedom with which they use the church building and their own homes. They come to the door (back or front) with a cheery, "Hello, I've come over to use the phone," or "to borrow your paring knives so we can get the potatoes peeled for the women's luncheon," or "to pick up the groceries we had delivered to the parsonage earlier in the day," or for any one of a dozen other reasons.

There are no doubt many values which can result from such informal and friendly "invasions" of the parsonage, but certainly privacy is not fostered. Add to the kind of thing mentioned above the many committee meetings, the informal conferences, and the conversations with the people who just drop in for a minute, and it is easy to see why many pastors might respond to questions about their private lives by saying, "We don't have any."

Insofar as this is true, it is unfortunate. Ministers and their families, like other people, need privacy. In spite of the values resulting from the parsonage being something of a center of religious and social life, the price is too great to pay if it deprives the minister and his family of privacy.

It is hardly fair, however, to suggest that the alternatives are to have the parsonage a social and religious center for the congregation with no privacy for the minister and his family; or, for the minister and his family to have their privacy, with the congregation feeling excluded from the parsonage. With a little attention given to the matter, it would seem that an adequate measure of privacy can be secured while at the same time the parsonage serves a significant function.

Perhaps the first thing to be done is for the pastor and his family to recognize that the last thing most members of a congregation really want to do is to invade the privacy of the parsonage family. Much of that which results in the "fish bowl" existence of many ministers and their families is the result of

144

friendliness and neighborliness. It becomes a problem only because no one of the individuals who stop in to use the telephone, or chat for a minute, realize how many other people do the same thing. A kindly reminder in connection with the matter will often work wonders. It is probably not wise for the pastor to voice this reminder publicly, but he is a poor pastor if he has not learned how to stimulate others in the doing of such things for him. Much can be done in this way when a new pastorate is entered upon. By suggesting that such a problem existed in a previous pastorate, and inquiring as to what might be expected in the new situation, the whole matter can be opened up for constructive consideration.

A second step which can be taken is that of leading in the providing of necessary equipment and facilities at the church. If there are a sufficient number of paring knives and pots and pans at the church, there will be less need for "invading" the parsonage for such. If there are telephones accessible to the public and rest rooms at the church, those at the parsonage will not be used so widely. And the parsonage will not have to be used so often for committee and small group meetings if comfortable facilities for such purposes are provided at the church.

A third suggestion is that the minister should, in the language of the Old West, "beat the brethren to the draw" by suggesting some place other than the parsonage for committee meetings, conferences, and the like. Some such meetings and conferences should, no doubt, be held in the parsonage, but certainly not a large number of them. The parsonage is first of all the home for the pastor and his family, and only secondarily an adjunct to the church building. Most meetings which are held in it should be on the invitation of those whose home it is, as would be the case in any other home. If others suggest the use of the parsonage and it is not convenient, or if it is done too frequently, occasional refusals for good reasons are in order. After all "Mrs. Parson" has days when she does her washing or ironing or cleaning; and at the end of them she is "dead tired," just as any other housewife is. And her being tired is as good a reason not holding a meeting in the parsonage as it is for its not being held in any other home.

Another step that can be taken in some situations is recommending that a parsonage not be located next door to the church. It is much more difficult to maintain the parsonage as a home for the pastor and his family when it is located next door to the church. It is too readily accessible to all those who come to the church. Even a few doors' distance makes a great deal of difference, and any distance beyond a block can work wonders when it comes to keeping "traffic" out of the parsonage. This should be kept in mind as new parsonages are located; the responsible leadership of a church should be advised as to the desirability of locating the parsonage at least a half block from the church, and even farther away in small communities.

On the more positive side, let it be said that the members of the congregation will not feel excluded from the parsonage (and it can still be a real center of life) if the pastor and his wife make it a practice to invite individuals and groups to the parsonage. It would be excellent if every individual in the church could be included, at least once a year, among those invited to some activity in the parsonage. In larger churches this would be practically impossible, but insofar as it could be approximated without destroying the privacy of the pastor and his family, it would be desirable. Members of the congregation should be invited to the parsonage to meet visitors, for social occasions, for prayer meetings, and the like. Open houses might be held and committees might have occasional meetings in the home of the pastor. Receptions for new members could be a yearly event. Almost all of these should be at the instigation of the pastor and his wife, however, and they should be planned and spaced carefully, neither interfering with nor destroying family life and privacy in the parsonage.

Just which of the above suggestions can be carried out in a given situation will, of course, depend upon the size of the church and other factors in the particular situation. Certainly a church of 3,000 members could not expect every member to be invited to the parsonage every year for anything other than a series of open houses, and even this might not be possible. Probably the only persons in large church situations who could expect to be invited to the parsonage with any regularity would be those in key leadership positions, and new members. Be that as it may, it would seem clear that if such suggestions as the above and others like them are followed, the privacy of the home life of the parsonage family can be protected while at the same time the parsonage serves a significant function.

MYRON TAGGART HOPPER,
Dean and Professor of Religious Education,
The College of the Bible,
Lexington, Kentucky.

A professor of pastoral care answers:

Jesus could accurately say of Himself that the foxes had holes, and the birds of the air had their nests, but the Son of Man had not where to lay His head. He was constantly on the move, and lived the life of a stranger and pilgrim on the earth. The pastor of a church can, in a sense, be said to have the same feeling. Usually the house he lives in is not his own, rarely is he at the same place long enough to have any "sure dwelling-place." This in itself lends a type of tentativeness to what he does. Further, the demands made on the pastor's time by his congregation are such that even in the short time when he is at any one given pastorate or charge, he still does not have much time alone with his family. He may be at home and "free," but his telephone quite regularly interrupts meals, breaks into private conversations, and intrudes even on family prayers. If his parsonage, manse, or rectory is near the church, it becomes a meeting place for recreational groups and church committees, and is often turned into a Sunday School annex to the church on Sunday mornings. He really has his work in the house with him.

A part of this is due to the carelessness of many pastors when they begin their relationships in a new community. Some ministers are quite inconsiderate of their families at this time. For instance, the minister who invites his official board to his home for a meal without even conferring with his wife thereby sets a pattern for others to follow: a pattern which thoroughly disregards his family's needs.

Another part of the problem arises from the lack of foresight of pastors who guide decisions on the purchase of property for the parsonage. Two extremes are evident: first, some ministers urge the people to buy property near the church, or even adjacent to it, because of the convenience. Others urge the church to buy property a great distance from the church so they will not be "bothered." Both extremes invite certain problems. A happy medium of distance seems wise.

A minister often does well to talk his problem over with his trusted leadership: the understanding thus attained will gradually communicate itself by the grapevine to a larger and larger number of people. The simplest rule is for people to visit his home on the same basis they visit each other's homes: either giving notice ahead of time, or by invitation from the pastor himself. Parishioners will usually observe this courtesy if the minister (in the beginning, in all his anxiety to be accepted by his people) did not over-react by offering elaborate invitations such as, "Just drop in any time, day or night, there is always room for one more!" or "We are *always* glad to see you, and want you to come right on in. And if we are not home, just go on in and make yourselves at home until we get there!" A little reserve at the beginning of a pastoral relationship will bring dividends in privacy later.

In addition to these precautions, the pastor can set a good example for his flock by letting it be known that he and his family set aside "a family night at home each week." This is a gentle way of telling his congregation that he is going to keep that night for his family alone, except in the most unusual circumstances. If a pastor lives under the close scrutiny of a small town all week, it does him and his family good to get in the car occasionally and go to another town for an outing. It is really refreshing to visit a strange town with one's family; to relax in a park, at a theater, a zoo, a circus, a farm-and-home exhibit, a fair—or just to eat out in a nice restaurant without being observed by the same people who stare at one as he preaches every Sunday.

Another suggestion that I have found helpful in my own home, which is also a much-visited place, is this: I have the home so arranged that a part of it can be shut off from the rest. My family can move around freely using other entrances, providing privacy for the visitors and for me, yet not disrupting their own routines at all. Every parsonage, rectory, or manse, therefore, should be built with a back passageway with such a need in mind. A minister's home should have some of the same kind of planning that goes into the planning of a doctor's home.

A minister's own personal attitude toward his home is all-indicative to his people. He should, without preaching at them, have such an innate attitude of reverence toward his home that his congregation regards it as a sanctuary of the church. Literally, the home of a pastor should inspire reverence; not, however, by being an unhappy, awesome, morgue-like place. His wife's serenity, her planning, and her organization of life have more to do with this than can be estimated. Obviously, both the pastor and his wife must avoid unloading their own private troubles, worries, and family problems on the public mind of the congregation.

The minister who writes refers to "young ministers" accurately. One of the mistakes that most young ministers tend to make is that of becoming too open and "chummy" with their people, thereby losing the certain amount of reserve and distance necessary if they are to evoke real confidence from members of the congregation.

WAYNE E. OATES,
Professor of Pastoral Care,
Southern Baptist Theological Seminary,
Louisville, Kentucky.

Faith Healing

A minister asks:

As I have studied the whole matter of spiritual therapy or faith healing, I find my most persistent question is "Why are not more of us ministers doing something significant with it in our parish ministry?" There is not a minister whom I have interviewed who does not long for some sort of technique which he can use with the sick and the dying in his church; and yet only a very few of them are willing to make an investigation of what is happening in our day through the application of prayers of faith to problems of illness.

Right in the midst of the twentieth century some ministers and laymen are being channels through which the healing power of God is flowing with miraculous effect, but I have as much trouble getting my brethren interested in such a program as I have getting some of my old-time church members concerned about a wholesome recreational program in the church for our high school youth. We are all so afraid of being thought "queer" that we will let some of our very finest workers in the church die off rather than believe that *materia medica* hasn't the last word and that God has a higher power which might be used effectively if only we would meet the conditions.

I am well aware of the fact that there are many aspects of this whole ministry of healing which raise problems for us, and I am anxious to go to the root of every problem and find what answers I can. However, in the meantime, I refuse to sit back and do nothing just because I do not know, or see, or understand all that is involved. I don't understand why electricity does what it does, but I thank God that it does it, and I mean to go right on throwing switches for my own and others' comfort and creative usefulness. I think it is right to say that we do not know all that spiritual therapy involves, but we—if we want to—can see what

150

it does and can become "ministrants" through whom it is doing wonders. I no longer call upon a sick parishioner without explaining what wonderful things are being done through spiritual therapy these days and asking permission to apply what simple principles I have thus far perceived. Without exception I have found folk responsive and not a one has told me—whatever he may have told others—that he thought I was "queer" for wanting to make available to him every device for healing known to man.

There are still some real questions with which I am struggling as I go forward in this healing work which is new to my ministry. Here are some of them:

(1) Is faith healing a "gift" which is bestowed by God to just a few, or is it a ministry available to any who will keep themselves in harmony with His laws?

(2) What sort of prayer brings healing?

(3) Do the "laying on of hands" and "anointing" have any real value in this ministry?

(4) Does the one to be healed have to believe that the process will be efficacious?

(5) Are there any sorts of disease which will not respond to spiritual therapy?

(6) Is fasting of any value when used in connection with faith healing?

(7) Why is it easier (so reported by some therapists) to effect healings among the Pentecostal church groups than the more conservative ones?

(8) What effect does the ministrant's (clergy or lay person) fall from a real fellowship with God have upon his ability to be a channel for the free-flow of healing power?

(9) Is intercessory prayer for faith healing effective across great intervening distances?

I am convinced that our best answers to these questions will not be found in the heads of men who think they know the answer, but rather in the case records of men who, believing that faith healing is possible, have gone out among the sick and the dying to put their belief into practice. I'm not interested in what anyone has to say who is not making a sincere effort to be as thorough and scientific as he can be, for I am convinced that what we have to work with in spiritual therapy is not a "setting aside of God's laws" but an application of a higher law than we have yet been able to comprehend in its entirety. It is a fallacy to say faith healing is unimportant, for there are too many people running around hale and hearty who were given up for dead to make such a surmise defensible. But we must not be satisfied to use this power without knowing more about it; and not from the standpoint of idle curiosity either, but with a view to becoming more proficient in the extending of the lives of those who are sorely needed in the building of the kingdom of God upon the earth.

A professor of Church History—a profound student of spiritual healing—replies:

I welcome the opportunity you have given me to remark on this interesting letter. I shall try to answer its nine questions.

(1) The New Testament and the Early Church recognized that the healing *charisma* was given to a fairly limited group of persons. From my observation and from the experience of the past, I should think that the healing gift is associated most often with people in whom the rational categories are rather undeveloped, and who have a closer, more direct relation to the subconscious. Long ago Origen observed that "it is the *uneducated* who do such things." I feel that, as in other instances of parapsychological phenomena, the most effective results arise with persons who have a capacity for "dissociation," and whose minds are more "fluid" than highly organized. That explains two things: why so many good faith healers are unreliable with regard to exact information, and tend to be romancers, uninterested in scientific research and statistics. It also explains why faith healing is more effectual among sectarian groups (answer to question 7). This does not prejudice the question of *sacramental* healing, which depends on different powers and methods (see question 3).

(2) The kind of prayer which brings healing of the "charismatic" kind is generally extempore. It springs more from the experience of *"being* prayed" than that of praying. One feels one is controlled by the Spirit. The subconscious finds utterance
152

in intense, often symbolic forms. Speaking with "tongues" occurs. From a rational point of view this is generally meaningless; from a religious point of view it is speech determined by the religious unconscious.

(3) Laying on of hands and unction can be used in two very different connections. As *charismatic* acts they are media through which a sort of "religious power" is transferred (this is especially true of laying on of hands). I imagine this power springs from the nervous system in some way. But what it is, who can say? We only know it is controlled by faith and belongs to our "depths." The healer experiences a power "beyond himself." He feels he is only a "channel," and he knows that conscious sin puts a barrier in its way (either his sin or the patient's).

As sacramental acts, laying on of hands and unction operate differently. The sincerity of priest and his particular moral state are not too significant. The power resides in the *tradition* (which I think of as an energy intermediate between our ideas of mind and body, i.e., "spirit" in its ancient sense. The nearest analogies are to be found in psychical phenomena). The *receptivity* of the patient is essential. He must place no conscious barrier in its way (the Roman Catholic doctrine of the *obex*). See further my article "Church Unity and the Ministry of the Sick" in *Religion in Life,* Winter, 1951.

(4) I do not think that the patient always has to believe. His faith certainly helps. What helps even more, in both kinds of healing, is his genuine *confession* of sins and his willingness to be relaxed and *receptive* (not so much actively as passively— putting no conscious blocks in the way. On this point Christian Science has some illuminating material).

(5) The evidence of Lourdes proves conclusively that no type of disease in principle is beyond religious healing. But some healers do better with some diseases than others (different *charismata*). Also, some diseases yield to such treatment better than others: e.g., psychosomatic diseases. The highest statistics for Lourdes are, I believe, for T.B. At Lourdes, I may mention, there is a blending of charismatic and sacramental powers, though the emphasis is on the latter.

(6) Fasting is of fundamental importance. This we learn from the Oriental world. But I am inclined to think it must be *rigorous* to be effectual. It would seem that such fasting makes profound physiological and psychological differences in a person, so that his relation to his subconscious becomes more direct.

(7) See my answer to question 1 above.

(8) "Real fellowship with God" on the part of the healer appears more important in charismatic healing than in sacramental. The blending of the two should, in principle, be the most effectual.

(9) Distance seems to have no effect. I should imagine that the same principles apply here as are in force with Extra Sensory Perception and other psychical phenomena. We are dealing with powers which belong to the realm of "spirit," which seem to transcend space and time. Qualifications will doubtless have to be made when we know more about these phenomena.

Let me in conclusion emphasize that all visitation of the sick should provide the *occasion* or *setting* for religious healing. But we should recognize that (a) we know very little about it, and (b) it is God who heals and not we. We can only be charismatic or sacramental *channels*. We cannot force the Holy Spirit. Hence we should never raise false hopes or pretend to be miracle-workers.

CYRIL C. RICHARDSON,
Washburn Professor of Church History,
Union Theological Seminary.

A pioneer scholar and investigator of spiritual healing replies:

Psychotherapy, if I may paraphrase a definition of social work by Richard Cabot, involves two steps: (1) To unlock and keep clear the channels of understanding within and between individuals, and (2) through these channels to favor (by action or passivity) the entrance of the spirit and bounty of God.

This definition may help us in answering the question. It stresses the importance of the interpersonal relations, the "channels of understanding," to use Dr. Cabot's phrase, and it recognizes that these include the internalized relationships with which religion is concerned. Expertness, then, has to do with these relationships and it involves understanding, i.e., comprehension of the nature of the difficulty.

Any one who works in a hospital has abundant opportunity to observe the part played by the interpersonal relationships in the healing of mind and of body. The successful physician must be able to do something more than administer drugs or remove tonsils. He must also be able to inspire faith and confidence in his patient. There are physicians who get results even though their knowledge of medicine is woefully lacking, all because they believe in themselves and their patients believe in them. For the same reason, many new treatments are effective merely because they are believed in by the physician with a faith which communicates itself to the patient.

There can thus be no question regarding the patient's frame of mind as a factor in his recovery; but this letter raises another question. How far in our attempts to help the sick is it necessary to have a true understanding of the causes of the ailment?

It was my privilege in the early twenties to be associated with Dr. Elwood Worcester in his work at Emmanuel Church in Boston. I can recall how deeply he felt on this subject. He had begun his clinical work in collaboration with the best medical support available; he and his associate, Dr. McComb, had at first made extensive use of hypnosis. As the years went on, however, he made less and less use of hypnosis and sought more and more to discover and deal with the underlying difficulties in the personal and social adjustments. And he looked with deepening misgiving at those attempts at healing which relied upon faith alone.

My own disposition is to strive first of all for true understanding of the patient and of his difficulties and to recognize that techniques of whatever sort, whether they have to do with methods of counseling, anointing with oil, laying on of hands, saying prayers or administering the sacraments, are secondary to interpersonal relationships of trust on the one side and understanding

155

on the other. I do not for a minute hold that a minister should sit back and do nothing before he has learned the current answers and acquired some recognized accreditation before he tries to practice the art of helping people out of trouble. I would only insist that he beware of trying to be a wonder worker and that he recognize that the art of listening is the basis of all true psychotherapy.

ANTON T. BOISEN,
Chaplain Emeritus,
Elgin State Hospital.

A minister writes:

The relationship of the Christian Gospel to healing of spirit, mind, and body has long had its place in the pulpit and parish work of the Fifth Avenue Presbyterian Church under the leadership of Dr. John Sutherland Bonnell. The growing interest within the congregation made a series of sermons on this theme advisable. These I gave on Wednesday evenings during the past fall and winter and centered them around the healing miracles of Jesus.

Since my emphasis was on the healing power of the *spirit* of Our Lord, it was necessary to indicate that this did not eliminate material aid, in the spirit of the Good Samaritan, to bodily suffering. One or two people professionally in the medical field regularly shared the conduct of the worship with me to counteract any impression that we were embarking on faith healing to the setting aside of sound scientific advance.

Nonetheless, the place of contagious faith, hope, and love in healing was shown to be as important as ever, if not more so. Many psychosomatic illnesses disappear steadily in the face of Christian serenity. Elimination of "hysterical" ailments is harder of achievement, though more spectacular, and cannot be accomplished apart from spiritual influences. Inducement of Christian attitudes often plays a large part in speeding recovery from organic illnesses and surgery.

In addition to showing the application of the power of the Christian spirit in one type of ailment after another, right pray-

156

ing was taught and engaged in. The more we brought spiritual force to bear upon specific situations the more we realized our need for the healing power of the risen Lord Himself if we are to know again today the miracles He wrought in the first century.

L. HUMPHREY WALZ,
Associate Minister,
Fifth Avenue Presbyterian Church,
New York, New York.

Evangelistic Calling

A minister asks:

I need advice on the subject of evangelistic calling.

Let me define more precisely what my problem seems to be. In every community there are a large number of people who do not go to church or care for it. On a minister's first call—which in my case seems to average about five minutes in length—how does he get a favorable response from such people?

By "favorable response" I mean any or all of these things. First—a friendly feeling toward the church and minister. Second—an attitude of receptiveness which will make further calling easier; and on the part of the people visited, even desirable. Third—an active desire to visit the church, its auxiliaries, or even some of its social functions; and a willingness to make use of its services. And fourth—confidence in the will of the church and the ability of its minister to "minister."

I feel that each of these points is important; I would most like to create an attitude of receptiveness, however, because I find it a near impossibility to achieve Point Three after only one or two visits.

The general reaction to evangelistic visits is courteous, but it seems to reveal a feeling on the part of those visited that the pastor is "after something": money or more members, for example. Even worse, I sometimes sense the feeling that these people believe that the minister's presence and visit is a sort of condemnation of them.

Here is a pretty accurate word-for-word report on what seems to happen in about half of my first calls:

MINISTER: "How do you do, Mrs. Jones." (Name from a friend, census report, etc.) "I am Pastor G—— from the Blank Church down the street. I have stopped by to talk about church. Do you belong to some church?"

ANSWER: "I used to." Or, "I attend once in a while." Generally this is a vague sort of reply.

MINISTER: "Do you attend church regularly?"

ANSWER: "No, but I think a person can be just as good a Christian staying at home as going to church."

Now the problem at this point is that I know a *number* of things a person misses by "staying at home." On the other hand, as soon as I start to mention them I find that my reply tends to be an argumentative one. And it is clear from my experience that arguing will never accomplish anything in this sphere.

My question is: what should I say?

A professor of religion replies:

In evangelistic calling, it seems to me, the approach should embody the same basic principles and same fundamental elements of good interpersonal relations as are involved in the techniques of "case-work," interviewing, and counseling. It should be as nonauthoritarian and permissive as possible.

The suggested phrase, "I have stopped by to talk about church," strikes me as violating about every canon of human understanding and empathy. Obviously, it puts the "addressee" immediately on the defensive and makes impossible for some time the necessary rapport.

The meaning conveyed in opening words should be that the minister comes as representative of a fellowship or community which is open, warm, and friendly. His own personality and speech should reflect a humble desire to help, to meet such needs as may be known, and to accept the individual "as is." Isn't that the role, among others, of the Minister which we find exemplified in the New Testament portrait of Jesus?

It should be kept in mind, moreover, that "church" is not a meaningful or relevant symbol for most people today and, accordingly, does not represent a "point of contact." Some areas of more immediate concern, e.g., the children, the health of the individual, or job, might be selected as a likely starting point.

Now, as for the reply, "I think a person can be just as good staying at home as going to church," this need not lead to an "argumentative" approach by the pastor. Why not make some noncommittal sound and then encourage the speaker to go on and say just why she feels that way? After all, that is a rather common opinion; but it is held for a wide variety of reasons. Maybe the speaker would be helped if she, or he, were given the opportunity to get it all out and could then see for herself that there are no particularly rational grounds for the attitude. Wouldn't it be better if a person made that discovery for herself? Better than if churchgoing were sold to her as though it were a vacuum cleaner?

The following suggestions come to me from a colleague:

(1) "Good morning, Mrs. Smith, you are one of my neighbors whom I haven't had the pleasure of meeting as yet." (Notice here that the minister has taken the trouble to find out the name of the person whom he is contacting. Furthermore, the approach centers on the person from the start.)

(2) "Good morning, one of our mutual friends has told me about you, and I do want to meet you." (There is a feeling of "rightness" in this call in that you convey the fact that a bond already exists.)

(3) "Good morning, Mrs. Smith. Your son Johnny and I have had a playground (or sidewalk) acquaintance for some time and I thought I would like to meet his parents." (Certainly you are establishing a bond here immediately and on a highly vulnerable level.)

(4) Any crisis situation which you know provides a golden opportunity to make new contacts. For example, "Good morning, Mrs. Smith, I have just learned that your husband is very ill. Is there anything I can do to help?"

(5) Children in the church school, in the choir, etc., are good entrees into families who "send their children to church." For example, "Good morning, Mrs. Smith. I am the rector of the church where Johnny sings in the choir. I thought it would be nice to meet his parents."

To sum up, *center* on the person being contacted. Try to establish a pre-existing bond. Be friendly. Do not push a program. Be interested in the person. "Love begets love."

ALDEN DREW KELLEY,
Dean, Seabury-Western Theological Seminary.

PASTORAL PSYCHOLOGY IN THE TOTAL MINISTRY

A professor of practical theology replies:

First of all, we must be concerned about those within and without the churches today who have never had a creative encounter with God through Jesus Christ. We cannot escape the necessity of bringing about this meeting. After all, this is evangelism; it is the business of so presenting the reality of the judgment and grace which are in Christ, that people, whether as individuals or in groups, will meet the Lord of Life and by consenting to Him start the great adventure of moving into the Life that is in Him.

This initial encounter must be made, and this encounter must continue. No one becomes a Christian and no one remains a Christian without this encounter. Pastors who have the shepherd's heart cannot help but be deeply concerned that persons shall meet Christ and through living faith in Him become progressively normal, as God intended them to be.

Second, if we understand this redemption process, we will make our calls upon people with the greatest of tact and the greatest of boldness. This sounds paradoxical, yet it is true. Too many of us are timid in raising the question with others about the meaning and drift of life. Perhaps that is because we have been reared in a conservative atmosphere in which religious "affections" were not openly expressed. Perhaps it may be an expression of revolt against the bold folks who go around asking people, "Are you saved?" We admire that boldness, but we question their tact.

On the other hand, the timid person who expects God to "make the contact" is to be reprimanded too. God reaches people through other people. There is no other way.

It is love for the neighbor, such as Christ had for people, which will make a pastor call upon people with great tact and great boldness. Too many of us are apologetic for the things of Christ; and too many of us are lacking in that identifying love which helps us treat a neighbor as a real person—not as a prospective church member, not as a prospective financial resource, not as one more statistic. Evangelistic calling must be *shorn* of all desire for getting "church members"; it must partake of the

161

truth and love that are in Christ, and extend it to those within and without.

But then—what happens when the pastor makes his call, with spirit right and message true . . . and finds that he has called at an inopportune time! I think it best to telephone the people upon whom calls are to be made; thus they will be prepared for the call. And the ensuing visit must be devoid of all sales talk; there should be no effort to get people to sign upon a dotted line.

The pastor must *know* the people upon whom he calls, and he must know the course he plans to follow. The process of the conversation will adhere to the rules of pastoral counseling, yet there will be no attempt to make this one visit serve the two purposes of evangelism and counseling, even though they have elements and objectives in common. It is the Christ, the reality, who is the center of conversation. The counselee is the one to make the decision and accept the responsibility for discipleship. High-pressure tactics can override people by sheer force of persuasion—and leave behind a great many questions. Much evangelism is ineffective because it is not thorough.

The pastor ought make clear on these calls that he is not the main issue, nor is it his church and organization. The main issue is the reality of God; and of man as seen in Jesus Christ. About this, persons must be clear and certain in their own minds.

The pastor making the call will greet his neighbors with "How do you do, Mr. and Mrs. Blank. I'm really happy to have the privilege of visiting with you this evening. I know it is an imposition on your time . . ."

They will then speak of several things; but in the course of the conversation the topic will eventually focus on the main purpose of the call. The major problem, remember, is not how these people stand toward the church, but how they stand toward Jesus and everything associated with Him. This is a far more realistic topic than the church!

Now if the pastor comes into a house "cold," he may be able to do some evangelistic work, but it will not very likely be effective. At best it can be a *pre*-evangelistic call. He ought to return later, after opening the subject with the persons in the home. Thus he might say after his greeting, "How are things going in this fine home of yours? I have often thought of calling here, but knowing how busy you are . . ."

After some conversation, he can say: "I've often wanted to discuss a serious matter with all of you. I mean this whole business of religion in life and in our community. I wonder if we could get together sometime to talk about Christ, the church, the world and life—perhaps one of these evenings when you're free. I shall be glad to be of service. Do you think it would be a good idea to have a small-group 'get-together' in some home or at the church to talk about these matters?"

I admit that individuals vary greatly. It may be that some persons must be confronted rather bluntly with the claims of Christ. But even in such cases, we will need to know our man and time and the condition of his soul.

Let me sum up. Evangelism is an urgent and a necessary ministry of every Christian. It is a ministry that must be done in the spirit of a certain boldness tempered with grace and tact. It must show the love borne for those on whom the pastor calls. Ministers will not be motivated by a desire to add people to the membership of the church; rather they will be motivated by a deep desire to make the reality and the claim of life in Christ plain, desirable, necessary and compelling to persons, so that all these people will want to be Christians. Relating such committed persons to the church is a *consequence* of commitment, and not an end in itself.

While my remarks may not give the pastor a variety of canned phrases or concrete approaches, my main aim has been to discuss with him the whole meaning and consequence of a call upon persons which has this as its aim: bringing them into that interactionary relationship of revelation-response, either for the first time or in a new and vital way, with Christ which "saves" persons from a false life to the true life.

E. G. HOMRIGHAUSEN,

Chairman, Department of Practical Theology,

Princeton Theological Seminary.

A Bishop answers:

These frigid home situations evident in first-time calls are baffling. Church interest has grown stale. Newcomers, as well as old-stayers-away, are frequently marked by a defensive apathy. The first visit can easily resolve itself into a short-durationed cold war.

What can you do to melt the ice? (Incidentally, a call of five minutes' length is indefensible.) Mainly, it is a matter of what you bring to the visit. What about a genuine disinterestedness?

To say, "I have stopped to talk about the church" may seem a likely thing to do. But how do you know that this person, who has never seen you before, wants to talk about the church? Why not say something like this, "We have noticed that you have moved here recently" or "We have felt for a long while that we would like to become acquainted with you." You begin from that point to manifest an interest in these people for themselves. This proves both pleasing and assuring—the best possible dissolvent of the "What does *he* want?" sort of mood.

Do you agree with the assumption that every home has a spiritual need? Religion and religious practice are indispensable to the family, where persons bring their depletions, where familiarity breeds all sorts of things, where struggle with emotional voltage seems so useless, where the threat of insecurity may be very real.

Motivated by disinterestedness, your sensibilities are alive to this home, to this family, how it lives, what it enjoys, what it needs. By indirection in conversation, the person called upon may allude to problems, ever so slightly, but nevertheless significantly. "We do not get out much in the evening. My husband prefers to stay at home." "Joey doesn't seem to get on in school." "How do you describe God to a five-year-old?"

At this and subsequent calls these ventured remarks become definite channels by which something of your ministry can flow back to the home.

Unless the people you visit develop a feeling of interest in you, a confidence in your pastoral gift, to urge church upon them will not help. Let them venture about your church.

The way to avoid an argumentative reply is not to precipitate an argument. When you ask "Do you belong to a church?" you have forced the person visited to go on record. Church for them may be a long-ago matter and it may bring a conflict into their thinking. You have created your own hurdle. "Do you attend regularly?" will impel the person visited to save face every time. People thus confronted will retreat miles from a favorable feeling about church, and you have on your hands the necessity of bringing them back all of that distance.

When you have established rapport you can then allude to the interesting things that are happening all the while within the church or in the lives of people who belong to it. You can refer to that very wonderful prayer of a little boy, to a Sunday School teacher recently honored by the town, to the men who stood by that layman through all the time that his life was drenched with trouble.

Let the church and the indispensability of it be an implication. Keep in mind, in and out of it all, that you are not there to sell or to compel, that you are interested in the spiritual possibilities of these folks upon whom you call for their sakes.

BISHOP HAZEN G. WERNER,
The Methodist Church,
Columbus, Ohio.

Pastoral Prayer

A minister writes:

I would like to have the pastoral prayer discussed from several viewpoints. What petitions should it contain? How should the petitions be phrased? How specific should the petitions be?

For example, should the pastoral prayer be modeled on a prayer like this one by W. E. Orchard?

O God, who has formed all hearts to love thee, made all ways lead to thee, created all desire to be unsatisfied save in thee; with great compassion look upon us gathered here. Our presence is our prayer, our need the only plea we dare to claim, thy purposes the one assurance we possess.

Some of us are very confused; we do not know why we were ever born, for what end we should live, which way we should take. But we are willing to be guided. Take our trembling hands in thine, and lead us on.

Some of us are sore within. We long for love and friendship, but we care for no one and we feel that no one cares for us. We are misunderstood, we are lonely, we have been disappointed, we have lost our faith in man and our faith in life. Wilt thou not let us love thee who first loved us?

Some of us are vexed with passions that affright us; to yield to them would mean disaster, to restrain them is beyond our power, and nothing earth contains exhausts their vehemence or satisfies their fierce desire.

And so because there is no answer, no end or satisfaction in ourselves; and because we are what we are, and yet long to be so different; we believe thou art, and that thou dost understand us. By faith we feel after thee, through love we find the way, in hope we bring ourselves to thee. *Amen.*

Or, should the pastoral prayer follow the more formal, more

166

objective petitions of the following prayer by Bishop Thomas Wilson?

Almighty God, who by thy grace and providence hast brought my great and crying sins to light, I most humbly beseech thee to continue thy grace and mercy to me, that my conscience being now awakened, I may call my ways to remembrance, and confess, and bewail and abhor all the sins of my life past. And, O merciful God, give me true repentance for them, even that repentance to which thou hast promised mercy and pardon, that even the consequences of my wrongdoing may bring a blessing to me, and that in all I may find mercy at thy hands, through the merits and mediation of our Lord Jesus Christ. *Amen.*

Another way of putting the question I am raising is: how should sins be confessed in the pastoral prayer?

A minister replies:

The secret of effectiveness in pastoral prayer lies in the ability and the habit to talk with God naturally and honestly about one's own problems and listen to people openly and affectionately as they talk about their problems.

The chief drawback of most of the pastoral prayers that I hear is the inability of the pastor to be natural in his public prayer. There are more forms of affectation and pretense in pastoral prayer than in almost any form of ministerial service. Unless a man can talk with God naturally and without affectation he cannot pray meaningfully for his people. There is no trick, device, rule, or habit of study that will bring a man to usefulness to his people in pastoral prayer unless his own prayers to God are meaningful and recreative for him.

Any person who leads others in worship is wise to study devotional literature, to be in a habit of memorizing scripture, and to keep his mind filled with great poetry.

A pastor is wise to take his full Saturday mornings, I believe, for the preparation of his pastoral prayer. After the week he has spent in service of his people, in listening to their problems, in trying to shoulder their burdens, his heart should be full of

167

their needs. I believe that he first ought to decide what he really wants to say in his prayer. Following that, he is wise to turn to the great devotional books and find the ways in which the great masters have put these same petitions into words. Such study should enable a man to develop a style worthy of prayer and without affectation. Whether a man then reads a prayer in the pulpit is not as important as whether or not he has read and re-read the prayer enough that he knows it well and it comes naturally from his lips.

The confession of sins in public prayer, I believe, should be just as specific as one's insight into human nature permits. Nowhere I think is a person more tempted to repetition. We all tend to confess our own sins when we speak of the sins of others. There particularly, any person leading in public prayer needs to watch being too autobiographical. Every confession of sin in public prayer should be a confession of "our" sins and not "yours," but a man needs very carefully to be on his guard unless he continues to confess the same sins week in and week out. When a man does that it is often because he is so preoccupied with his own inner difficulties that he is not aware of the wide range of troubles which are visited upon his people.

The confession of sin in public prayer should, of course, be direct and earnest but it should also be spoken in an abounding confidence that, if we confess our sins, God is faithful and just to forgive us our sins and to cleanse us from all unrighteousness. Confession will not cleanse without a confidence that God is eager to cleanse. Here is one of our chief failings. We find it easier to make the reality of sin vivid to our people than we do the reality of God's forgiving grace. Every confession of sin in public prayer, I believe, ought to be integrally related to an equal confession of faith in God's eagerness to cleanse us from our sins.

EUGENE L. SMITH,
Executive Secretary,
Division of Foreign Missions of the Board of Missions
and Church Extension of The Methodist Church.

A professor of Christian theology answers:

The pastoral prayer, if it is to be truly pastoral, will doubt-less include from time to time a confession of sins. This essential element in all prayer cannot be adequately cared for by formal collects or unison prayers printed in the order of service, since these become more perfunctory with each repetition and cease to stimulate the mood of honest repentance which is after all their real intent. In the pastoral prayer, with its more personal and intimate address to God, something incisive and self-searching can and should be said.

Several practical suggestions may be made looking toward this end:

(1) The pastor must identify himself closely with his people in confession, as Orchard's prayer succeeds in doing. He speaks for them, not to them. He accepts and so articulates for his fellow-worshipers the conscious bitterness of need.

(2) The confessional portion of a worthy pastoral prayer should be stated in specific, graphic form, capable of arousing in the congregation both penitence and a desire to be forgiven.

(3) Nevertheless the pastor should avoid making his prayer of confession merely a catalogue or listing of sins-in-particular. In the act of prayer we ought to be made aware not only of sins, but of sin and of ourselves as sinners. No "check-list" or "run-through" can achieve this.

(4) There is required in every prayer a certain amplitude of statement which lifts us out of the rut of self-concerned subjectivity and the moralistic balance sheet; the General Confession in the Book of Common Prayer is a good example to follow in this respect.

(5) This spacious, universal note of reference is best secured by bringing more vividly into the prayer the sense of God as hearing and heeding it, as Bishop Wilson does by the device of repeated address to God in the second person. It ought never to be forgotten, most of all in confessional prayer, that we are not meditating on our state alone but conversing with God. This keeps the pastor in his place before God, reminds the people of

the prayer's true purpose, and puts sin in its proper perspective as something to be overcome.

So far as the theory of confessional prayer goes, the major accent must be upon God's own power to save rather than on our weakness or alienation from Him. Notice how the Lord's Prayer achieves this. It is not insensitive to the range and depth of sin in human life, but it puts the emphasis throughout on God's resourcefulness and guidance. A prayer of confession is primarily one of petition; that is probably why it best fits the litany-form, as in the great Southwell Litany of Bishop Ridding. It might be better if more pastoral prayers were cast in this mold; in fact many litanies of confession may be adapted to this purpose quite easily and appropriately. Or the penitential psalms may be employed as a source-book of phrases and ideas in this regard, giving a note of authenticity and poignancy which our prayers usually lack.

ROGER HAZELTON,
Abbot Professor of Christian Theology,
Andover Newton Theological School,
Newton Centre, Massachusetts.

How Can a Rural Pastor Improve His Work?

A minister writes:

I am a pastor who is working in a rural area a good distance away from metropolitan centers with facilities for psychiatric or other clinical consultation. There are a great many problems which are brought to me by my parishioners and it is most important for me, a rural minister, to find some way whereby I can get help with my counseling—at least to share my problems. I am sure that this must be a real problem to a great many other ministers in my situation, and I will appreciate the help of your panel of experts.

A minister replies:

First of all, let me say that it is a real compliment to you that people come to you. That they feel free to come means they are close to you, that there is a rapport between you, and that even in your sermons you are not talking at them but thinking with them.

However, we all understand that in some cases such difficult problems arise that the pastor needs expert psychiatric advice to help him in his counseling; or, he may even need to make referrals to competent psychiatrists when he finds himself out beyond his depth.

A good start for any of us in your situation is to grow in insight as to effective counseling methods. As long as you listen objectively, entering into the experiences of your people, you are not likely to make mistakes, and you stand a good chance of helping them grow in insight and understanding of their own problems. Reading again and again books such as Carroll Wise's *Pastoral Counseling, Its Theory and Practice,* and Karl Menninger's *The Human Mind* will be of inestimable help to you.

Another thing that would be helpful would be to get a few

171

other ministers (as many as you can) to join with you in making a study of counseling. You would share your experiences and insights. You would pool your resources, often getting from others leads that would help you in troublesome cases.

Some attempt should be made to get physicians working with the group, to assist in particular cases where medical help is needed, and to help promote a more vital teamwork between our men of medicine and clergymen in general.

If there is a mental hospital within reach of you, you might have one of its psychiatrists join with your group in studying the needs of the people of the community. From the psychiatrist the ministers would learn how to make referrals when necessary, and from him also they would learn much about the factors involved in effective counseling. A closer relationship with the psychiatrist would make it easier for the pastor to consult with him by telephone over difficult cases.

A final suggestion is for you to build up church nurture groups, or groups fostering growth in the life of the spirit. In these groups members will not only learn how to keep themselves in healthy frames of mind but also they will, by entering into and sharing each other's experiences, extrovert their attention and help each other in the solution of individual problems.

ROY A. BURKHART,
First Community Church,
Columbus, Ohio.

Another minister and teacher of counseling replies:

Concerning psychiatric and psychological resources in a rural community, several observations may be noted:

(1) The pastor should contact the county health department for specific advice. Often these departments have access to traveling clinics, visiting psychiatric social workers, and the like. Kentucky is a predominantly rural state, but we have five or six clinics in operation over the state through the Mental Hygiene Division of the State Board of Health.

(2) The pastor should be acquainted with the regional resources as well as immediate community resources. For instance, one man, in a rural church of which I was pastor, received

172

reasonably inexpensive and very beneficial help in a clinic 112 miles away. Another received similar service from a distance of over 500 miles.

(3) The pastor will do well to join his efforts with other civic-minded persons in a quiet and tactful manner to seek to bring to the community a young and energetic medical doctor, a general practitioner, with plenty of common sense and some psychiatric training. He can do much to prevent mental illness by detecting it early and giving common-sense suggestions to his patients, their families, and their associates.

(4) For acutely psychotic persons in a rural area, a pastor needs to realize that a thinly populated area and a relatively simple culture can more easily absorb psychic peculiarities than can a thickly populated and culturally complex city. People tend to be less hurried, more patient, and more indulgent.

(5) Also, the pastor needs to pay more attention to the improvement of state hospital facilities. This would do much toward enriching his resources for dependable psychiatric help. In many cases of chronic and dangerous psychotic disorders, the pastor can do no better than to cooperate with the family in committing the patient to a state hospital. This is always difficult emotionally for the pastor as well as the family, but it is the only alternative in many cases. The rural pastor, more than others, longs to see psychiatrists working with people who need them most—state hospital inmates.

WAYNE E. OATES,
Professor of Pastoral Care,
Southern Baptist Theological Seminary.

A minister-chaplain writes:

In many large urban centers the number of men receiving seminar training for pastoral counseling is considerable.

But what of the vast majority of the clergy serving in the country—men in town and country parishes? Seminars of this type are beyond their hoping. *Are they?* A good idea is capable of many modifications. A state council of churches can set up one-day demonstration clinics in strategic centers about the state. Resource men with a national or state reputation can be

173

present. One of these persons can present a case and have others comment upon it, asking him questions. The clinical method can be demonstrated. State boards of health have already held similar meetings. In Wisconsin, two of the resource leaders were drawn from the field of religious counseling. It would be but a slight yet significant step forward for demonstration clinics to be church sponsored and devoted specifically to cases of religious counseling.

Without waiting for a demonstration clinic to come their way, a group of like-minded ministers could begin to meet for a study of verbatim reports on counseling situations. Let us assume that you know just two ministers in your area who might respond to the idea. Start talking it over with them. Each should know another. Four or five are not too few for a beginning. Groups can soon become too large, for a clinic is not a clinic if it is so large some members never contribute a case.

Your enthusiasm will have to be high or your idea may die. Others will agree it is good, but they are *so* busy. Never relent. If the four of you are golf enthusiasts you will meet as a foursome several times during the year. If you fish, you have your fishing partners. Clergymen who have a concern for the care of souls will not be too busy to meet with other clergymen who want to learn "how they really function" in the care of souls.

Before you set a time for the group to meet, think through what is to be attempted. If you are the spark plug, none of the rest may be ready to bring in, right at the start, a verbatim record. Should you provide a verbatim report drawn from your work in pastoral care? If you bring in a display piece in which the movement was almost ideal, don't be surprised if the group compliments you and fails to meet again! Keep your ego down. If you start with a case of your own let it be your worst failure. Let the others tell you where you failed. The group will then have a chance to survive.

Possibly the group will feel that this idea of meeting to study clinical material ought to commence with materials being used that have been gathered elsewhere. Hiltner's *Pastoral Counseling* has a variety of case material that could be employed by a group. PASTORAL PSYCHOLOGY carries a Consultation Clinic. It

174

does not provide verbatim records, but there are replies to questions submitted—replies from men with wide reputations. Warming up on such material may pull the trigger and fire someore to volunteer a case he is having trouble with.

As you already know, if you have made any extensive search for verbatim reports of religious counseling, the material published in this field is so slight as to be almost nonexistent. In the secular field there is Snyder's *Casebook of Non-Directive Counseling*. It is the best known of much similar material found in books or journals. The field of religious counseling is quite bare in comparison. In each seminary where counseling is taught the instructor has his extensive collection of verbatim records that have been assembled both by himself and his students. Some of this material in mimeograph form is probably being used elsewhere as well, in groups such as I am describing. But we are still a long way from where we ought to be.

D. M. STERLING,
Minister of the Congregational Church,
Spring Valley, Wisconsin.

The Minister and Law Enforcement

A minister writes:

I am in my first resident pastorate and a question that has bothered me for some time is this: how far should a minister go in law enforcement? Should he say nothing and pray that the moral influence of his sermons will right a problem by causing the membership to do something about it? Should he go to the other extreme and swear out complaints with the county attorney, or use other legal means to halt a violation of law that the community willfully permits?

To cite one example: In our state gambling is against the law. Each year the public school holds a carnival in which a lottery (which is unlawful) is held. Clearly you cannot teach future citizens respect for the law when it is violated openly. What should a pastor do?

A psychiatrist replies:

The minister's responsibility is to lead and teach his people in the Christian way of life, trusting that Christian knowledge will enable them to distinguish between right and wrong. When a group of individuals in a community feel that law enforcement is weak, it is generally best to meet the situation through normal democratic processes.

A minister may well take part as a citizen in movements for civic reform, or if the people wish it, as their representative. To swear out complaints leading to legal action presents the danger of weakening the ultimate great power of moral suasion, and of emphasizing the use of force rather than spiritual influence. The minister's individual task is to change lives, not to enforce laws.

R. H. FELIX, M.D.,
Director, National Institute of Mental Health,
U. S. Public Health Service, Bethesda, Maryland.

176

A minister replies:

Jesus made no direct attack on human slavery. But His teaching of love and brotherhood and the sacredness of personality eventually doomed slavery. People gamble because of some inner dissatisfaction. To sense the need which prompts gambling and endeavor to meet it in a more satisfying way is the real problem which is implied in the question whether a minister should do more than pray that the moral influence of his sermons will right the wrong.

But the gambling interests are organized. They have money, and spend it freely for the protection of their interests, often contributing heavily to the campaign funds of both leading political parties to insure friendly relations. The organized element, though a small minority, will control the situation if the majority who oppose the permission of organized gambling in violation of the law sit idly by and do nothing.

The knowledge that laws are not being enforced with respect to any form of illegal activity is an open invitation to other forms of vice or crime, and a single minister's moral effect upon his congregation will rarely make a great impact upon the situation. On the other hand, neither will his efforts to secure a few convictions in flagrant cases. Experience has shown that broadsides spotlighting the evil, or even reform waves, change the situation only temporarily at best.

To be effective, I believe, a minister must become a part of an educational program which will make known the facts and eventually inspire the action of an aroused majority. Study groups must know the extent of illegal gambling if they are to seek the enforcement of anti-gambling laws in a community. The extent of influence through political machinery must be investigated. The apathy of the public, which may see no danger in a few $2.00 bets in a handbook, must be awakened to the real dangers of continued connivance. How great is the political corruption? What are the ties with prostitution and other criminal activities?

Armed with this information, groups may be effective in investigating the connections of candidates for political office, and

177

elect responsible persons. One of the most effective tools is the support and encouragement of good men in public office who are doing their duty.

What to do in the case of an illegal lottery held by a public school is difficult to say unless more specific data is obtained. In general, however, it would seem that rash and hasty condemnation might be unwise. Such action is often ineffective.

Before any steps are taken it would be necessary to know how long the carnival has been accepted in the community without question. Who supports it? Are other forms of lotteries accepted in the community? If this is the first question to be raised about the propriety of the lottery, it will have a profound bearing upon the method of approach. If the community as a whole is overwhelmingly in favor of such enterprise, long-term educational methods will be necessary.

It may be that no one has ever gone to the superintendent of the school or the persons directly responsible for the lottery. That would undoubtedly be the first step after surveying the community climate with respect to lotteries: to go to these persons to discuss the influence upon youth of condoning illegal gambling. It may be that simply urging the abolishment of the lottery, for its value in teaching respect for law, may be sufficient.

In any event it would be well to go to the persons responsible for the lottery armed with a more acceptable plan for raising money.

ORVAL H. AUSTIN,
Institutional Chaplain,
Louisville Council of Churches,
Louisville, Kentucky.

A specialist in mental hygiene, with a ministerial background, answers:

The very way the questioner phrases his question suggests both the conflict he has about the matter and the direction of his own thinking in trying to arrive at an answer. He poses two extremes, suggesting that the answer may be somewhere between the two. In commenting, "clearly you cannot teach respect for

178

law when it is violated openly," he further suggests that educational methods may have to be used more than legal means.

A fuller verbalization of the questioner's own feelings and thoughts would probably run something like this: I have strong personal convictions that some things are right and others are wrong. As a minister I am expected always to stand on the side of right and to oppose that which is wrong. Both my own conscience and my professional position therefore compel me to take a stand on all major issues of right and wrong, but one wants to take his stand in such a way that it will really bring about desired results. There is no virtue in merely banging one's head against a wall, for that results in nothing except a bruised head. This is one place where the exhortation, "Be ye wise as serpents and harmless as doves" may be applicable, but just how does one proceed to be both wise and harmless in this problem?

What a minister should do in this kind of a situation will depend upon his own convictions and the motives which prompt his action. I am assuming that the questioner is fairly free from neurotic motivation and does not have to take action which will advertise his moral superiority or compel him to become a martyr. And I assume that he really wants to do whatever will work toward the ethical well-being and social good of the people of his community. If so, he will realize that he cannot count on his listeners automatically converting the moral tone of his sermon into appropriate social action. Neither can he have much confidence in single-handedly making a complaint to the officer of the law.

If the action of his parishioners is to be ethical and make for social good it will have to be a considered, conscious choice on the part of the people. Moreover, just because there is force in numbers, appropriate action is apt to be taken only if a very sizable number of people want the action to be taken, and take their own part in it. In other words, the minister who is really concerned to see his people respect the law fully will have to do some teaching, very specifically getting them to analyze the social reasons behind the laws, the psychological reasons why they are too often observed in the breach, help them to see what is involved in reference to each specific law, such as the law against gambling, and invite concerted action on the part of those who come to hold similar convictions in the matter. If enough of them come to believe that lottery in the public school is bad they can easily take steps to do away with it.

The chances are that the head of the school is no more consulted on the method of raising funds than is the minister, and he would more than welcome some more wholesome method of raising funds, such as through added taxes, voluntary contributions, or legitimate profit from the sale of goods or service.

In brief, the minister should go far enough in law enforcement to teach his people the positive values to be achieved and served by obeying the laws, if they are just and acceptable, and the ill effects from disobeying those laws. If laws are unjust or unacceptable, either because initially ill-conceived, or because social conditions have changed so that they are unethical or impractical, the minister should proceed to educate his people in the interest of changing the laws so as to make them acceptable. In either instance he has an obligation to engage in further education of his people, helping them to see what is involved and to arrive at sound conclusions and take active steps to bring about enforcement of the law if it is good, or change of the law if it is not. The minister will accomplish much more by educational methods which enlist the thinking and active cooperation of people than by trusting either to vague moral influence or mechanical legal means.

LUTHER E. WOODWARD,
Coordinator of Mental Health Activities,
State of New York, Department of Mental Hygiene.

How Can a Psychiatrist Best Serve His Church?

A psychiatrist asks:

I would like to have some advice regarding a project which I am about to undertake. In many respects this project is new to me, and I would like to have a little help or advice from you or someone whom you could designate to answer this letter.

First, I might say that I am a psychiatrist in private practice in this city. I have been interested in many community projects and have a fairly well-balanced social outlook upon community needs. I also have a fairly solid religious background, but have at times been in conflict with many of the fundamental teachings and dogmas of the various denominations. In my psychotherapeutic work, I endeavor to be very tolerant and do not attempt to undermine any religious beliefs which my patients might have. I am also very careful to explore those beliefs which do enter into any emotional problem. I might say I am a very conservative, modern religious believer and quite active in church work. At the present time I am a trustee in a Presbyterian church, which has a membership of approximately 300.

For about a year now, the men of our church, a group of fairly progressive, average-income members, have been asking me to start a Men's Bible Class. There has been a definite need in our church for this type of class, but I have been very reluctant to accept this responsibility because I feel I cannot teach some of the dogma and fundamental teachings of the Presbyterian church, or one might even say of the Protestant faith.

From reading your issues of PASTORAL PSYCHOLOGY and from other sources, I am beginning to realize that the church itself is beginning to come closer to psychiatry than ever before. I have consented to take this class and have talked the situation over with the minister. I have laid down some stipulations which I feel will be necessary in order for me to become a leader of this group. Stipulation number one is that I am not to be ham-

181

strung or compelled to follow routine lessons, as prescribed by the heads of the church. The subjects I shall discuss will deal mainly with making Christianity practicable in man's everyday life. Under that classification, of course, many subjects will be discussed with which the layman is constantly coming in contact. Using the Bible as a textbook, I would like to be able to choose a subject and then permit the men to air their views on all points. Of course it would be my job to steer them along sound fundamental lines of thought. I would be glad to receive any suggestions or criticisms you wish to offer in building up my group.

I might say our pastor has agreed to these stipulations. I realize this is going to be a big responsibility in addition to my community work and my practice. However, I feel there is a definite need for this type of action.

A minister replies:

It is heartening to know of a situation in which a psychiatrist is volunteering his leadership as teacher of a Men's Bible Class. I hope that his minister will use him fully.

In our church in Columbus we have made extensive use of the professional services of various psychiatrists who have a Christian point of view. They work closely with our program of guidance in many areas:

(1) In helping guide the clinic sessions for expectant parents, for parents of pre-school children, primary children, junior-age children, and adolescents. Each age group meets once a month with the church school teachers, and we invite a psychiatrist to interpret how to care for the child so that he will feel secure; how to love him so that his needs are met in his first year of life. The psychiatrist helps the parents understand the child's first five years of experience, what the emphases should be, and how guidance should be given. Other topics include: helping the child become wholesomely independent; helping the parents become free from hostility and anxiety which distort their own approach to their children; understanding the basic periods of childhood; preparing parents so they can guide their young people in an interpretation of biological maturation and the various experiences of adolescence.

182

(2) Psychiatrists participate in various other groups of the church from time to time, helping our people understand the requirements for sound emotional health as well as the causes and indications of emotional illness. The nature of treatment required when a person does become mentally ill is interpreted, so that there will not be the feelings of shame and guilt usually experienced by a family if one of their members is hospitalized. We work with psychiatrists in helping persons who *have* been hospitalized by mental illness make an adjustment in everyday living.

For discussions concerning personality growth, creative human relations, and the problem of vocational choice, psychiatrists lead meetings with youth groups of various ages.

We use psychiatrists with groups of men and women in an effort to help people discover how fears can be overcome, how a state of depression can be relieved without hospitalization, and how one can grow in that way of thinking and feeling which makes life whole. An interpretation of the climacteric is another phase. People live to be older today than ever before, and they need to be prepared for the change of life even as young people must be prepared for puberty.

Psychiatrists aid in supplementing our pre-marital counseling program. If we discover a deep fear block, or a homosexual pattern, or some other factor where a hidden element is involved, we send that person to a psychiatrist for help.

In our church, the ministers consult many times with psychiatrists about various behavior situations. Then, in line with their guidance, we can carry on the counseling without using more of the time of the psychiatrist.

We believe that such teamwork between the minister, the psychiatrist, and the physician is a most fruitful one. In the past seventeen years we have seen the results—increased emotional stability, lasting marriages, happy and healthy children, less and less need for hospitalization.

ROY A. BURKHART,
Minister, First Community Church,
Columbus, Ohio.

183

Volunteers in Parish Work

A minister writes:

Could we have some discussion concerning the handling of volunteers in parish organizations, or how to provide intelligent leadership with trustees and vestry groups? As you probably know, many of our active workers in parishes are neurotics, and it is extremely important that young clergymen understand some of the difficulties which they will face in parish organizations. You probably also realize that many women become interested in churches and assume active responsibility as the result of being rejected by secular women's groups such as women's clubs, etc. A church by reason of its Christian motivation permits these women to become active, thereby creating serious problems with the clergy and the organization generally. Could we have some discussion concerning these problems?

A minister replies:

In essence it seems to me that the solution of this problem of volunteer visitors is to be found in carefully selecting the persons desired for this kind of work and then in using the most effective methods in enlisting those particular individuals. If the minister should issue a general call for volunteers to do parish visitation, he should not be surprised when the response comes from the type of individual suggested in this inquiry.

How this works out in practice may be a rather long story, but a single illustration may indicate what I mean. The woman who directs the program of visitation on the sick and shut-in members of one church is known as the "courtesy chairman" of the women's council. Each circle of the council also has its courtesy chairman, and these constitute the "courtesy committee of the council." Additional workers are enlisted as they are
184

needed, but these, too, are selected on the basis of their abilities rather than being a group of people who respond to a general call. All of these workers do their visiting in the name of the church and under instructions from the church. Every opportunity is taken to magnify the importance of the courtesy work in the eyes of all of the members of the council.

When there was a vacancy in the general chairmanship a few months ago, the nominating committee selected the woman whom they felt could serve most effectively. She was generally respected for her Christian character, intelligence, and ability. Not long before this she had been selected as the city's "Woman of the Year." The chairman of the nominating committee, with the president of the women's council and the minister, called at her home and discussed the opportunity with her. They made no attempt to minimize the amount of work that would be involved but did emphasize the significance of the kind of service for the church and for the individuals who would be aided in times of personal need. She responded favorably to the challenge that was offered.

This particular procedure, of course, is not a prescription for all cases. The general principle is that people should be carefully selected because of their ability to do this particular work, and their cooperation should be sought by the methods which are likely to be most effective in each case. Additional time and care expended in securing the right leadership may save hours which would otherwise be wasted with incompetent leadership.

FRANCIS W. PRITCHARD,
New Providence Presbyterian Church,
Maryville, Tennessee.

Another minister writes:

Each minister is faced with the problem of how to choose the kind of people who are emotionally mature enough for effective leadership in the church. There are those persons who are obsessional neurotics who get into the church often as a means to find solutions to their problems. Persons rejected elsewhere turn to the church. Unless they get help with their difficulties, they become a problem. Hostility, guilt, rejection, and anxiety may be manifested in many ways, and when people are afflicted they can create serious problems.

Here is one example: a woman active in church affairs apparently had fundamental emotional hesitations which made her frigid. She sought a solution to her problem by taking up a study of Unity. Within its philosophy she seemed to find authority for the idea that if people lived by the truth, they never would die; and thus they would not have to "commit the sin of having intercourse" to have children.

This woman became a problem in the choir, in every Bible class and study class. She was constantly forcing her point of view on the group and on the teacher. When the minister spoke on marriage, she would carry on a constant argument with those sitting next to her in the choir.

Her problem was of such a deep nature that she would not submit to counseling, and finally when a new choir season began, she was not invited to join. She was now requested by the minister to submit to a counseling program or to no longer attend the various groups in the church. She withdrew, somewhat hurt, and is now quite active in Unity. While she was not helped to solve her problem, she finally was influenced to withdraw and thus permit the groups to proceed without the constant annoyance of her particular point of view.

It is important for the church to have a policy that will protect boards and committees from people who have anxiety or other types of compulsive tendencies. In one church, persons serve only three years and then they are automatically taken off the board or committee. This saves the church from becoming a victim of a sick person.

Another suggestion is that the nominating committee needs to be very careful in the selection of people for various jobs. Those with major problems should be gently guided into study groups and nurture groups. Individuals should be chosen for various jobs in light of their background and training. Nominees for the board of trustees should have a certain background; those for the board of deacons and board of women, another;

those for the board of ushers, another; church school teachers, another.

The smaller church, of course, has a different problem here from that of the larger church. However, persons should be selected carefully and then given adequate training.

A fundamental procedure is the developing of the spiritual life in the church in order to help all people become more free. Discussion groups, nurture groups, and group therapy procedures will be helpful. The people with major difficulties can get help in these groups; and as they do, will become ready for more constructive leadership.

ROY A. BURKHART,
First Community Church,
Columbus, Ohio.

A psychiatrist with ministerial training writes:

I doubt that there are any blanket rules for handling "neurotic women" in church because there really is no such thing as *neurotic women*—there is only a series of individual neurotic females who must be treated individually either through the aid of a psychiatrist or through pastoral counseling. If the right person were available, a little group therapy might be tried in addition.

FLANDERS DUNBAR, M.D.,
New York City.

A psychiatric social research worker writes:

Most of us seem to need to be needed, to feel of value in and for ourselves, and to be a welcome and integral part of a group, no matter how small.

To the church, as the writer of the question points out, are likely to come those who have been denied the gratification of these three wishes. Some of them can be helped, some can be supported, and some must be tolerated and protected by their more fortunate companions.

Crippled and unhappy though these maimed ones are, they have something to contribute if their offering can only be chan-

187

neled in the right direction. They are faithful in attendance, sustained in purpose, almost frighteningly tenacious in endeavor, capable of great sacrifice, and able to work like dogs for something which has caught their will and attention.

Unfortunately, they are likely to get the emphasis on the wrong thing. Seeking fellowship, they fail to see that pursued it eludes, that it is not a pouring in of attention and interest on one individual by a group of people, but the result of a shared task, a journeying together toward a common goal, a joint sacrifice for the sake of a prized ideal.

Yearning for a sense of achievement and worth, they press for reassurance, for praise, for denial of their statements of their own inferiority, and obtrude their weaknesses or lacks constantly upon their fellows. They fail to see that pity—a wry mixture of revulsion and compassion—is but thin brew for the thick broth and breed of love for which they wish and which, with a different approach, they *could* evoke. Craving of personal value, they completely misinterpret the Christian doctrine of man and see it as applying to others but not themselves; look upon it as potentially available to them if they were only someone other than who they are; or cut it small and look for its fulfillment in too mundane and concrete terms. Wishing to be needed, they seize upon unnecessary or unwanted services or over-give that which is requested; and then present a high due-bill for recompense in recognition, praise, or—most embarrassing—for sharing in areas of life, emotion, and activity not thrown open to them by the relationship.

Insecure, they demand—as do the child, the sick, and the aging—a predictable environment. Any hint of change is a danger to them, presenting a challenge which they feel they may not be able to meet; and carrying with it the threat that the thing they prize is to be abandoned; and that they, along with it, will be regarded as "being of no value." A good number of the fights which come to vestries and take place in women's groups are related to the phenomenon that a challenge to the object for which one has fought and worked may be interpreted as a rejection of one's self, one's sacrifice, and one's cherished dream.

A further difficulty comes from the goal chosen by the group or its leader. If the task in hand is buying a carpet or shingling a roof or reinvesting the endowment funds; or changing the order of service, or inculcating a dogma, the clamorous or needy one becomes an obstructionist and a source of irritation.

On the other hand, if the goal is the helping of individuals who are children of God and heirs to His Kingdom seeking to know and work out His Will in time, the hungry ones are less annoying, the possible delay for the immediate pursuit is less frustrating and often, amazingly enough, the job gets done more quickly and more smoothly than it would had the human values been overridden.

Nevertheless, these people are a problem. They threaten the needs, interests, and gratifications of the others in the group, who also require a sense of achievement, of value, of belonging. Each must be treated as an individual and they cannot be handled *en masse*. To each must be granted a measured endowment of the nutriment he is seeking, always within the bounds of that which the relationship permits and in the form it makes appropriate. For each, the leader (or the one responsible for the well-being of the group, or the outcome of the task) must perform a highly creative act and arrive at a vantage point from which he is able to see that this person, troublesome though he is, has a unique gift to contribute . . . can find the channel through which this gift can most productively be poured forth . . . and realize that he has truly contributed something of value which only *he* could give.

INA MAY GREER,
Massachusetts General Hospital,
Boston, Massachusetts.

Another psychiatrist replies:

Many intensely active and useful people in every walk of life have neurotic traits: parish groups certainly have no monopoly. In spite of the personality difficulties encountered, many ministers would perhaps not care to lose the neurotic, over-meticulous, but invariably accurate treasurer; or the unstable but artistic lady who contributes so much aesthetically to the church; or the fund-raiser whose neurosis won't let him take "no" for an answer. The point is to find a niche for these people which will not irritate the jagged edges of their personalities, and will keep them from hurting others. This can be accomplished only by extreme sensitivity and patience on the part of the minister, who must observe, counsel, and then devise activities which will be appropriate. This implies a church program which is varied and adjustable, and the building of groups which can tolerate some deviation among their members.

The more deeply neurotic may be unable to function creatively even in this permissive kind of environment. They may require more intensive pastoral counseling (Seward Hiltner's *Pastoral Counseling* will prove a most helpful guide). Sometimes a discussion group around personal problems, a mental health film, or a thoughtful sermon on emotions and mental conflict may effectively pave the way to such counseling.

The pastor has to resist the impulse to treat every case himself. Some of the referral-determining factors with the more seriously neurotic are: the pastor's competence and experience in counseling, time limitations, and the availability of community resources for psychotherapy. Not to refer to a psychiatrist when one is available and the case is severe may do a great disservice to the patient, and may result in the pastor's activities becoming part of the community's mental health problem.

DALLAS PRATT, M.D.,
National Association for Mental Health,
New York City.

The Minister and the Overdominant Parishioner

A minister writes:

I have in my church a group of people who, it seems, would make an ideal psychological demonstration of almost every type. They live on tradition and the past and are very much *for* themselves. In their attitudes, no one knows anything about anything but themselves. The pastor is just a figurehead who knows nothing about his job; he is never considered or consulted in anything; and often when he or others endeavor for leadership, the attitudes against them are almost, if not quite, abusive.

Among these is one in particular who feels and displays an excessive attitude of superiority. He treats all others including the pastor as "worms." He refuses to discuss or explain any actions or activities anticipated, despite every attempt to attain such. The proper church officials do nothing, and evade the responsibility of dealing with him. He is a most dominating individual determined to carry through his plans irrespective of how they may interfere. Again and again, the pastoral office is invaded without as much as a word of information.

(An example: A group has been undergoing training for a permanent part in church services. Although some expressed opposition to placing this man in charge as sponsor, they actually approved it when the issue was brought to them. Now, the group is about ready to appear in worship service but the pastor finds it impossible to get information or to have consultation to plan properly. It could be a great advantage, but if not handled properly could disrupt the whole service.)

After more than seven years of this, I have been forced to take an attitude of tolerance. I find that this reacts within me in a manner which it ought not. I resent it because I know it is wrong, but I must be tolerant.

As you see, there is a double psychological problem, one that

191

affects the condition, and one as it affects me as a pastor. I may say that others have faced the same thing, and the condition is very common in this area.

A minister answers:

This is an unfortunate situation. We feel we are entitled to more cooperative attitudes on the part of those who profess to be religious leaders than are shown by this layman. However, there will be no improvement in this situation unless we are able to isolate the illusions behind which tensions are accumulating.

Our first illusion, shared by the pastor in this case, is that in Christian circles this sort of thing should not happen. We feel we are entitled to better treatment by our laymen. We can hardly call him Christian, acting the way he does. Also, we cannot understand how the church group can support him as it does. The fact is, this is a real life situation brought about by living, growing individuals, each and every one of whom have psychological needs to be met. We are not always in a position to know just what these needs are. Each person, trying to meet his own needs, contributes to a situation of this type. When we find ourselves in one, however, there are three possible courses of action. We may take flight—go to another parish, or in some way run away. We may attack it. Less genteel people hurl epithets and sometimes more material objects. Neither of these courses is acceptable to this pastor. There is only one other way of meeting the situation. That is to accept it. This does not mean that he is to sit down beside it and ignore it. It means that, without emotion on his own part, he will seek to recognize it as a fact. He will try to understand the motivations which have led each participant to this impasse. He will know that heaven on earth can only be won by hard work, emotional control, and slow growth on the part of all concerned. The illusion about the situation must be dispelled and the situation accepted.

The second illusion is that the layman is wrong. This is a moral judgment which does not adequately describe the layman. He believes he is right. He is meeting certain needs of his own. He gains ego satisfaction and perhaps satisfies a power drive. He finds in the church a most compatible field for his activities.

192

His needs may be personal, they may be infantile and immature. However this may be, the group sees that he is somewhat of an asset in spite of his liabilities and they continue to choose him to lead them. So, we must learn to accept him. We cannot flee, we cannot attack. We must get over the illusion that he is "wrong" and accept him as an immature person who is not growing up and who is more eager to satisfy his own personality needs than first to build the Kingdom and let all these things be added unto him.

The third illusion blinds the pastor to his own immaturities. Childish traits are residual in all of us. Who is free from trying to meet his own psychological needs? We must accept ourselves as we are. This situation has resolved itself into a contest for power. The resulting frustration within the pastor is causing symptoms. "I find this reacts within me in a manner which it ought not," he writes. The festering matter within the pastor is resentment. The resentment rises from repressed wishes to flee or attack. As neither of these is acceptable to him, he resorts to "tolerance." To tolerate is to accept under protest. It is the "protest" which is causing the pastor's own psychological difficulty.

Losing our life for the sake of Christ may not mean utter self-denial. It may mean that we have learned not to flee, not to fight, not even to repress desires to fight as in tolerance, but full acceptance of other people, ourselves, situations and God Himself.

GEORGE H. PARKER,
First Methodist Church,
South Braintree, Massachusetts.

Another minister answers:

One wonders why the minister has stayed on in such a church for seven years, the opportunities for service being what they are, with the great need for ministers in other churches. Realistically, which I am afraid this minister's attitude is not, *nothing* can be done to help such a group as he describes, especially the man he writes about who has an "attitude of superiority." Actually the man is not "superior" but suffers from a deep sense of frustration and emotional insecurity; since he does not understand this fact there is nothing that can be done for him. The minister confuses Christian tolerance with lack of emotional fortitude in himself. He speaks of "resenting" the position of tolerance which he has been forced into. I'm afraid that his feeling of resentment is toward himself because he has been forced to accept and work with "a bully" of whom he is basically afraid.

There is no need to condemn oneself because of being unable to help someone who needs help but who refuses to accept it. One of the hardest things the minister has to accept—and this is something that many of us are never able to admit—is the fact that we often fail when we work with people. I am told by medical instructors that this same lesson is one of the hardest the medical student has to learn: that the doctor makes mistakes. I often hear ministers argue, "But how can you know you have failed?" I am a little impatient with this argument, because it is too easy an escape hatch. The minister who does not know when he has failed in his work with individuals needs a basic lesson in honesty.

RUSSELL DICKS,
Divinity School,
Duke University.

Another minister replies:

The pastor has presented one of the most difficult and typical problems confronting us as ministers. Every church, as well as every group, has to wrestle with the disruptive domineering person.

In handling the difficulty the writer has rightly indicated there are two facets to consider. The first deals with the external situation of the man himself. The second focuses on the pastor and his reaction to the conflict.

The first aspect is the domineering individual himself. It is important to have as clear an understanding of the man and his dynamics as possible. The striving for power is conspicuous. He constantly must seek to fortify his own position. His excessive superiority and degrading of others enables us to make some safe generalizations. We see reflected an insecurity arising from deep-seated feelings of being unwanted. There is, therefore, a

194

low self-esteem with accompanying repressed hostility. His aggressiveness is a protection against his anxiety over his feeling of helplessness. It provides an outlet for the repressed anger. It enables him to shun any appearance of helplessness. He doesn't need help. He is afraid to give in, for to do so would be regarded as a sign of impotence. He controls others and despises their weakness. Consequently, he desires to humiliate them. We must go behind the façade of aggressiveness and superiority to his underlying fear and anxiety, namely, helplessness and low self-esteem. On this subject I refer you to Karen Horney's book, *The Neurotic Personality*, especially Chapter X.

Within a group setting, certain considerations are important to remember. Although crippled in their effectiveness by their anxiety, these people are usually quite capable. They can assume responsibility. Even if the minister isn't consulted, he can be reasonably certain such a driving person will carry through. It may not be quite in the manner the minister desires, but such an individual *needs* to be successful. He will bend efforts to accomplish that end. Only in rare exceptions would one clash with him in a meeting. If such an occasion arises, one must be certain it is a basic issue. So often clashes come because we are responding from our own distorted needs. We react from weakness instead of strength. At those times when a confrontation is required, it would be good to first recognize his leadership contribution appreciatively. Then you would indicate that on this particular issue you feel a different course might be wiser.

Primarily, such domineering individuals need to be handled on an individual basis. Counseling is almost prohibited. Only under severe crisis do they recognize and admit their need. However, the minister can lessen tension by casually consulting them outside of meetings. The seed of an idea can be sown in that way. Perhaps weeks or even months later the individual will bring it out as his own. In such informal discussion the minister should keep his emotional investment to a minimum. For example: "I don't know whether this has any merit or not but it has been mentioned. I just thought I would tell you about it in case you ever thought there might be something in it." An approach like that avoids the appearance of weakness. You are not giving the impression of groveling hopefully so that he will be favorable to your pet idea. At the same time you are utilizing his need to feel wanted and important.

The second aspect of the problem is the minister's own reaction. How does it affect him and in what way does he respond? As to the external factors, the minister has only partial control. The one point he can really do something with is his own feelings. Some people do usurp leadership that we feel ought to be ours. They do fail to consult us as we feel they should. We are given the feeling we are unimportant and unnecessary. Quite naturally we are resentful and hostile. We want to strike back. When we find that such reactions only aggravate the condition, we settle back into a hostile and bitter tolerance.

If we find ourselves bristling, it is a wise procedure to examine whether some sore point of our own is being touched. Which needs of our own are being threatened, preventing us from responding helpfully to the underlying anxiety of the other person? Perhaps our own problems distort what our role as leader ought to be. Instead of helping others find their creative fulfillment we are preoccupied with being the one to carry the ball. Actually the strongest leader is the one who encourages others to develop initiative and responsibility for themselves without having to be dependent on the minister. The focus of our concern ought to be on others' ideas, feelings, and reactions. When we find ourselves overly concerned with how others are treating and responding to us, then it behooves us to do some self-analysis. It might even mean that brief professional therapy would be helpful in untangling our emotional involvement in the situation.

JAMES B. ASHBROOK,
First Baptist Church,
Granville, Ohio.

196

Preaching as an Opportunity in a Rural Church

A minister sends this challenging statement:

Preachers who read book on book by professional or ministerial counselors may get as puzzled as this writer. After turning the last page we say: "What's wrong with me? Don't they trust me? Where are all these people with problems?"

Common sense should tell us that most articles and books written by effective minister-counselors are written out of situations which do not and never will hold true for most Protestant preachers. Barring a few exceptions, here are the conditions under which our best-known religious counselors operate: A city parish situation which gives anonymity to callers. A private study located so the caller can slip in rather inconspicuously. A female secretary whose presence makes private talks with women visitors possible. Nearby psychiatric, social, and medical services. A term of pastoral service by the minister exceeding a get-acquainted period of one to three years. The small church rarely holds a minister five years, and people just don't unburden to a new minister of a couple of years' stay.

These and other conditions make possible a counseling situation not attainable in a small town church where Aunt Susie Smith can peek through the curtains and see the young divorcee Marie Jones going to Pastor Smith's study, and him all alone. Hmmm!

That's why so many books and articles on counseling which start off with "Recently there came to my office a young man evidently in great distress" don't apply to the vast majority of Protestant ministers. The big majority of Protestants are in the small town or country. Counseling is done there over the barbed-wire fence or kitchen table, but rarely in a book-paneled study. City boys going into the rural parish should not worry too much when that couple in the most disrupted home in town fail to ask for his help. If they do, he should consider it a remarkable tribute to his own reputation.

Then how can the average Protestant minister talk with people about their broken hearts, adulteries, selfishness, and eating crackers in bed? Don't be discouraged! Every Sunday we have our chance to help.

Without turning the sanctuary into an aspirin tablet dispensary, the Protestant clergyman has a whole hour every week when he deals with his parishoners' souls and soul problems. If he doesn't so deal, he has not only failed to counsel—but failed to preach, also. For preaching, like effective counseling, is talking with people about our common sins and about the deepest issues of life—heart to heart, face to face.

There they are, in the fifth pew back. Ralph Jones and his wife. Regular church goers, but their marriage has fizzed out. A few good sermons on the ideal Christian family might reveal their own situation and its remedy so vividly they won't need counseling, or perhaps will never say directly to you or to each other just how they got back on the track.

Mrs. Anderson goes to the doctor thrice weekly for her "nerves." She's afraid of her own shadow, of old age, of everything. The good old doctrine of assurance, well preached, effective public prayers, and good hymns may combine to tide her over until next Sunday. But, you say, she's just eking out, that way. Remember, many psychiatrists would feel complacent if they could do as well with some of their patients. Anyway, the church must help the weak to keep going as well as stimulate the strong to live dynamically.

Deacon Brown would be the last to come to a minister for counseling but, oh, what a case! Stingy, self-righteous, tyrannical in his home, foot-dragging in church meetings. You might yearn for a funeral, but he'll outlast you. Maybe nothing will jar him loose. Try shock treatment. Jesus did. Show him the yawning mouth of Hell, with flames reaching out for him and his money. He doesn't need soothing salve or aspirin, but he does need the most vivid portrayal possible of Hell.

Perhaps the whole congregation feels self-righteous about war. With social protest so easily neglected, who but the preacher will raise his voice against war and militarism in your community? Congregations saturated with the communique terminology of "neutralize enemy positions," "mopping-up operations," or "slight casualties" need a detailed sermon on the actual meaning of war. Those who came to be comforted may go away disturbed. What of it? We cannot be saved and undisturbed simultaneously.

In every pew (those occupied) are people with sin on their hearts. A time of confession to God, set apart in the prayer, will unburden many a soul. How better can the Protestant minister lead in the soul-cleansing process of confession and forgiveness?

The whole Sunday morning worship service, it goes without saying, should be planned and aimed at leading the congregation to the worship of Almighty God. If the people actually worship God this one hour a week, then the minister may feel that he has been a privileged participant in a process which cannot be glorified enough by the word "counseling," yet is counseling in its grandest sense. For the chief sin of all the sinners in any congregation is the worship of self. If the congregation, by whatever means—comfort, shock, hell fire, assurance, fear—can be lifted out of its prison of self and into a real worship of our Father, then it has been counseled. Many a professional counselor would like to tell the self-pitier seated before him—Aw, forget yourself! The preacher can actually do this, without saying it. By prayer, hymns, and by the spoken word, he can release the prisoner from self. In his sermon he can be blunter than the private counselor, for he can state facts without pointing the finger.

What about the danger of "directing the patient" in a worship service? You have heard: Never direct, let the patient find the answer for himself. Every "patient" who comes to a psychiatrist or clergyman comes because he needs human help outside himself. He needs some kind of direction. Anyway, professional counselors are not as strict as they were about the dogma of "don't direct." They know that somebody should have tried-and-true answers.

The Christian minister has those answers. Just how he presents them to soul-hungry people and those who don't want help but need it, is the big question. If, Sunday after Sunday, he presents the Bread of Life, then lives will be changed. He must show that he understands the sinner, yet hates sin. He must show a way of salvation from sin. He must lift men out of the prison of self and into the worship of God. To drab lives he must offer a life of abundance; rivers of fresh waters. To lives lived in the shallows, he must offer the depth of God's love. To those afraid, he must offer eternal assurance. To the stingy he must paint horrible pictures of the Dives and Lazarus.

What if Jim Jones doesn't come at midnight with a tale of an "affair" and ask your help? If you serve an average Protestant church you have no study at the church itself, and Jim doesn't dare come to the house, for the parsonage is next door to the worst gossip in town. But there's Jim out there in the pew next Sunday, just as eager for help as if he sat across from your desk. Take over from here.

A minister replies:

Personal counseling can never be a substitute for the ministry of the pulpit. By the same token the preaching ministry cannot eliminate the necessity for personal work. Our Lord's ministry emphasized both preaching and counseling, and His ministers will do well to follow this example. The pastor's sermon is an excellent preventive and remedy for many problems. Some of his members with difficulties, however, may not be present to hear it. The percentage of problems among the inactive church members is usually higher than among the regular attenders. This is because people often are ashamed of their problems and feel hypocritical in coming to church. (They shouldn't, of course, but often they do.) Even if a member becomes delinquent in his attendance due to no special problem, he may soon run into difficulties simply because he is without the influence of the weekly service.

People with long-standing and deep-seated personality problems usually need the individual attention of the counseling process to get to the bottom of their difficulty. The interchange of conversation in the counseling relationship is invaluable for the achievement of self-understanding and for the development of emotional stability. Preaching and counseling ought to complement each other in a balanced ministry. In fact, the kind of
200

preaching that gives people help in their problems also moves them to desire to talk to the pastor personally.

Although many of the authorities in pastoral counseling speak from a backlog of experience in a metropolitan church or institution, the counseling ministry can be adapted also to the small town and rural parish. I think I understand the small town. I have been living in one for the past few years. People in both large and small towns have not as a whole been accustomed to taking their problems to their pastor. It is the pastor's task to educate them to do this. The lack of anonymity in small town life does not prevent people from taking their problems to their doctor or their lawyer, because it is the customary thing to do. They can be educated to feel the same way about their pastor. I have discussed the ways and means of doing this in, "How to Set Up a Counseling Program in Your Church," in the January, 1952, issue of PASTORAL PSYCHOLOGY.

While some small town churches—as well as metropolitan—have had a pastor in their history whose conduct has been reprehensible, a pastor who is known as a consecrated Christian can counteract this memory. The life of a pastor who is obviously a man of God is not conducive to gossip. Jesus did not hesitate to counsel with questionable women in towns large and small, and even His enemies raised their eyebrows only in snobbery and never in suspicion. I am unable to see why His ministers should fear to do likewise. The fear of gossips should move us to take the precautions of wisdom, but should not be allowed to handcuff our ministry.

There is also a difference between the counseling ministry in a large and in a small church. I served a small church for three and a half years. It had no study and I had no secretary. (Personally I would consider the presence of a secretary a hindrance rather than a help to counseling.) Usually with ingenuity some sort of a counseling place can be arranged and made modestly attractive. I used a small sacristy entrance-way that led to the chancel. Even if some remodeling has to be done, the counseling ministry is surely worth the bother and expense. If the congregation invests a little in the counseling program, members may be more inclined to make use of it.

THE MINISTER'S CONSULTATION CLINIC

I can say from experience that the pastor in a small church *can* have a flourishing ministry in personal counseling. But it won't all be within his counseling room—at least not at first. In the small church counseling begins as an extension of the calling ministry. The pastor does not wait for his people to come to him. In his house-to-house calling he goes to them. The calling ministry takes the pastor into the home. It takes him also to his inactive members. If he is alert to the symptoms of problems and his conversational approach is sympathetic to counseling, he will meet up with opportunities for counseling. And he can do this in his first year in the parish.

Once he has counseled with a person in the home, the pastor can encourage him to come to church for the follow-up interview. If this is not feasible, the pastor can continue to go to the home for these sessions. In the meantime this individual, as well as others whom the pastor has counseled in a similar manner, will meet up with other people who need help; and so will recommend to them that they talk with Pastor Brown. When these people ask Pastor Brown if they can see him, he can make appointments with them during his regular hours at the church. Although he may never succeed in transferring even the majority of his counseling to the church, he nevertheless is doing personal counseling. And where he does his counseling is not so important as that he does it.

WILLIAM E. HULME,
Wartburg College,
Waverly, Iowa,

202

The Relationship of Preaching
to Pastoral Counseling

A minister asks:

I would like to see a discussion on the application of "client-centered counseling" or "non-directive counseling" to preaching. I have read many attacks on preaching as being too authoritative, and causing unnecessary and harmful guilt feelings. I can see how one can use the client-centered method in individual work, but I don't see how it can best be used in preaching.

A minister replies:

What does acceptance of non-directive counseling premises and method do to our preaching? What does it do to the pastor as preacher? These are pertinent questions and confront us with what may become a perennial problem. At the risk of appearing a champion of grossly directive counseling, let me suggest some considerations which may contribute to a working solution.

First of all, let a rank amateur as a counselor give his frank opinion that complete application of non-directive counseling procedures to preaching is doomed to failure. Slavish devotion to the principles of such counseling in the pulpit might provide an interesting introduction to a homily. For example, such a pastor might begin, "There was a man who had two sons; and the younger of them said to his father, 'Father, give me the share of property that falls to me.' According to the familiar parable the father then divided his living between them. What the father should have said to this immature son, was 'So you want me to give you your share of the property . . .?' Eductive counseling was indicated. Consider with me the reasons why."

Conceivably such a sermon would be interesting and might even prove edifying to a congregation of consulting psychologists and psychologically adept pastors. How long could the preacher keep

203

this up? If he followed some such tactic week by week across the years, would he be faithful to his commission to preach the Gospel? Does not Christian preaching include exposition of doctrine, biblical interpretation, ethical and evangelistic emphasis? If so, how can a measure of clear guidance and appeal be avoided? Someone has suggested that a doctrinaire advocate of unqualifiedly non-directive counseling would prove provocatively unhelpful to a stranger in his community who asked how he would go to Times Square. "So you want to go to Times Square," the single-minded counselor might respond, as he boarded his bus and left the inquirer to work out his own itinerary!

Are we then to discard all the insights gained through our study and practice of eductive counseling when we prepare and deliver a sermon? Patently it creates a dichotomy in the minister's "office," separating his preaching and pastoral functions in an arbitrary and unfortunate fashion. Twenty years ago it was said in Baltimore that the late Dr. John Rathbone Oliver, a well-known psychiatrist and author, deliberately did something like this week by week. Monday through Friday he was the medical psychologist; Saturday and Sunday he was the priest, discharging his duties as leader of worship and preacher. As far as one man could, it was alleged that Dr. Oliver assumed one role for his consulting room, another for the sanctuary, and saw no reason why the twain ever should meet. It is not even a good trick if you can do it; and one begs leave to question the possibility. No informed and conscientious Christian pastor willingly discards the insights gained in counseling, whatever type this may be, simply because he has entered the pulpit to preach the Word.

How then can we apply what we have learned from our eductive counseling to our preaching? In the first place we can proceed on the assumption that in preaching we have a significant opportunity to help men and women help themselves. Our teachers in the field of counseling have assured us that preaching, together with the other activities of our vocation, can be a precounseling activity. By conveying insight, understanding and love of human beings, the preacher will awaken drowsy emotions and drugged consciences. Such awakening, combined with the forceful impression of wisdom and friendship created by the power and empathy of enlightened preaching, frequently leads the hearer to seek a "confidential talk" with his minister. Others will experience a kind of group therapy as the result of listening to and receiving the words of the pastor-preacher. To the more intelligent among such auditors the preacher's role will be more than "supportive," it will be that of a competent guide pointing them to goals of Christian maturity and uncovering resources for their journey thereto. If, as I think, the most effective and helpful preaching is the pastoral kind, knowledge of the principles and experience of the results of eductive counseling is almost indispensable to it.

Again, counseling experience of the kind described by our questioner, should clarify for the pastor this fact: pastoral counseling cannot be the exclusive concern of the Christian minister. He must seek ever to avoid the dangers of "specialism" and also realize that by "the foolishness of preaching" the spirit of God still operates to save men from their confusion, failures and fears. What I am saying is that we must hold both major aspects of our task in balance.

What kind of preaching shall the pastoral counselor do? All kinds except the authoritarian, the egocentric, the extremely dogmatic, the coercive and moralistic kinds! Preaching, as I see it, is the communication of truth in love, by a man committed to the Gospel, to individuals in their known needs, that such individuals confronted by the good news of God in Christ may be enabled by God's Spirit to grow into fullness of life within the community of Christians.

This definition, although tentative, provides scope for the most skillful and conscientious pastoral counselor. How can a man know individuals in their actual needs without psychological knowledge of their deep motivations, hungers, perplexities? How can he communicate the Christian answer and reassurance if he does not love them and the Lord in whose stead and by whose grace he speaks—as well as listens? "Psychologizing" in preaching may be indicated; "theologizing" must be behind it. In any case, application of the principles of non-directive counseling to the total task of the minister must never (here I am blatantly dogmatic and unscientifically directive!) inhibit him as he acts as a "herald of God."

Already the results of clinical training and competent instruction by teachers of pastoral counseling appear to be bearing fruit in preaching. The best of our younger preachers "preach for a verdict," but with profound respect for the rights of personality and the basic needs of persons. They assume that a Christian minister can proclaim the truth as it is in Jesus, define the human situation, and unmistakably, if often indirectly, appeal for a decision. Are they not true to the spirit of our Lord when they leave the actual decision to the hearer? Our Lord did not bludgeon His way into the inner sanctuary of personality. The last New Testament book reports Him saying, "Behold, I stand at the door and knock; if any man hear my voice and open the door I will come in . . ." But our Lord did confront the man behind the door with Himself, and He did speak of Himself as the Way, the Truth, the Life. Can we do less than to help His Spirit do likewise? "Permissive" does not mean passive.

Non-directive counseling within reason contributes to preaching by inducing in the preacher attitudes and a spirit whereby he can function as an agent and instrument of Him whose Son Jesus Christ came that all of God's children might have life full; free in the sense of responsible freedom, united, purposeful. The New Testament writer put it more simply and adequately: that they might have life and that they might have it more abundantly.

Davɪᴅ A. MacLᴇɴɴᴀɴ,
Brick Presbyterian Church,
Rochester, New York.

A teacher of homiletics replies:

Every year brings a growing realization of the new resources for preaching disclosed in the development of the whole field of personal counseling. This new interest has helped the preacher develop and retain what easily becomes lost—the high art of preaching directly to individuals in the congregation. The preacher who has followed the amazing development of personal and pastoral counseling is aware of a new model for his preaching. That model is in the words used in briefing airmen in the second world war, "Target for tonight." The preacher realizes that his target for this morning is not the human race, but individuals. When that sense of the destination of the message in an individual is lost, preaching may become just spraying the solar system with words.

Moncure D. Conway was a young minister in the last century. A woman in the congregation once said to him, "Brother Conway, you seem to be preaching to the moon." Most of us know just what she meant. The moon has been a well-evangelized planet, but the preacher's commission does not say, "Go ye into all the moon and preach the gospel." It says rather clearly, "Go ye into all the earth . . ."—a much more demanding place. Preaching without the sense of the individual hearer and of his pertinent need follows the pattern of the address of Lord Byron to the sea, "Roll on, thou deep and dark blue ocean, roll." After that stirring message the blue ocean undoubtedly rolled on, though it is not certain whether Byron's good advice had anything to do with it or not.

Counseling enables the preacher to move nearer to a better model for meeting spiritual problems than Byron's address to the waves. The better model is found in the conversation which Jesus held with a woman at a well in Samaria. Dr. Harry Emerson Fosdick, who has been both a great pioneer in this field and its effective exemplar, said many years ago that there are four common types of preaching—where real preaching, directly to individuals—is not done, and consequently misses its mark.

These four preachers are: the man who is preaching a system of theology; the man who is getting something off his chest; the man who is trying to solve a world-wide problem; and the man who is charmed with his own literary style.

With a strong feeling of the sense of debt, I am moved to raise a question whether there is not at present in preaching the danger of an over-compensation for a former neglect of the whole realm of personal counseling. What I have in mind is the danger of the preacher's failure to bring the full resources of the Gospel to bear on personal needs through a too-slavish devotion to the dictum that indirect counseling is far more effective than direct counseling. There is no question about the truth of that basic principle. There is no question about the great debt we all have to Professor Carl R. Rogers, who has stated that principle so persuasively. He did not contemplate making a contribution to preaching, but he made a big one which has been increased by the insights and explorations of others.

Of course, it is the chief place of a minister to deal with persons. Where other people saw things, Jesus always saw persons. When He came up to Jerusalem, His disciples were deeply impressed with the buildings. They cried, "Look, Master, what a size!"

But Jesus saw persons. He saw a woman casting two coins into the treasury. Coming up to the city with the whole issue before Him of His witness and execution there, He nevertheless saw along the roadside what no one else paid any attention to: a person, blind Bartimeus. Even when cleansing the temple He saw persons, those who were wronged by being deprived of a temple as the house of prayer for all people.

Indirect counseling in preaching, as in personal contact, becomes a cooperative search for the solution of the problem. It makes preaching more interesting and it brings a live clash of ideas. It avoids the danger of creating an undue dependence on the counselor-preacher.

But there may be such a complete adaptation of the principle of indirect counseling that man may lose the affirmative quality of his Gospel. There may be an over-correction of a former fault. Some preachers have become so reluctant to appear dogmatic, so hesitating to give direct advice, that they end up by giving no help or too little help. The message becomes a sort of Delphic Oracle—a holy noise issuing from a cave and impossible to interpret. There can be no greater calamity in preaching than to lose or mislay the great direct positive affirmations of the Gospel. Many deeply troubled souls can be nerved with great affirmatives.

There are two kinds of counseling, both to the individual and in the preaching ministry. One is the indirect counseling, often in the form of raising questions which throw a person back on his own resources. Jesus did this very often. He asks again and again, "How does it seem to you?" (In that connection, I wish that the extreme neo-orthodox theologians and devotees had paid more attention to that question of Jesus, which is an appeal to the validity of human reason on religious questions, an appeal too often disdained.) Jesus did ask, "What do you think about it?" and "Which is greater, he that sitteth at meat, or he that serveth?" But also there was the direct exhortation and counseling. At the conclusion of the story of the Good Samaritan He said, "Go and do thou likewise." That looks very much like direct counseling. He said, "So, if you are offering your gift at the altar and there remember that your brother has something against you, leave your gift there before the altar and go first, be reconciled to your brother, and then come and offer your gift." That is specific and direct, telling a person just what to do. Again to the woman at the well in Samaria. As the climax of a conversation full of a marvelous indirect appreciation to her personal need, Jesus gives this direct word, "Go call your husband and come hither." When the disciples made a direct request of Jesus, "Lord, teach us to pray," He gave them a very direct answer. He said, "When you pray say, Our Father, which art in Heaven."

The use of these two kinds of teaching is a continuing mark of Jesus. To the preacher the word may well come in this matter, "What God has joined together let no man put asunder in the pulpit." Years ago, during the excessive vogue of the discussion method, when to its many devotees it seemed the final method of education, Dean Willard L. Sperry made a pertinent comment about it as applied to religion. He said in effect that, if in St. Paul's day the discussion method had been in full flower when the Philippian jailor asked Paul the question, "What must I do to be saved?" Paul would have said, "Well, what do you think about it?" That would have left something to be desired. After all, Christianity is a religion of tremendous affirmations. It is that which saves it, as Dorothy Sayres has pointed out, from being a pale pageant of aspirations and good advice. It is a drama of redemption and the dogma is the drama. Hence, Paul could answer the jailor and give him some very direct counseling, "Believe on the Lord Jesus Christ and thou shalt be saved."

All this is old stuff. It is simply the manifold wisdom of the

New Testament. The pastoral counselor in the pulpit has many ways of ministering to a soul diseased. God fulfills himself in many ways, lest one good custom should become exclusive. The debt of the pulpit to psychology and its use in enriching the pastoral ministry cannot be overstated. It has contributed greatly to the decline and fall of Sir Oracle. "I am Sir Oracle, and when I ope my lips, let no dog bark." Sir Oracle has been the blight in the pulpit too often and too long. But indirect counseling is not another legalism. Along with it must go at the proper time the clear word of direction in which much preparation is caught up. For without the direct word on occasion, and indeed without specific exhortation, the work lacks saving direction.

HALFORD E. LUCCOCK,
Professor Emeritus of Religion,
Yale University Divinity School

Another minister replies:

There was a time when I looked upon the preaching and pastoral roles as two incompatible activities. I get the distinct feeling that Dr. Luccock and Dr. MacLennan still look upon them in this way.

To be sure, they suggest some compromises, but in essence they suggest compromises between activities which they feel are really incompatible. The reason why they feel such a disparity between counseling and preaching roles, and find it necessary to admonish against too much carry-over of the counseling role into preaching, is that *they both consider client-centered counseling a matter of techniques and procedures.* Both look upon client-centered counseling as a role: something one does . . . a set of ready-made responses one can apply to all situations.

Client-centered counseling is not a "role," it is not something a counselor *does,* it is not a ready-made stack of phrases like "you seem to be saying" or "it would seem you feel this way." Client-centered counseling is a matter of *attitudes held by a counselor and expressed in an intimate interpersonal relationship.* These attitudes are ones of acceptance—the deepest kind of human feeling one can offer to another human being; of understanding—that constant human challenge to depart from one's

210

universe of meaning and enter into the universe of personal meanings of one who stands against us as a "thou"; and of respect—that attitude so rarely found, which is based simply on the non-transferable quality of human existence and which accepts the fact that each of us must make our own accounting for the lives we are living.

Seen in the light of these attitudes, client-centered counseling is not a thing to be compromised with when it comes to preaching. It is not a thing to be cautioned against taking in excess. As if attitudes of acceptance, understanding, and respect were a poisonous threat to the Christian Gospel! Rather than stand fearful of too much closeness between client-centered attitudes and the preaching role of the pastor, let us see their more conspicuous blending.

It seems to me that the blending of client-centered attitudes with preaching may take the following form. I have been impressed with how much of a personal transformation occurs when one holds and develops attitudes of acceptance, understanding, and respect in one's counseling work. These are *imperial* attitudes fully as much as the attitudes of rejection, hostility, and hatred are. These are attitudes which seek to extend the domain of their influence. Somehow or other, a consistent life of acceptance and warm understanding in the counseling relationship does wonders not only for parishioners but also for counselors. The pastor who begins to hold attitudinally that people need deep, sensitive understanding, who begins to find experientially that people have responsive strengths beyond our power to imagine, will also be the pastor who finds it no longer fitting to address other human beings in dogmatic tone and no longer necessary to speak of moral matters moralistically. It is this kind of personal transformation at an attitudinal level which a consistent and developing experience of client-centered attitudes in counseling can bring to the man who would be the spokesman for God. A friend in the ministry who has a rich and rewarding client-centered experience in his pastoral counseling work, indicated that preaching had become increasingly a matter not of preaching the Gospel, but of *being* the Gospel while preaching.

Does this mean that preaching will lose its evangelical and ethical qualities? And Christianity its character as a divine judgment on our lives? Not at all. But there can be a world of difference between a judgment spoken in love—where respect and acceptance of the other as a person still exists—and a judgment spoken in the mood of disrespect at the level of interpersonal feeling. The former is the honest statement of one human being to another human being offered in terms of one's own perceptions of reality and of one's own ethical sensitivities. The statement spoken in the mood of personal contempt is felt as a statement of one human being who believes he has acquired the perceptions and sensitivities of God Himself. The world of difference is in the attitude of the preacher, and it is precisely at this point that client-centered counseling focuses its attention.

Client-centered counseling is caricatured when it is treated as Professor MacLennan did, as a means of circumventing direct communication. Client-centered attitudes are actually the means by which a more direct communication, in the sense of a real understanding of another person, takes place. The carry-over of attitudes which are basically facilitating of communication and understanding in one interpersonal relationship, in such a way as to make them barriers to honest self-expression in preaching relations, would seem to be a perversion of the client-centered interest in the deepening fullness of personal and social existence.

RUSSELL BECKER,
Associate Professor of Psychology,
The College of Wooster,
Wooster, Ohio.

Specific Counseling Problems

delphia, Pennsylvania; Chaplain Granger E. Westberg, University of Chicago Clinics, Chicago, Illinois; and Dr. George V. LeRoy, Associate Dean, University of Chicago Medical School, Chicago, Illinois.

cussed by: The Reverend Wesner Fallaw, Professor of Religious Education, Andover Newton Theological School, Newton Centre, Massachusetts; the Reverend Leland Foster Wood, Marriage Counselor, New York City; Dr. David R. Mace, Professor of Human Relations, Drew Theological Seminary, Madison, New Jersey; and the Reverend Russell Becker, Assistant Professor of Psychology, The College of Wooster, Wooster, Ohio.

When Is Grief Healthy or Morbid?

A minister asks:

A family lost a strapping twenty-four-year-old son in Alaska when he fell from an airplane, and the body has never been located. It has been about a year now.

The family belongs to this church. The mother has gone through various episodes since: lack of a satisfactory explanation of it all, a sense of nearness of her son, frustration, a what's-the-use attitude, a resolve to live as she considers her son would have her live, a feeling of duty toward the community, a stoical acceptance, and maybe some thoughts of self-destruction. May we have a discussion of the psychological and counseling implications here, and some information about the phases through which an individual may pass when tragic death has come into the home?

A minister answers:

"Emancipation" is the key word here. The mother still seems to be tied to the son, even though he has been gone for more than a year. There is need that these ties be broken. To break these bonds the mother must talk—talk about the accident, about her son and his relationship to herself. If a counseling relationship can be established so that the minister can meet this woman for an hour once or twice a week for several weeks, that would be best.

There is need for the bereaved to cover her whole relationship to her son back through the years. She should be encouraged not only to give a recital of events, but to express her *feelings* about her son and his relationships to her. The minister will remain permissive, and not seek to evaluate or to judge feelings,

219

either positive or negative. The important thing is how the bereaved feels. She may, for example, express certain guilt feelings which the minister knows or believes are unjustified. Their objective reality is beside the point. How does the bereaved feel, that is the issue. If there are justified guilt feelings, the minister will neither want to blame nor condemn.

As the bereaved talks, she will undoubtedly have spells of weeping. She should be encouraged to feel that these are natural and are not a matter for feeling ashamed. Nor are they a denial of faith.

"Consolation" is a second important word here. When the bereaved has been emancipated, then she can be consoled. There is danger in trying to give assurances too soon. By his sympathetic understanding the minister will have brought some consolation, but formal consolation can now be brought. The minister can remind the bereaved of the implications of the doctrine of the resurrection or of immortality, and of the strengthening presence of the Living Christ. We don't know why these things happen, only how a Christian should meet them.

"Socialization" is a third word to remember. When the bereaved has been freed from ties to the deceased, then there is need for new interpersonal relationships. There is need to realize that an individual can be in a crowd without being *of* it. The minister will have started the process of socialization in his counseling. Beyond this he can help the bereaved to find her way into close fellowship in small groups.

Here are some suggested readings:

Ina May Greer, "Grief Must Be Faced," *The Christian Century,* February, 1945.

Erich Lindemann, "Symptomatology and Management of Acute Grief," *The American Journal of Psychiatry,* September, 1944. Technical and basic.

William F. Rogers, "The Place of Grief Work in Mental Health," unpublished Ph.D. dissertation; Paul E. Johnson, Major Professor, Boston University, 1948.

William F. Rogers, *Ye Shall Be Comforted,* Westminster Pastoral Aid Series, Westminster Press, 1950. Popular, but suggestive for ministers.

WILLIAM F. ROGERS,
Protestant Chaplain,
St. Louis City Hospital,
St. Louis, Missouri.

A psychiatrist answers:

The loss of a son in war can be a harrowing experience. It is usually intensified if the person is missing a long time before death is established, or if the body is never located. Fears and hopes are constantly at war in both the unconscious and the conscious mind, and delay the resolution of the grief.

From the description provided in the question, the mother of this young man has suffered a difficult grief reaction. None of the individual episodes described are in themselves pathological, and any or all may occur in a normal grief reaction, yet the very fact that the question is asked strongly suggests that these "episodes" have been more intense, more prolonged, or more vacillating than usual.

A normal grief reaction represents the painful experience of separation from a loved one which is experienced as the loss of a part of oneself. It is usually done bit by bit and is perhaps never fully accomplished. What is important is that a sufficient amount of the investment of life interest and energy be gradually weaned from the memory of the loved one so that it can be reinvested in living persons and current and future activities. The death-centered mind must be life-centered again.

Difficulties in carrying out this transition may result from many causes, among them suddenness and unexpectedness of separation; excessively prolonged period of uncertainty regarding the reality of the separation (here, for example, one may even have accomplished one's separation and may then discover that the person is going to live after all and that the relationship henceforth is an altered one); mixed feelings for the person occurring particularly on the unconscious level and resulting in the feeling or acting as if "the score had not been settled" with

221

the person who has departed; or identification with him in continuing his work, purpose, or personality.

The pastor's role in these situations is that of relating in an understanding manner to the woman in all the vacillation and alteration of her moods; admitting with her the fact that we as human beings do not have satisfactory explanations of why some individuals are taken now and others later; assuring her of his understanding of her feeling of her son's nearness, and perhaps interpreting it in terms of the experience of the communion of saints; acknowledging during periods of frustration his understanding of how thwarted and blocked one must feel when one's hopes are dashed and one must begin to rebuild from ashes. The pastor, while he probably avoided indulging in Pollyanna preachments during periods of discouragement and defeat, nevertheless represented one who expresses his strength through understanding even if it be entirely silent and tacit.

There is room for successful application of resolves to "live as her son would have her" or "feelings of duty toward the community," provided they do not partake of martyrdom or fanatic zealotry. Only time and love can heal the stoical attitude. If it approaches self-destructive thoughts, psychiatric consultation should be undertaken for the protection of both the woman and her pastor. However, no psychiatrist can replace the pastor's function in the majority of separation and grief reactions of his parishioners. It is only his own maturity and faith and understanding that will enable the minister to share in the rehabilitation of the bereaved. It must be remembered that the process of "grief work," as Freud termed it, is a slow one, and what has been said is not meant to imply that it can necessarily be accelerated to any great degree, or that time alone will not heal the majority of grief reactions. Nevertheless, much comfort can be brought to the bereaved, and their usefulness to the community and themselves can be enhanced, by helping them in relating their lives to persons and activities as early as possible.

During counseling sessions mourners should be freely permitted to describe in great detail their past relations and experiences. (Some Irish wakes have provided a cultural setting for this phenomenon.) What gradually occurs seems to be the recognition and acceptance, bit by bit, of the fact that the loved one really was, but is no more in this life; and that one is oneself still here and has both work and joy now and in the future. The Christian hope of immortality can provide a cheerful contrast to an otherwise somewhat stoical acceptance of death's finality.

EARL A. LOOMIS, JR., M.D.,
Associate Professor of Psychiatry,
Western Psychiatric Institute and Clinics,
Pittsburgh, Pennsylvania.

Fatal Illness

What is the role of the minister or chaplain in telling a parishioner that his illness is hopeless and death is imminent?

A chaplain replies:

This is a basic question which always is raised in a terminal
illness by those who care for the patient; and it is of particular
significance to the minister, who is primarily concerned with the
meaning of life and death. It would seem to me that no definite
rule can be established. No statement is possible which stipulates
that there is always inherent good in telling the parishioner that
death is imminent, or in always avoiding telling him. The primary role of the minister is to meet the spiritual need of his
parishioner. And this in actuality is not too different when a
man faces death than it is when he attempts to face life, and
in particular, his own life.

Whether he is told or not should depend upon his desire to
know; and this desire is usually based upon his conscious or
unconscious ability to accept the fact of imminent death. In some
instances he will indicate his desire to know either directly or
indirectly; in other cases he will deliberately avoid any remarks
which might involve gaining this knowledge. It is important at
this point that the minister let him have the privilege and dignity
of making his own choice. Above all, the minister must accept
it with due respect.

When a patient does want to know the truth about "his
chances," the role of the minister is plain: he must help the
patient face death without feeling overcome by it. He must help
the patient face death in *faith* rather than in fear. A dying man
can still feel that he has some command of the situation and its

224

significance for him, if he will sense and understand life's meaning for him in relationship to God.

If the parishioner does not want to know the truth, the task of the minister may prove more difficult. Yet in essence it will not be very much different than it is when the patient *is* prepared to consider the possibility of death and its involvements for him. The role of the minister is always one in which he helps his parishioners face life in terms of their personal relationship to man and God; thus it is always a difficult and painful role, since all our human relationships are imperfect, and since they all involve good and bad, attainment and failure, fulfillment and frustration.

Nevertheless, the need is to see life as it really is, not as one tries to convince himself it is. The patient's acceptance of his life helps him experience the need of forgiveness for himself; and it creates a desire in him to forgive others.

When this primary work has been accomplished, the patient is able to proceed to more direct consideration of his relationship to God and God's acceptance of him in life and in death. It is on the basis of such work that the parishioner does himself that the minister fulfills his role so that the patient faces life and death, not in fear and despair and bitterness, but in faith, hope, and love. Oftentimes the minister can further fulfill his role by offering the parishioner whatever ministrations of the church he has been accustomed to, or which now would prove meaningful to him. For example, the Holy Communion, in which the requirement is "that he do truly and earnestly repent him of his sins and is in love and charity with his neighbors," and ends on the triumphant thought that "he is an heir, through hope, of God's everlasting Kingdom."

ARTHUR G. ELCOMBE,
Protestant Chaplain,
Bellevue Hospital,
New York, New York.

A psychiatrist replies:

It is assumed, first, that there is full cooperation between the physician and the clergyman, and that the physician has indicated that the patient needs to be told that his illness is hopeless and death is imminent.

Second, it seems important that the clergyman consult with the patient's family to make sure that they know that he is going to deal with this emotional problem.

If both physician and family are in agreement, it may then be well to remember that in most cases—possibly four out of five—the patient is already aware of the seriousness of his illness. But, like the family and the physician, he has not wanted to introduce the subject of hopelessness or death to those around him. Consequently, the clergyman can usually do the patient a favor by being the one to bring the subject up for discussion. He can say, "Have you thought about the nature of your illness?" Or, "Have you thought about how seriously ill you are?"

Asking the patient, "How do you think you are progressing" may give him a chance to express his misgivings, particularly since it is likely that until now others have permitted him only buoyant, hopeful ideas. Should the patient not follow one of these leads into a discussion of the seriousness of his illness, the clergyman might proceed further and say, "Have you thought that your illness might have a serious termination?" If this does not bring the subject into the open, then it seems appropriate for the clergyman to say, "Your physician and family have commissioned me to talk to you about the seriousness of your illness and the possibility that it might end fatally." Or, "I have spoken with your physician and family and they would like me to talk over with you the seriousness of your illness and the possibility that it might end with death." By this time the clergyman has come to grips with the question unless the patient is mentally sick in some way and showing some denial of his sense of reality.

It then seems important to find out how much in the way of religious help and consolation, such as prayer and Bible-reading, the patient wants or needs. It should be kept in mind, however, that these things may possibly make the patient more apprehensive and that he may prefer to have them later after the initial shock of breaking the news has been dealt with. However, once having opened the discussion, the clergyman can say, "Do you wish to talk with me about the fact that this may be your last illness? Are there some things that you would like to do that I can help you with? Are there letters you wish to write? Are there people with whom you wish to communicate?" If the clergyman knows that the patient has not made a will, he will wish to raise this matter.

Some patients will discuss the whole situation quite calmly and matter-of-factly, and will even wish to discuss funeral arrangements and other things at the first interview. Others may be much more anxious and awe-struck if the idea of death is new to them, and they may merely want to think about it or talk about the fact that this is their last illness. They may have to show some emotion through crying or expressing their regret. If this is all the patient can do at this point, then a later session should be arranged. The clergyman will have to judge how much the patient can deal with in this first visit.

The giving of consolation, strength, and courage to meet death are techniques which the clergyman has been taught, and they are many and varied. Some patients may wish to discuss the coming of death in considerable detail. Other patients may not wish to discuss the problem at all, but prefer to let death come without verbalization of its meaning or of what attitude to take toward it. The clergyman will need to use intuition, coupled with experience, and if he is very young in his ministry, some actual trial and error will be necessary until he knows how to be of most help to the patient in this situation.

O. SPURGEON ENGLISH, M.D.,
Department of Psychiatry,
Temple University Hospital,
Philadelphia, Pennsylvania.

Another chaplain answers:

The minister must always remember that the doctor is committed to keeping life going. He will do nothing that will cut down the force of a patient's will to live. The doctor never wants to call any case hopeless—and neither should a minister. Many older doctors recall that during the period of their practice they have seen a number of "hopeless" diseases like diabetes, diphtheria, pneumonia, and smallpox become curable. Some of the patients who were being "starved to death" in the old manner of diabetes treatment were actually kept alive long enough by this somewhat brutal method to be miraculously healed by the discovery of insulin.

If to "tell a patient" means to imply utter hopelessness, then a minister will certainly not encourage such telling. If, on the other hand, it is thought of as being in the same category as telling the T.B. patient the truth in order that he may work cooperatively with those who could help him, then it serves a valid purpose. The suspected T.B. patient who is waiting for the diagnosis usually says that even though the news may be bad, he can hardly wait until he gets a definite answer. Living in doubt and uncertainty is worse than knowing the truth. Once he knows he has T.B., he learns to face it realistically. If all malignancies were contagious, then these patients too would have to be told and perhaps the problem confronting us would be quite different.

Most of us would agree that the decision to tell the patient that his illness appears to be hopeless lies with his family. Our guess is that seventy-five percent of doctors would rather that the patient not be told he has a malignancy, because it might cut down his ability to fight against it. They suggest this to the family and soon they all enter into a conspiracy of deceit. Unless the patient presses his family or the doctor for a specific answer, contacts with him are on a superficially cheerful basis. He is treated as if he were a small child and conversations are confined to small talk (which often means inane trivialities). Obviously there are many patients who are not fooled by this ruse. There are others who desire to be fooled, and it is not at all easy to tell in advance what attitude is best to assume around any particular patient.

The minister finds himself in some sort of dilemma at this point because he has always been opposed to deceit in any form. Yet the majority of the so-called "hopeless" cases with which he deals are handled by the deceit method. This naturally irritates him, for the mood created runs contrary to the Christian concept that it is always best for man to face life and death realistically. But most ministers have shied away from facing up to this problem. We think there are at least three reasons why they have.

(a) They do not want to be like a very small percentage of ministers who seem to take delight in making people squirm by holding over their heads the threat of death, judgment, and hell.

(b) They respect the tremendous advances in scientific medicine and want to work closely with the doctor, and so have been willing to abide by his orders even though the matter of telling patients the truth may not be solely in what can be called a medical category.

(c) They know that the family puts more trust in the doctor during illness than in the minister. Because the minister has not been at all sure of his value in the sick room, he has been too timid even to question some of the customs dictated by a materialistic culture.

Now that people in general are beginning to appreciate what a minister can accomplish through pastoral care, he has taken courage to ask whether deceit is ever justified—even in a sick room. He wonders if it is quite fair to expect a man to fight against the most difficult of foes, the unknown. He has long believed that if a problem is repressed, it will cause the person more real suffering than if it is taken out of its hiding place and faced with the help of loving friends. If it is true that children can bear and handle all sorts of tragedy much better than they can handle lies, deceit, and pretense, then perhaps the same can be said for adults.

All this gives the impression that I personally believe every patient with a malignancy ought to be told. I doubt that I shall ever say "every," for I can immediately think of a number of patients who I am sure could not have handled it. But I think there are more people than we realize who would have had a more meaningful last few months if they had been treated like adults. Some of them have confided to ministers that they "played the game" because their doctor and family wanted it that way.

Is there anything that can be done about this problem? We think there is. We are now in a position to ask medical and theological educators to meet together from time to time to address themselves to the many problems which they face in common. The patient is the center of attention of both of these disciplines. As they both attend to the needs of the patient they cannot help seeing how these professions overlap. In the give and take of such discussions new insights are bound to develop and new ways of dealing with particular problems will be explored. It is to be hoped that such discussions will stress the "wholeness of man" and see in problems such as this more than the physical dimension.

If we are to set down some principles for ministering to those whose illness is apparently hopeless the following things might be said.

(1) The minister must always think of each patient as an individual for whom the usual methods of pastoral care may not be appropriate.

(2) The minister must consider each problem in the light of his own personality. If he tends toward being the "brutally frank" type he must attempt to understand the dynamics underlying his behavior. If he is often overly cautious it may be that he never has sufficient conviction on any issue to stand up and be counted.

(3) The minister must be willing to take the time to talk with responsible members of the family about the religious and psychological implications of facing the future realistically.

(4) If the minister believes it would be best for the patient to know the truth, then he ought convey this information to the doctor. If sufficient medical reasons can be given to show that this course should not be followed, then at least it is clear that the withholding of the truth has been decided upon with the patient's best interest in mind.

(5) If religious and psychological reasons for telling the truth seem to outweigh the medical reasons for not telling it, it is to be assumed that the physician will understand this.

(6) If the family, the doctor, and the minister are in agreement that the patient should be told, there will, of course, be no formal announcement. If the patient asks if he has a malignancy, the answer is simply "Yes" *with an immediate description of all the possibilities for counteracting it.*

When an atmosphere of honesty prevails, the air seems much clearer. All conversations carried on in the patient's presence are free, easy, and open. No one has to be on his guard to remember the last lie told the patient. The minister is his same hopeful self, encouraging and strengthening the patient with the resources of the Christian faith. He is no longer fettered by being unable to discuss with the patient all aspects of the Gospel. He does not have to avoid certain passages of Scripture which deal with death and the hope of life eternal. He now speaks frankly of both life and death with the realism so characteristic of the early Christians. He is a minister of the religion best equipped to help people die victoriously. It would be unkind to withhold such a faith from most terminal patients.

GRANGER E. WESTBERG,
Chaplain, University of Chicago Clinics,
Chicago, Illinois.

A doctor writes:

It is unlikely that early in the course of any but a few diseases the word "hopeless" should be used. At the time the average *incurable* disease is recognized (with few exceptions), "hopeless" is the *wrong* word. There is always hope for relief of pain, for palliation, for daring surgery, for unusual reactions to drugs, or even for the advent of a drug that can control or cure.

Life itself can be called an incurable disease. The cardiac or the diabetic or the hypertensive is more incurable than the cancer patient. Each knows with more certainty than the rest of us what will be the likely cause of death. Although it is true that such knowledge is hard to bear, uncertainty is intolerable.

Although any patient will experience anxiety when he has to face the reality that he is not immortal, he has really always known this—and his faith can be a powerful support at this time.

GEORGE V. LEROY, M.D.,
Associate Dean, University of Chicago Medical School,
Chicago, Illinois.

The Pastor and Suicide

A minister writes:

I would appreciate a thorough analysis of the pastor's duties at the time of a suicide. I had the funeral of a suicide recently and could find very little helpful material on the subject.

I think the trend away from the funeral "message" is the loss of an opportunity to do some helpful group counseling in ten to twelve minutes of guided meditation. If references to the dead person be kept at a minimum, this part of the service can be especially helpful.

Another minister asks:

The funeral of a suicide is one of the most difficult tasks of the minister. It is a situation where counseling is desperately needed by the bereaved. What should the pastor keep in mind while conducting such a funeral?

And, more important, what elements should be taken into consideration when counseling with the family? Often such folks shut themselves away from the minister because of a feeling of shame. Can the pastor make himself available to them without forcing himself upon them? If he is able to make contact, how much of the counseling is likely to deal with what is behind the act of suicide?

A minister replies:

In ministering to the family of a suicide, a pastor would not, as a rule, push back too deeply into the things which caused the tragedy. If, however, he knows the situation well, he may be able to interpret the significance of causes which are known to the family. It will be helpful if the minister can clarify the intolerable strain under which such a person must have been living, a strain which warped judgment and made escape seem the only solution.

232

I have found one helpful approach to such a situation in the prayer which G. A. Johnston Ross offered at the funeral of a friend of mine who took his own life. The prayer, in part, was:

Lord God of our fathers, whose undying life encompasses and enswathes the little fragments of experience which we call living, hear us, we entreat Thee, when we repair to Thee as our fathers did, when overwhelmed and vexed with the mystery, and sore with the agony, of amputated life.

We are here to mourn the loss of a beloved comrade, snatched from us by some power to which we can give no name.

We remember with wistful thanksgiving the generous opening of his manhood as we saw it here: his brightness, his cheerfulness, his gentle courtesy, his loyalty to his comrades, his diligence in study, his hunger for affection.

And then we remember the mysterious shadow of the later days, which we so little understood and alas! did so little to relieve: the shadow which, despite his smiling courage, gradually reduced his life's hopes and purposes to confusion and frustration, made thought more and more difficult and sleep impossible; until at last the tired will resigned its directive office, and the life went out in tragedy swift and dark.

O God, whose endless resources of life rebuke the penury of our confidence, increase our faith! Give us to believe that Thy love has triumphed; and that our brother lives in Thee with all frustrations over, all maladjustments past, with faculties fully released and opportunity infinitely extended— taught no longer by frail mortal men who knew so little more than he—but growing and serving, under the immediate tuition of the Mind and Heart of God.

HAROLD LEONARD BOWMAN,
First Presbyterian Church,
Chicago, Illinois.

A psychiatrist writes:

In the private practice of psychiatry, suicides constitute the principal cause of mortality, and prevention of suicide is the principal direct lifesaving effort of the psychiatrist. In the out-and-out case of threatened suicide, the psychiatrist makes every effort to get the patient under hospitalization and treatment at the earliest possible moment. However, there is always a border-land of suicidal possibility in which a great many patients inevi-tably are to be found. Occasionally, but fortunately rarely, one of these patients will attempt to take his life. Sometimes he will succeed. A psychiatrist has a difficult problem in handling the families of those threatening suicide and an even more painful task in dealing with those who have been bereaved by suicide, since so often the psychiatrist may be blamed or misunderstood. It is particularly difficult if he does feel to blame and guilty about the unfortunate outcome of his therapeutic attempts.

I have not had experience in directing any such families to their ministers, and have not seen firsthand any examples of how best a minister might perform his function in such a situation. Therefore my remarks are somewhat theoretical. I hope they will provoke confirmatory or contradictory statements from those who have had such experiences.

In conducting the funeral of a suicide, a pastor should keep in mind the following:

(1) The family probably feels very guilty and very much to blame (as well they may be, or at least as the suicide may well have wished them to feel). To deal with the terrific forces of submerged hostility, part of which is turned inward and part outward, challenges the skill and understanding of the most capable minister. Despite the fact that words are painful and that there is little that can comfortably be said about one who has taken his own life, a great effort should be made to express in plentiful speech as much as possible of one's freedom to face, feel, and discuss the question of suicide. Too often it is shrouded in a dank silence and fetid gloom.

To recognize and express one's conviction that most suicides are the result of illness, and may be thought of as the terminal event of an emotional sickness which was not cured in time (just as physical disease frequently ends in death) is to lay the ground-work for a less anxious, guilty, and depressed attitude. It is to be hoped that if suicide can be presented with conviction as a fatal illness rather than an act of blasphemy, it will be better understood and its mourning can pass more naturally through the usual sequence of grief work. (See Freud: *Mourning and Melancholia;* Lindemann: "Grief," PASTORAL PSYCHOLOGY, June, 1950.)

(2) The same applies to the community, especially including those who hear the service. Too frequently they are attending out of mixed loyalties, guilts, and perhaps even morbid curiosity. To reflect the naturalness of life's inevitable end and the recognition that the forces of health and disease are at war within the mind and emotions as well as in the cells and tissues will possibly begin to have a salutary effect upon the community's attitude toward suicide. Just as it has been possible to rid the community bit by bit of the bulk of its superstition about insanity, tuberculosis, and cancer, so too, in time, suicide may be appreciated for what it is: the consequence of illness. To be sure, there are suicides which result from causes other than direct mental illness, and many psychiatrists and psychoanalysts disagree with the statement that suicide occurs only in the psychotic. Nevertheless, the concept of inner warfare ending in the defeat of the life forces is helpful in viewing suicide as a whole. One must, however, recognize that it may be the result of numerous causes, each of which deserves individual study.

The principles to be taken into consideration in counseling with the family seem to me to stem from the same roots as those elaborated above. Providing, with patience and both through listening and talking, the opportunity for full ventilation of grief, remorse, guilt, and shame over a period of time, will serve to hasten and amplify the grief work. These folks can be helped to avoid shutting themselves away from the minister if he has already prepared them in previous contacts for a more Christian and scientific attitude toward life and death. Certainly, if he is unwelcome at any moment, he should delay his return until the door is more likely to be ajar, and then patiently wait until he is invited in. His attitude should be more one of permitting expression of feeling than of explaining and interpreting, although the latter should be safe if limited to the general principles applying to all bereavement. Naturally his focus should

235

be more upon the bereaved than upon the psychopathology of the departed.

EARL A. LOOMIS, JR., M.D.,
Associate Professor of Psychiatry,
Western Psychiatric Institute and Clinics,
Pittsburgh, Pennsylvania.

Another minister replies:

In all that he does the minister is attempting to interpret the Christian view of life, here and hereafter, including the place of death in making the transition from one to the other. At the same time he is trying to bring comfort and hope to others, and to lead them into a more mature Christian life. The question here is how he is going to bring this ministry to someone whose beloved has taken his own life.

There are at least three phases of this ministry—the minister's personal contact with the bereaved, the funeral service, and the healing which comes from the interpersonal relationships in group activity. These are all inter-related, and all dependent upon such other factors as the minister's previous relationship to the family and the circumstances of the suicide.

Chronologically the minister's personal contact with the bereaved will normally come first, as he goes to them immediately upon hearing of the death. The degree of his acceptability to the bereaved will depend upon his previous relationship to them, as well as on their feelings about the suicide. If the minister has not been close to the family in the past, or the bereaved feel that he will be judgmental in this situation, then he may have difficulty in reaching rapport with them. Even if there has been a good relationship in the past, the family may withdraw because of their own shame or guilt feelings.

The fact that the minister may have a difficult time making emotional contact with the bereaved does not mean that he will not try, nor that eventually he cannot succeed. If he is himself emotionally mature, and comes with the desire to bring help to the bereaved, they will come to realize this, and will accept him. Failure to establish rapport often comes at the point of the

236

minister's own embarrassment because he feels he ought to say something, but isn't quite sure what he should say.

The minister's first task is to discover the emotional state of the bereaved. Do they feel guilty because they know or suspect that their own actions or failures contributed to the state of mind which led to suicide? Do they feel hurt because the act of suicide seems to be an act of aggression against them? Are they ashamed because someone connected with them has demonstrated a great weakness of character? Are they angry at someone else because they feel this other party is responsible for the act? The only way the minister can find out is to get the information from the bereaved themselves. If he comes in with a prepared plan of assurance he may miss the need of the bereaved altogether, and raise a further barrier to rapport by convincing them that here is one person, at least, who doesn't understand.

Discovering the emotional state of the bereaved does not mean probing or cross-questioning, but rather leaving the initiative up to the parishioners. When the minister comes, following a suicide, the bereaved will know the event that brings him, although they may not know what the minister's intentions are. If he comes in the spirit of sympathy and with a desire to help, this will communicate itself to the bereaved eventually, if not on the first visit. One should not be surprised, however, if his personal ministry before the funeral is largely a matter of standing by, with effective counseling being postponed until later. Eventually, though, the bereaved should have an opportunity to work through all their emotional tensions relating to the deceased.

What one does at the funeral depends somewhat on the relationship he has had with the bereaved and their particular need. If he has been unable to have any real communication with them, then he will have to go on general principles. The first point is that the funeral is a ritual of separation. One thing it should do is to help the bereaved to accept emotionally the fact that this "bad dream" is real, and that they are now going to have to adjust themselves to getting along without the physical presence of the deceased. The presence of the body aids in actualizing the experience. Readings or remarks can also further this.

237

THE MINISTER'S CONSULTATION CLINIC

The message of the Resurrection and of the comforting Presence to strengthen the bereaved also are basic in the funeral service.

Whether one brings his message by formal readings or through informal remarks will ultimately depend on the way in which the minister can best express himself. Talking to a formal group is not counseling, which is a give-and-take relationship between two or more people. There may be a place for teaching here, but one needs to remember again that intellectual formulations and verbal assurances probably won't register with the emotionally disturbed. If the minister has had an opportunity before the funeral to hear an expression of the bereaved's feelings toward the deceased, these might be reflected in a review of the deceased's life. Unless he has this expression, however, he will do well to proceed with caution as he might praise one with whom the bereaved are angry for disgracing them, or about whom they feel guilty because they have failed him. This may serve only to increase their distress. In many instances it would seem better to keep the funeral formal and brief, and to depend on personal counseling to do the necessary grief work.

When the minister himself has made emotional contact with the bereaved, then he can begin to help them make wider interpersonal contacts through other members of the parish, and groups in the church.

WILLIAM F. ROGERS,
Protestant Chaplain,
St. Louis City Hospital.

A professor of pastoral care replies:

The pastor who is called upon to officiate at the funeral of a person who has committed suicide, and to minister to the bereaved family, has both a unique opportunity and a difficult task.

The pastor needs a word of guidance about his function in *preventing* suicide. His own inadequate feelings may very easily be associated with the fact that he was in close rapport with the deceased, and condemns himself for not having detected signs of the disaster before it happened.

The most obvious sign of a possible suicide is the verbalized threat on the part of the person. It is a common adage that the person who talks about suicide never does it. This is, like most popular opinions, not necessarily true. When a person tells me that he is contemplating suicide, I take his word at face value just to be on the safe side. Of course, the open threat of suicide is not as common as the covert threat which comes in the form of hesitantly expressed "death wishes," such as "I wish I had never been born," "I am at the end of my wits and there's nothing left for me except the crazy house, the poorhouse, or the grave," "Sometimes I just don't see how I can go on living," or "I am afraid I will do something desperate."

Especially significant are such expressions if the person also shows definite signs of depression along with these threats. A pastor should read the psychiatric literature in such books as Menninger, *Man Against Himself;* Henderson and Gillespie, *A Textbook of Psychiatry;* and D. B. Klein, *Mental Hygiene,* on the subject of depressions. The person may have real causes for depression, i.e., it is a reactive sort of thing, caused by a plainly evident loss of some kind—the death or defection of a loved person, a reverse of financial fortune, a shock to personal self-esteem. Or, again, the depression may be what some doctors call a "true psychic depression," arising from internal inadequacies of a long-term duration. Regardless of the structure and function of the depression, the pastor needs the help of a dependable medical doctor, preferably a good psychiatrist, in sharing with him the responsibility of counseling and caring for the person. *Analysis* of the roots of the depression can best be done by the doctor, while the pastor can supply a *supportive* ministry of carefully placed reassurance, rather generous amounts of personal companionship, and skillful but covert use of such recreational and occupational facilities as he has available.

Careful planning with other trustworthy persons within the church can provide appropriate social opportunities for "propping the person up" when the blows of adversity have him "perplexed unto despair." The use of carefully chosen Scripture in "prescription" form can serve as mental pegs for the person to hang his hopes upon. (Example: I John 3:20; I John 4:18; John 16:33.) Carefully worded, reassuring prayers—both written and spoken—are of invaluable aid. An example of this kind of prayer is found in Ephesians 3:14-21. So valuable is this prayer for all occasions that I have had it printed separately on a card for use in pastoral work. I have it entitled: "Your Pastor's Prayer For You."

But too many are the instances in which the person with suicidal intentions does not come to the attention of the pastor until the act has been completed and the damage done. What can a pastor do at this point? It is a situation in which counseling is desperately needed by the bereaved. What should the pastor keep in mind while conducting such a funeral?

Of course, the care of a bereaved family in the event of suicide follows the same principles as any other grief situation:

(1) The pastor's approach is determined largely by the degree of "closeness" he has with the family. The more intimately acquainted a pastor is with the family, the more emotionally involved he is and the less he has to depend on "formal" approaches.

(2) The amount of shock and surprise in the death determines the kind of attention the pastor gives. For instance, a suicide occasionally comes after a long siege of acute mental illness and repeated unsuccessful attempts. This type of funeral has a different emotional frame of reference from the one in which the person's suicide came as a sudden surprise, "out of the clear blue sky," from the point of view of the family.

These two considerations should be kept in mind at all funerals. But more specifically, several facts need to be reckoned with both in the conduct of a funeral of a person who has committed suicide and in counseling the bereaved family.

(1) Each member of the family is privately—and sometimes not so privately—trying to affix blame for "causing" the suicide. This may take the form of self-recrimination and depression, or it may take the form of projection and hostility toward others who were related to the deceased.

(2) The question usually arises in the thoughts of relatives: "Was he in his right mind?" For non-sophisticated people the conclusion that the loved one was mentally ill and "beside himself" provides a "psychiatric out" for their guilt feelings. But for some sophisticated persons, the same conclusion might add to

240

the shame and stigma rather than relieve it. They likely will feel that "it's hereditary—in the family," and their own personal security will be shaken all the more by this.

(3) Since time immemorial persons who believe in heaven and hell as eternal realities have also tended to believe that the person who commits suicide is eternally condemned to hell. Many hold the superstition that suicide is "the unpardonable sin." Some ministers may also be the victims of this way of thinking. It is an interesting cloaking of a universal taboo against self-destruction with theological sanction.

(4) With the weight of the above considerations in their minds, the most likely response of a family to a minister—unless he is intimately acquainted with them—is to ask him only for the traditional and perfunctory duty of "conducting the funeral." They tend to want to "let it go at that." The minister's greatest task is that of establishing entrée into the private thoughts and discussions of the different members of the family.

My own experience has been varied at this point. I have served families who carefully concealed the cause of death with deceptions and deliberate camouflage. I have served other families who took it stoically and said: "Well, it's just one of those things no one can do anything about." There have been other families who fell into severe conflict with each other as to "who caused him to do it." They treated the minister as a sort of referee. Also, I have dealt with families who had called upon another minister for the traditional function of the funeral and later called upon me for specialized counseling help in working out a subsequent adjustment to the tragedy.

In any kind of post-funeral counseling, the minister follows the same pattern of counseling procedure that he would follow in any other bereavement situation. In an atmosphere of permissive acceptance he seeks to enter into the feeling tone of the person's emotional conflicts.

In counseling bereaved persons it is more important for the person to feel that he is not alone in his suffering than it is that he hear some clichés such as Job heard from his counselors. The pastor will depend upon the careful management of his own personal relationships to the person, rather than upon having

241

the "right answers" for the imponderable questions which will be somewhat aggressively put to him by the person who is bereaved. Of course, *honest* reassurance is a supportive therapy, one in which the first aim of the minister is to move with the spirit of the bereaved through the various stages of grief, and toward the acceptance of reality and their own finite limitations as human beings.

What Seward Hiltner has said about the determinative nature of the convictions of the counselor is especially appropriate in dealing with bereaved persons whose loved one committed suicide. If the pastor believes that suicide *is* the unpardonable sin, that it does consign the person to hell; if he believes it is the result of a hereditary taint in the blood stream, it isn't likely that he can keep this from the person to whom he is ministering, whether he says so or not. On the contrary, if he feels that suicide is something which could happen to anybody, given sufficient taxation of his frustration tolerance; if he has acquainted himself with the scientific literature concerning the structure and function of depressions; and if he has read the Bible with intelligence and without superstition, he will have a much mellower and discriminating kind of tenderness to impart to a suffering family, regardless of how incompletely he may answer their questions.

As for going into the cause of the person's act with the family, this tends to follow the same pattern as does all intelligent counseling: the pastor is more concerned with the inner achievement of personal insight on the part of a person who is confronted with a problem than he is in foisting upon him his own personal convictions as to the dynamics of the suicidal act. This is determined largely by the amount of time that the pastor can spend with the person, and the type of relationship the person is willing to afford him. Whether the person came seeking help or whether he had to be visited and have help offered him is an index to the kind of relationship that the pastor has.

By all means the minister's most valuable function as a counselor is to detect signs of the suicidal intent before they become full-grown. In the actual conducting of a funeral of a person who has committed suicide, the limitation of the service to the

242

use of scripture, prayer, and music as a means of melting the middle walls of partition that separate the family from the rest of the community, seems to be the best. Of all the funeral situations imaginable, the funeral sermon is the least appropriate in the event of a suicidal death. And finally, as for counseling a bereaved person whose loved one did commit suicide, the pastor's best approach is to deal with the person on the same basis of acceptance and understanding as he would if the person had died of some natural cause, i.e., that the person should not feel odd or different because of the thing that has befallen him and the one whom he lost.

WAYNE E. OATES,
Professor of Pastoral Care,
Southern Baptist Theological Seminary,
Louisville, Kentucky.

The Minister and Attempted Suicide

A minister asks:

Within the past year or so I have been called in on two cases of attempted suicide, neither of which resulted in death but did result in severe injury. In both cases these men are now working again and are apparently getting on. In neither case was regret or penitence expressed, but instead there was a kind of emotional apathy. I would appreciate a discussion of how to deal with persons after an unsuccessful attempt at suicide. Usually the family will insist that psychiatric help be rendered, and the patient submits to this; but what is the minister to do, and what steps are recommended to prevent recurrence?

A minister replies:

A discussion of this question will have to be on a vague and general basis because no insights are given regarding the patients' ages, occupations, backgrounds, families, education, religious life, biological heritage or previous medical history. Any, some, or all of these factors may contribute to a patient's retreat to suicide.

An attempt at suicide may be the patient's resort to the most drastic escape mechanism, a "way out" he feels driven to accept. For that reason, the patient should be given psychiatric treatment under the care of a competent, qualified psychiatrist. Unfortunately such psychiatric help is not always available, but an allusion in the question leads me to believe that this minister's parishioners have had such care. If that is the case, then I think it is advisable that the minister consult the psychiatrist or psychiatrists in question, outlining his reasons for being interested. Thus he might obtain some insights which will help the minister in his relationship with the parishioner.

The questioner mentions that both cases are "apathetic" and

"express no regret or penitence." This attitude is rather characteristic, but does not necessarily indicate that the patient *feels* no regret or penitence. Perhaps a deep-seated feeling of guilt is what causes the apathy. The church has always frowned upon suicide and regards it as sinful unless it is caused by mental derangement. (Just what is meant by "mental derangement," the church has not [to my knowledge] defined.) There is also in the race a deep-seated aversion to suicide, since if uncontrolled it could lead to racial extinction. Consequently, the patient may neither want to talk to the minister (who, he believes, will condemn him) nor to others (who may show their instinctive fear and distrust of one who has attempted to kill himself).

The minister's ability to help him, then, will depend upon the rapport which can be established. In this case the psychiatrist may be helpful, if he is able to persuade the patient that the minister's attitude is not one of condemnation or pity (or fear or distrust). If the psychiatrist suggests that the patient talk with his minister "because the minister understands," then the way is open for assistance.

Another way to reach one who has attempted suicide is through his family, if the minister has their confidence. Suicide is usually a retreat, and sometimes members of the family—inadvertently and otherwise—deepen the stress. Often they are in need of help themselves. I am reminded of the woman who came to my office and asked me to visit her alcoholic, hospitalized husband. During the conversation I thought I smelled liquor on *her* breath, but I was not certain until I asked whether her husband used whiskey "as a bracer when he thinks he needs it to relieve a feeling of tenseness." She answered that he not only did, "but went farther than that, while she herself stopped right there." The ensuing conversation showed that she needed guidance about drinking as much as her husband did.

Perhaps, then, the minister can help the patient's family; and through them, the patient himself in his adjustment. Those who attempt suicide often have a deep feeling of personal inadequacy; if it has its origins in their home life, their sources of tension can be somewhat relieved by working with the others in the home. All too often the patient alone receives psychiatric treatment, whereas in fact it should also be given to those who are driving him beyond his abilities. Yet since so many circumstances can contribute to a patient's stress, the pastor must be cautious in all of his efforts even after he has the confidence of the man and his family.

The very act of "acceptance" of the pastor by a patient—no matter which has made the approach—is in itself of psychological help. That help will increase as the relationship increases. The minister's attitude can represent the love which God feels and offers; and if the patient does attend church services, he should hear positive preaching there—preaching which will help him regain confidence in himself, and which will restore or reinforce his faith in God.

In any event, until such rapport exists, pastoral calling upon the patient (with the cooperation and approval of the psychiatrist)—and upon his family—should be continued as heretofore. This may at least serve to convince the patient that his status in the minister's regard has not been altered by his act; and this in itself will have a salutary effect.

CARL J. SCHERZER,
Protestant Deaconess Hospital,
Evansville, Indiana.

A professor of religion replies:

On the face of it, this question assumes that psychiatric treatment is indicated. The immediate issue for the pastor, then, must be seen in terms of the sort of relationship he may establish with a person undergoing medical care.

Some of the elements of pastoral responsibility would seem to be clear. First, the pastor will recognize that for the duration of the treatment his role is subordinate to that of the physician. Second, he will support the person in accepting treatment, and interpret the necessity of it to his family. Third, the pastor will refrain from discussing the suicidal behavior with the person while he is under the care of the psychiatrist. (In the instances cited, this is made especially obvious by the reference to the "emotional apathy" of the persons, indicating that they simply do not wish to talk with the pastor.) Fourth, while the pastor may not serve as therapist in any technical sense, there is another role he may use if his relationship to the person allows it. He may be an understanding friend who meets the person on a natural social level. The meanings associated with the pastor will be present and will have their effect, but the matter of importance is that the pastor shall accept the person *on equal terms and without judgment on the behavior in question.* In the psychiatric treatment, the person will be gaining insight and reconstructing his feelings about himself. Social acceptance by the pastor will reinforce the feeling of self-renewal, belonging, and forgiveness. In this way may the pastor make a positive contribution to the restoration of the person.

If the role of the pastor that has just been outlined is to prevail, the pastoral judgment implied in the reference to "emotional apathy," lack of "regret" and "penitence" must be avoided. Without doubt a sense of guilt contributed in large measure to the suicidal act. The terms used by the pastor reflect a disposition to intensify that guilt, or to view it as somehow necessary to a cure. Precisely the opposite is true. Actually it is guilt, morbid guilt issuing in self-punishment, that has led to the wish for self-destruction. Plainly this is disease and must be treated as such. Moreover, this pastor will do well to consider the part which guilt in the cases cited is playing in setting up a barrier between him and the persons he wishes to serve.

OREN H. BAKER,
Dean, Colgate-Rochester Divinity School,
Rochester, New York.

A psychiatrist replies:

When a person attempts suicide he shows that he no longer feels that life has any positive meaning. He feels that he has been so incompetent to meet life, so deeply hurt, so badly disappointed or frustrated that there is no other solution to his problems but—death. Therefore, as soon as his immediate physical needs have been met, the enigma of why life has lost so much of its meaning for him must be solved. The meaning of life must be redefined on a more constructive basis so that the sick man can again believe in the values and importance of living.

Attempted suicide should be recognized as a manifestation of serious mental illness. The understanding clergyman will neither reproach the individual nor seek penitence from him. He will, rather, try to understand why the individual became so emotionally disturbed. And the only real path to that door is to get the patient to talk about himself and why he did what he did.

The clergyman can do this much more easily than most. His position as spiritual confessor, adviser, leader, and friend makes it easier for him than anyone else to approach the sick man. But his success will depend largely upon his approach. If his approach be reproach, he may fail. One who attempts suicide is often regarded with a sense of awe because something violent, destructive, and unconventional was attempted by him. Also, one who has attempted suicide has admitted a certain kind of weakness, and it is not always easy to talk about demonstrated weakness or unconventional behavior. If, however, you somehow can let the sick man know that you understand unhappiness, despair, and futility, you have won half the battle. You must show willingness to listen, without censure or criticism. An approach from the level of the man's unhappiness will bring the most likely response. Let the patient know that you want to help, that you believe in him and in his grief, and that you honestly feel that unhappiness, if shared, can in some degree be dissipated.

We must realize that one who has attempted suicide is aware that by his very attempt he has let everyone know how very little they have meant to him as help-mates and supporters in his despair. He feels great shame for having thus revealed himself, and for the unspoken reproach he has given. Most suicidal attempts have in them elements of reproach to friends, to relatives, to life, to God. Getting the patient to be articulate about his reproaches—call them hostilities, if you will—is the only way to get him to release them and then be relieved of them.

Thus, the first and most important problem is to establish a rapport that makes verbal communication about emotions possible. Once this process starts, the clergyman need only listen, for a while at least. The patient may still believe he has many reasons why he should again attempt suicide. He must be listened to and his attitudes and ideas given respectful ear. After he has unburdened himself, it is up to the clergyman to point out to him where and how his attitudes can be altered with better results. He can tactfully direct the discussion toward the true meaning of life, its infinite possibilities for love, for service, for usefulness, for real personal satisfaction. The sick man, having been permitted the fullest possible expression of his personal despair, may, in the hands of a skillful clergyman and counselor whom he believes truly understands him, slowly pick up the threads of hope and, properly nurtured, once again live a full, meaningful life.

O. SPURGEON ENGLISH, M.D.,
Department of Psychiatry,
Temple University Hospital,
Philadephia, Pennsylvania.

Counseling with an Alcoholic Who Does Not Ask for Help

A minister asks:

There are times when people come to me with the request that I talk with someone else. Most often such requests have to do with alcoholics. In many such instances, however, the alcoholic has no apparent wish to be spoken with by the pastor; yet out of loyalty to the relative or friend who raised the question, he does agree to come and talk. Can such situations be handled without damage or, on occasion, with helpfulness?

A minister replies:

In the back of the parson's mind he does well to ask the question, "Why has this friend or relative of the alcoholic come to me?" As he listens to the person describe the situation, he may learn many things by wise direction of the conversation. One is whether the person himself is involved in the situation. *Would this person face the facts of his involvement if it becomes necessary in order to correct it?* In so doing would the person get into more difficulties than he can handle? Or is this person unwittingly looking for sympathy for himself about his own predicament? A simple request often involves many things.

These considerations are not meant to indicate that the parson should adversely suspect everyone who comes to him seeking aid. Rather, by skillful conversation with them he may get clues for himself by which he can make a judgment as to how helpful he can be in the situation. He need not indicate what is going on in his mind. It is enough that people be assured of his interest and good will. Wise handling of a first interview may be of the greatest help to the pastor.

From this first interview the pastor may also get a clue as to whether the unwillingness of the person to come to him is an unwillingness to talk to anyone, or just an unwillingness to talk to a minister. If it is the latter, that difficulty may disappear when he comes. If it is an unwillingness to talk to anyone, and the person doesn't like the minister, probably nothing will come of the interview. One of the first essentials is that the individual *want to do something about the situation and will let someone help him.*

When a reluctant person does come at last to the pastor, it may indicate a willingness to do something about the problem confronting him. It indicates at least a certain amount of decision and determination. The right approach on the part of the pastor may stimulate him to come again or seek further aid elsewhere. If the individual has come only to please someone else, the whole matter may end with one ineffective interview with the pastor.

This question raises the subject of the pastor dealing with the question of alcoholism. Usually it is difficult for a relative to face the true implications of it. A wife often cannot face the fact that her husband is involved in a disease which is affecting his whole emotional and mental life. She cannot believe he is not a normal person and cannot react as such. If the pastor has looked into this subject of alcoholism and knows what he is talking about, he can help the relative greatly by giving her a deeper understanding. This may be the pastor's greatest contribution to the situation. Without being any less loving she may be enabled to take a course of action she could not have embarked on without deeper understanding.

The parson ought to think out what his role is to be with alcoholics themselves. It seems that a reformed alcoholic has better luck in helping an alcoholic than a minister does. Alcoholics say they talk each other's language. The pastor may awaken the desire in the alcoholic to talk with a member of Alcoholics Anonymous, and then, while the time is ripe, secure such a person to talk with the alcoholic. The minister can play a vital role as a supporter of others as they do their work. The minister should not make the mistake of feeling that his job is to do everything himself. Often in a supporting role he is doing an even better job.

CHARLES F. BROOKS,
Dean of The Cathedral of St. John,
Providence, Rhode Island.

A psychiatrist replies:

This question recognizes the cardinal truth that, in all counseling, the unwilling individual derives little or no benefit from the counseling experience. Unfortunately, this truth too often hangs like a sword of Damocles, paralyzing all effort and, even worse, blocking thought on the problem. The facts are that even the adamantly resisting person is likely to have his Achilles heel; it is the task of the counselor to find it and to use the opening it affords as an avenue to the real person.

Of course, stone walls are encountered and when they are, two points are to be kept in mind. First, try to avoid making the defenses more impenetrable; and second, do what you can to soften them up in the hope that someone, sometime later, at a more propitious moment, may breach them. The important thing to remember is that the process of breaking through the crust may be long and that your interview will be one of many. Your function is to further the process of softening. Sledge hammer tactics rarely work; better a quiet word or two which will be mulled over later.

For instance, at a recent A.A. meeting, a man came up and thanked me for the help I had given him. Although his face was vaguely familiar, I was more than mystified and quite frankly told him so. He replied, "I'm not surprised you don't remember me but I came to see you nearly four years ago. My wife insisted I come and I did, but I didn't want to see you and you knew it. But you got me to talk about my drinking and when I asked you if that made me a drunk, you said 'not necessarily, but you still wouldn't want to be in my shoes.' That stuck because you didn't argue and get me mad. I felt you knew what you were talking about and it started me thinking, really for the first time. Oh, I had some more trouble but it wasn't too long before I began going to A.A. It didn't work right off but

252

I've been sober three years now and feel great. I couldn't have done it without A.A., but I always tell everyone that a psychiatrist gave me the first shove." Obviously not all such remarks are so fruitful, but you never know and, in fact, never need to know. If you do the job at hand, that is all that can be expected. There is no need to be completely hamstrung because your services are not met with open arms.

The "stonewall" diagnosis, however, should never be made without considerable searching for weak spots. For instance, one seemingly unassailable front was penetrated when the individual, who had proudly asserted his ability to quit after the fourth drink any time he put his mind to it, was asked, "Why do you have to keep proving to yourself that you can stop at four if you aren't anxious about the times when you don't?" Startled, he replied, "You know, I never looked at it that way; I guess I was busy showing myself I didn't need to be worried because underneath I really didn't like the way things were going." At least, the first line of defense had been pierced because the man could feel that his drinking was causing him real inner discomfort.

Trick shots like that which happen to hit the mark are not to be counted upon, but careful uncovering of the situation will often prove illuminating even to the person being questioned. To illustrate: with a person known to be recalcitrant, the interview (after the customary amenities) will proceed with the counselor saying something like this, "I suppose you are wondering a bit what this is all about and where I fit in. I'm not sure myself, but when your wife came to me, I couldn't be sure whether she had a right to be alarmed and upset, or not. So I told her I had better talk to you to find out how you saw the matter." Some sort of opening statement like that is necessary and, if not said in too judicial a tone, generally discloses the individual's real attitude toward his being there. Once the man starts talking, some kind of loophole is almost sure to be revealed so that first, the legitimacy of the wife's seeking help may be pointed out, and second, so that the possibility of his needing help may at least be commented upon. This may tend to remove or reduce any hostility which may have been aroused by the wife's action in going outside of the home, and can lead to freer discussion of the problem itself, which is all that can be asked.

Counseling with a reluctant person is never easy, but it should be remembered that every individual is reluctant at first about being counseled. We always have the job of overcoming initial doubts and uncertainties. It should be an accepted part of the task of counseling.

HARRY M. TIEBOUT, M.D.,
Chairman of the Committee on Psychiatry and Religion,
National Association for Mental Health.

A specialist in alcohol education writes:

The situation described can, I think, be handled without damage, and even, on occasion, with helpfulness *provided* that the pastor is properly equipped to handle it. Talking to an alcoholic who comes under such circumstances should never be confused with other types of consultation. It must be realized that alcoholics present a very special problem, for which a specialized approach is just as important as specialized medical treatment.

Anyone attempting to help an alcoholic under any circumstances whatever should have a basic knowledge of what alcoholism is and what it does to an individual in terms of behavior and attitudes. Without this knowledge, well-meaning efforts to help can do as much damage as if a butcher attempted to perform delicate surgery.

Today there are many sources of such knowledge: literature distributed by the National Committee on Alcoholism, and by the Quarterly Journal of Studies on Alcohol; books like *Primer on Alcoholism* by Marty Mann (Rinehart $2.00); *The Other Side of the Bottle* by Dwight Anderson (A.A. Wyn $3.00); *Drinking's Not the Problem* by Charles Clapp (Crowell $2.50). All serve to inform and instruct anyone who has to deal with an alcoholic.

Armed with accurate information, no one should be able to perpetuate the old mistakes which made such interviews turn out badly so often in the past. The alcoholic may approach the pastor unwillingly, even resentfully, but if he meets an attitude of enlightened understanding and a total lack of moralizing, preaching, or sentimentality, he may well respond with an outpouring of his deep fears and hopes, and his underlying desire to recover. What the alcoholic needs is the same information as to the nature of his illness and what can be done about it as the pastor must have in order to deal effectively with him.

If he can be brought to recognize the true nature of his problem—that he is a desperately sick man, in need of expert help—and to accept the responsibility he has *to himself*, as well as to his family, to make every effort to recover from his progressive and possibly fatal disease, he will have made the first steps toward recovery. And if the pastor can help him take those first steps, that pastor can justifiably feel that he has accomplished a tremendous job.

MRS. MARTY MANN,
Executive Director of the National
Committee on Alcoholism.

Another minister replies:

Your first impulse in a situation like this is to turn thumbs down, for there can be no real help unless the person wants it. We are faced with the practical problem, however, that persons who really need help are those least likely to seek it. How then can we bridge this gap between the need and the possibility for help? Or more pointedly, how can we change a negative counseling situation into a positive one?

Resistance to help will vary. To some, the asking for guidance symbolizes failure on their part. In order to ease feelings, therefore, a person may have to deny that there is a problem. At the other extreme is the person whose maladjustment is serving some useful purpose for him, and he prefers not to change. Then, too, there may be the fear that the minister will moralize about the problem or that the minister will identify in his feelings with the relative who made the referral. If the person comes in spite of these or other objections it may be to show that he is willing to try anything, but in reality hoping to prove that there isn't any help possible.

In dealing with negative feelings, an understanding and accepting attitude on the part of the minister will be a step in the right direction. It may not bring about change, but it is the approach by which changes are effected. The alcoholic experiences considerable rejection through loss of friends, loss of his job, and through conflict with relatives. If the individual can have an experience of being treated with respect, it may open up the way for further help. The experience may ease tensions so that he can think more constructively regarding his problem. This can lead to a real interest in doing something about his situation so that the minister or some counseling service in the community can be of help.

Going back to the original question, we must not overlook the possibility that the person who comes in the first instance may be seeking help for himself. Freedom to express his feelings may bring this out. Then, too, there are requests that come to the minister's attention that should be handled with caution. For instance, ministers are sometimes urged to do something about a family in which the children seem to be neglected. Such situations may be bad and usually are, but there are limits as to how far you can go in interfering in other people's private affairs unless they themselves are interested. If legal steps should be taken for the protection of children, then the proper social agency of the community should be consulted.

John L. Mixon,
Executive Director, All Nations
Foundation,
Los Angeles, California.

The Church and the Homosexual

I

A missionary from India asks:

It has been suggested to me that you might be able to help me to obtain some helpful materials on the subject of friendship. I am a missionary from India on furlough this year. There is a great deal of homosexuality among both the boys and girls with whom we work. It appears to me at the moment that this stems from a wrong conception of friendship, and I feel we should be doing something about this in our boarding school.

I would appreciate it if you could suggest some articles or books that might be helpful.

A psychiatrist replies:

The term homosexuality has acquired special stereotyped significance in the mind of the general public which bars the way to a sympathetic and constructive attitude toward individuals who at one time or another engage in intimate physical relations of a sexual character with one another. The term covers such a large variety of attitudes and practices, and has such different meaning when applied to members of different age groups, that its general use to cover all these phenomena is greatly to be deplored.

Overt and continuing sexual activity restricted to partners of the same sex, while inevitably constituting serious problems in the lives of people who have no other sexual outlets or interests, is regarded with critical attitudes of varying intensity among different groups in our society and among peoples of different races and cultures. It need hardly be said that in the United States the penal code considers such behavior as felonious, a fact which both does serious injury in many cases to victims who are

257

apprehended by the police and brought before the courts, and makes it very difficult to devise proper means for the protection of sick people and for the rehabilitation of those whom they may victimize.

The love impulse, or, in other words, the tendency in all human beings to have, among other emotions, warm feelings for other human beings which tend to draw them into close personal contact, has a long developmental history. This is never just the same for each and every one. In the majority of cases the goal of these natural feelings, and the direction which they take in the course of development, is toward a mating relationship with someone of the opposite sex. This natural course of development has its roots in the differing biological structures of the two sexes.

The first object toward whom such feelings are dimly experienced is the infant self. Gradually, the infant becomes aware of the existence of a protective figure, usually the mother, and in return, so to speak, for the favors received, as well as to insure their continuance, the infant begins to show love feelings toward this protective figure. Gradually, as the father has warm interests in the child and is capable of expressing these feelings through physical contact and play activities, a further investment of love is made, this time in the father. At this point, then, the main lovestream has two branches, as well as the original channel. In this way the first beginnings of love feelings for members of the two sexes make their appearance. In some instances one branch grows much wider and more powerful than the other.

If this analogy is understood, it will be readily seen that these two branches of the main love stream differ in their direction and under normal conditions never meet. Feelings for members of one's own sex are not the same in such cases as feelings for members of the opposite sex. When the more sexual elements make their appearance, this differentiation becomes clear, and individuals of the opposite sex become the object of sexual interest.

Sometimes, however, through frustration in relationships with members of the opposite sex, which arise, as they usually do, from fear and feelings of guilt that have originated in childhood, the natural direction of one branch stream may become blocked.

The force of the stream may then force a cross-channel to the other stream so that an intermingling of waters takes place.

The need to love and to be loved is basic in human nature. If there is too much frustration of this need from the side of parents, or, later, from others who exercise power and hold authority over the individual, the main stream of self-love gains strength as the branch streams dry up.

When individuals are closeted during adolescence in segregated, monosexual groups, there is greater danger that this natural need to express and receive love will become confused by the arousal of sexual feelings, and the ground may be laid for a permanent deviation of the sexual aim. Usually, however, the underlying biology of the boy or girl makes it possible for the natural direction to be resumed as soon as the proper opportunity appears. Problems of this sort that arise, therefore, in such groups, should be looked on as phases in the growth process which call for understanding and for full explanation by a sympathetic, knowledgeable, and unprejudiced counselor.

"Crushes" are frequently the order of the day in such groups, and may be considered "smart." These are basically due to the need for finding an idealized self to whom absolute loyalty and love can be expressed, because the individual is as yet unsure of himself and of his powers to attract the other sex. Hero-worship is a mild form of this phenomenon. Certain types of overt homosexual practice derive from this need to idealize some object of one's own sex to whom one can make a more or less complete surrender of the self.

Friendship between members of the same sex is naturally based, to some extent at least, on the finding of similar feelings, similar interests, similar problems in someone else. That person is then "simpatico," and is nearly enough the same as oneself as to create no anxiety. Such close friendships are always especially important in adolescence, when the individual has not yet learned the full measure of his own strength. If these friendships come to include a direct sexual intimacy, this may prove to be little more than an attempt to satisfy curiosity in a safe quarter.

In our society, however, the obvious dangers that the knowledge of such relationships bring to the door of those who continue to engage in them, are of such magnitude as to require sympathetic intervention at the earliest possible moment, before a faulty pattern of sexual practice becomes habitual. Free group discussions under competent leadership may be of great assistance in solving such problems.

JOHN A. P. MILLET, M.D.,
Chief Psychiatrist, Rehabilitation Center of the
American Rehabilitation Committee.

A psychiatrist-marriage counselor replies:

My reading of this question leads me to feel that the inquirer has a somewhat ingenuous concept of the meaning of homosexuality. I judge he looks upon it as a "morals" problem and one that might be overcome through skillfully directed management of friendship among young people of the same sex. This point of view is quite different from that of present-day psychiatry.

First, it should be emphasized that a certain amount of homosexual love feeling (and even sporadic homosexual physical contact) is not *necessarily* of morbid significance among young people who have very limited social relations with the opposite sex. Homosexuality becomes morbidly significant when it is a compulsively dominant tendency and then its real meaning lies not in its being a "bad habit" but in the much deeper proposition that it is a symptom of severe personality disorder, involving arrested psychosexual development in infancy and very early childhood.

The problem of the compulsively homosexual person lies in his (or her) fear of accepting a heterosexual role. He, the homosexual, has been conditioned in early childhood to intense fear of attempting to follow his own natural sex role in life. On this account it is useless to give him moral lectures or to believe that marriage will "cure" him (or her) as he reaches maturity. Also it should be noted that experiences during school life do not create a compulsive homosexual; rather, they are simply an expression of latent tendencies that were firmly established in early childhood.

Regarding remedies for the school situation described by our

Indian missionary, I am forced to observe that the roots of what he faces go so deeply into local family and cultural life that it would be irrational to expect him to do very much about correcting the situation in a hurry. He could easily make the problem more serious and individually traumatic by imposing harsh measures and I strongly advise against that.

For a more detailed discussion of this subject I refer the inquirer to pp. 213-242 of Dr. Edmund Bergler's book, *The Basic Neurosis,* published by Grune and Stratton, Inc., New York. Here he will find a rather technical but up-to-date presentation of psychiatric views on the meaning of homosexuality. It will be clear from a reading of Dr. Bergler's material that a *definitive* dealing with homosexuality is quite beyond the capabilities of school personnel. Tolerant and kindly attitudes are to be recommended and sublimation has a limited value. But little of a really effective nature can be accomplished without prolonged psychiatric treatment, and that is not always acceptable or successful even when available. And fundamental elimination of the factors in cultural and family life which cause homosexuality is a large social project that seems likely to be solved only after many new centuries of cultural progress.

WALTER R. STOKES, LL.B., M.D.,
Psychiatrist-Marriage Counselor,
Washingon, D. C.

Another psychiatrist writes:

All behavior has meaning which can be intelligible, and homosexuality is no exception. But in order to be even approximately accurate one must have all the facts at his disposal.

For some people homosexuality means merely the conscious preference of a person for the company of members of his own sex. For others it means erotic pleasure gained through genital stimulation by a person of one's own sex. For others it means unconscious strivings toward one's own sex and rejection of the opposite sex. However one looks at homosexuality, to me it must be further clarified beyond its outward manifestations by what its *symbolic meaning* is for the specific person under consideration.

261

For one person it may simply mean being "in the swim"—doing what everybody else seems to be doing—like the food or clothes or language fads of youngsters. Not to be doing what is the "smart" thing would be socially dangerous through failure of identification with them. The approbation of one's associates is often far more valuable than the approval of one's seniors.

It may mean that adolescent sex strivings must be checked or modified in order to comply with external demands, but that since these strivings are strong they emerge in the safest outlets as well as the ones most easily available. I understand that sex was an open subject in India long before it was in American culture, and the practice of homosexuality might be in part due to efforts of people trying to mold the children into a set of behavior values stemming from the traditions of the foreign culture.

Sometimes behavior of any nature can be clearly demonstrated to be an unconscious attempt to express hostility or rebellion toward the people in authority over them, or it may be an expression of resentment about having been frustrated in some sense of entitlement. Homosexuality is often an attempt to find a sense of togetherness with some person, and if one has acquired any assumptions which indicate some degree of danger from sexual association with members of the opposite sex, it would be logical to try to find closeness with one's own sex. For some, sexual experimentation with one's own sex is a kind of preliminary exercise preparatory to playing the grand finale of heterosexuality. As we know, babies creep before they walk, and their first efforts at walking do not resemble the later sureness they have as they go about, unconscious of their movements.

No matter what the standards of any culture, one can say with assurance that homosexuality is an incomplete stage of sexual development since it is not biologically sound. If we can look upon it as an incompleteness rather than as something to be judged morally, we may be in the best possible position to "do something about it," for we do not become frightening then to the people on whom we anticipate working, but only inquiring and objective. A truly objective attitude on the part of those who want to "do" something about anything stimulates objectivity in those on whom one is focusing, and it minimizes the defensiveness which can destroy all possibility of true growth on either side.

If we would encourage true friendship we must ourselves be friends or friendly people—that is, people with whom others are not afraid, or with whom they do not feel a need to be defensive. Only in this emotional climate can people reveal themselves freely, and this lack of fear is the essence of friendship.

Homosexuality may in some measure represent this effort toward friendship, in which they now, finally, reveal the last secret parts of themselves to some other person. Different cultures have different secret parts and places and it is always important to understand.

Whatever be the symbolic meaning of their patterns, they must be understood before it is possible to hope to effect anything but superficial changes. Is there any substitute gratification which can be held out to them which has a comparable symbolic value to them? Also, have you been free enough in your own thoughts and words concerning sex so that you have been able to talk with them about their patterns that are worrying you?

Camilla M. Anderson, M.D.,
Salt Lake City, Utah.

II

A minister inquires:

Would it be possible to give some guidance on this problem? There are two women who hold positions of leadership in the church. By personal observation, by word from a minister who has reason to know, and by a committee from the church, I have come to realize there is a situation of "unnatural affection" here.

These two women "hold hands" in church service. It is believed that their constant association is characterized by one acting as a man and the other as a woman. The one who acts as a man is "mannish" in dress and deportment. She is married. The other is small in stature, and has never been married. Both are about forty years of age. We think there is an unnatural sexual relation existing between these two women.

Assuming that there is, we have some questions to ask. If the facts are established, it will be my responsibility to handle the problem. The questions are:

(1) Could there be this unnatural affection between women? (I know there is between men.)

(2) Does holding hands in church, sleeping together, and constant companionship indicate a possibility?

(3) Is the "mannish" woman the aggressor? Would a small-in-stature maiden lady permit sexual advances from a woman who does not have the charm of a lady, but the strength of a man?

(4) If I do enter the situation, it will be with the maiden lady, and not the other. What is the wise way?

I recognize that this is a large order, and may be asking too much. But some guidance would be most helpful.

Another psychiatrist comments:

There could be and likely is an "unnatural affection" existing between the two women who are "hand-holders, who sleep together, and who are constant companions." Among women, display of amative affections is socially more acceptable than is corresponding behavior among men. But here we have two women whose relationship appears to be out-of-bounds; and the roles assumed readily identify which is playing the man and which is playing the girl.

The questions submitted imply that some kind of physical sexuality is practiced and that the smaller and more feminine one succumbs to the advances of the other. This touches on an element which is inferred and not established by evidence or admission, but its existence is not the important object of inquiry and it would be unwise to pursue it.

If the minister chooses to enter the situation, he should settle: (1) what the nature of the problem is, (2) what his objectives are, and (3) his estimate of his resources in dealing with it. His objectives are twofold: (a) to effect treatment of the parties involved, and (b) to relieve the tensions of his parish. I should counsel that this kind of relationship is a surface manifestation of deeply rooted psychic conflicts in both women, who fortuitously find in each other attempted complementary resolutions and momentary relief of tension, the sources of which they have no conscious awareness.

This phenomenon can be regarded as a kind of mental illness and not as a willful perversity. Psychic forces behind such relationships are imperative and repetitive and even with skillful handling are difficult to modify. The minister should hope to exploit any opportunity to get either party into competent psychiatric hands. He can achieve little unless either party can feel an incentive to use help. This incentive can be smothered if the minister engenders too much anxiety and especially if he makes a condemnatory moralistic attack upon the problem. Assuming, however, that he can reach neither party and no incentive is forthcoming, he has little recourse but to act in the interest of his parish group.

For the minister, I suspect the way out of this is to pursue a course which does not focus on the obvious sexual implications of the relationship, but rather on the motivation inherent in the display which has attracted the notice of the parish group. This imparts a curious, irrational color to the relationship between the pair and the group. Both women must know that their affection is illicit, at least unseemly; but they have continued to expose it in their gestures and to provoke a situation of uneasiness. It seems to me that if the minister approaches either party in the spirit of protecting reputation, he can confront the women with the fact that gestures have created notice and attention in others; he should avoid asking for the *meaning* of these gestures since he already divines it as indeed do also the women. But he will have achieved a unilateral tacit communication. He can expect that an insinuation of himself between the women will invoke anxiety in both, and with such, there is the risk that in either it may be disabling.

At best, I think the minister will be on safe ground if he first approaches the issue as a psychiatric problem, mindful that the roots of the relationship are anchored in the unconscious, and that moral insight alone is insufficient to deal with it.

PHILIP Q. ROCHE, M.D.,
University of Pennsylvania Medical School.

THE MINISTER'S CONSULTATION CLINIC

A minister responds:

From the information and interpretation given by the questioner, it seems altogether likely that a homosexual relationship exists between the two women he briefly describes. But saying this tells us very little about the relationship, and still less about what the pastor ought to do about it. It is a bit like the fable which Shailer Mathews used to tell. When Eve asked Adam why he had named a certain animal a "tiger," Adam replied, "Why, because it *looks* like a tiger!"

This looks like homosexuality, which can exist between women as well as between men. But what is homosexuality? Does it become such only when the interest of one woman extends to the sex organs of the other? In other words, is it to be defined biologically? Or is it to be understood in terms of affectional attachment, with or without mutual sex stimulation? Or is it to be understood, in still more general terms, as meaning such an antipathy to the opposite sex that one can have affectional relations only with one or more persons of his own sex?

Society in general is inclined to think of homosexuality in biological terms, especially in relation to women. Two women can get all the affectional and emotional satisfaction they wish from each other, provided they do not stimulate each other sexually—and provided they don't give hints of this in public. The same basic criterion is applied to two men, the difference being that less effusive behavior by them in public would be considered a hint of sex interest than in the case of two women.

I believe we must recognize that there is profound wisdom in this unspoken definition by society. There is a real and very important social difference between the person with what we might call homosexual impulses, or the person who has most of his affectional needs met by persons of his own sex, and the person who engages in sex behavior with his own sex. At the same time, if we look at all this from the standpoint of motivation, the differences may be much less than the similarities. The social difference is very real, and here society is correct. The psychological difference may be very small, and here society needs to do some rethinking.

266

Let us suppose, as seems unlikely in this case, that these two women who are cited never engage in any sex behavior with each other, or with anyone else of the female sex. Suppose that their relations are innocent of conscious thought or overt activity in relation to sex. What would the community say if it discovered this to be true? It would say, in effect, "We apologize. Here we thought all the time you might be homosexual. We're so happy to find you're not." The community would have understood the social difference but overlooked the psychological similarity.

But in that case, we, unlike the community generally, would have to ask ourselves these questions. Why can this married woman not gain her deeper emotional and affectional satisfactions from her husband, or at least in some woman-man relationship? Why can this single woman move into an intimate friendship only with someone of her own sex? Whatever the answers specific to these two people, we would surely have the following as a general answer—that, in the development of their respective capacities for interpersonal relationships, both these women have been unable to reach the kind of maturity in which the most deeply-sought love object is fundamentally different from oneself, of the other sex. It might be that one was reared to believe that the female functions in life are degrading, and that men are the agents of that degradation; or that the other was so brought up as to be comfortable only in the presence of one who looks like herself but makes all decisions for her. Whatever the specific elements in the background, the result would be a distortion and fixation at some early stage of development.

Thus, sex relations or no sex relations, the connection between the two women would be homosexual in this motivation sense. They would be fixed at a stage prior to maturity. They would not have attained the goals of adult human growth. Socially speaking, we might consider their behavior an offense. But viewed motivationally, we would see them as in some sense victims.

Anyone who would help in such a situation does well to recognize that society does have a stake, that there is a social difference between actual sex behavior and affectional attachment. But society tends to be harsh—closing its eyes to such things as long as it can, then emerging with an almost sadistic harshness which should find no counterpart in the outlook of the Christian pastor.

What can the pastor do? I doubt that he can ignore this situation. If he does, community hostility may be heaped upon these two persons in a thoroughly destructive way. But he will hardly help if he goes to them, or to one or the other, and pleads with them to stop. It seems to me his chance of helping might best be taken if he goes to them, says he believes they ought to know what the community is saying, that he is less interested in information about the situation than in whether they feel they need help. That is, he can exercise his function as community representative and Christian counselor without inherent contradiction. If they want help, he can either give it to them or help them get to someone who can. If they do not want help in the sense of possible change in themselves, they may at least learn to be less self-destructive in flaunting their relationship in the community's face.

I cannot resist asking another question suggested by this story. Suppose that our maiden lady came to church and held hands, not with the married woman, but with a bachelor from the congregation. Would the community judgment be easier or harsher on her than it is now? Although the two attitudes would not be the same, there are some respects in which it might be harsher if the hand-holder were the bachelor—at least if his intentions were clearly other than marriage. As long as this kind of attitude exists, it is an open question whether we do not make homosexuality an easier out than heterosexuality for some people. This is no simple matter, but one deserving more thought and attention.

SEWARD HILTNER,
Associate Professor of Pastoral Theology,
Federated Theological Faculty,
The University of Chicago.

Children and Sex

A minister writes:

A member of my congregation, who has a daughter some three years of age, called me last week to tell me that a boy of thirteen who was "sitting" with her daughter had been indulging in sex play with the child. The mother discovered him exposed and making shocking suggestions to the little girl. The mother promptly dismissed the boy, but because his parents are very fine people whom she regards highly, she is at a loss whether to reveal this incident to her husband, or to the parents of the boy. She called me for advice and I am completely stumped.

The boy in question had an eye removed a few years ago and unquestionably has been very high-strung as a result.

I shall be very grateful to you for any assistance you give me.

A minister replies:

It would seem from this pastor's description of the problem of the thirteen-year-old boy who was engaging in sex-play with the three-year-old girl, that the boy is in need of some help. There seems to be enough evidence that this lad is going through much more than the usual problems associated with adolescence and the maturation of sexual interest. It would therefore appear helpful if he could be seen by some wise and understanding counselor who could help him discuss some of his rather indiscriminate curiosity.

My own feeling is that if such help were to be forthcoming, then it might more easily be obtained were the parents of the boy to know what had happened. Here the main concern would be to discuss this with them in such a way as to be as minimally threatening as possible. One would wonder whether this could be done by the mother of the little girl, who herself appears to have been made so anxious that she wonders whether she should tell even her own husband. Here an understanding pastor might be a real help in assisting her to talk over these anxieties and relieve some of the necessity for concealment. Such an approach seems very much needed by this mother, who must have other concerns about her role as a parent which she does not feel free to discuss with her husband.

That she has already told her pastor about this problem might augur well for a good counseling relationship between them. However I would caution the pastor that unless he felt relatively comfortable about hearing this woman out, he ought not to proceed further until he himself has had an opportunity to discuss the problem with a fellow minister or other professional colleague.

ERNEST E. BRUDER,
Protestant Chaplain,
St. Elizabeths Hospital,
Washington, D. C.

A counselor with ministerial training replies:

Both the little girl and the boy need help to correct the impression made by the experiences to which the boy subjected the girl and probably also by the attitude of the girl's mother in dealing with the situation.

We might guess that the words: "Making shocking suggestions" indicate how the mother took the discovery. If she was shocked, then both the little girl and the boy were also. This may leave wounds that will be partially if not wholly repressed and can cause trouble later.

It would seem that the little girl has no brothers. She needs her father's help. She should be led not to be afraid of the male body, and to talk over the experience sufficiently to keep it open till it is assimilated free from shock.

The boy needs help much more. He is now handicapped not only physically but also emotionally. Since his parents are "very fine people" whom the mother "regards highly," they should be able to help their son. He is frustrated by the loss of his eye, probably feels himself somewhat isolated from other boys of his own age, inferior, and is tending to regress to infantile satisfactions.

It would seem to me that the minister is the person to initiate these healing processes by approaching the parents of the boy and by suggesting to the mother of the girl that she bring her husband into the problem. If he approaches the boy's parents, the problem will be raised to a higher level from that where it might remain if the girl's parents went to the boy's. He can help the boy's father and mother see that the mother of the girl was not complaining about a neighbor so much as she was perplexed.

The boy's minimum needs, besides opening up again the particular tragic experience, would appear to be understanding; being made to feel more secure with his parents; finding his place with boys of his own age; and gradually discovering new and healthy outlets for his desires.

ALECK D. DODD,
Counselor,
Toledo, Ohio.

A psychologist answers:

The question of whether or not the husband of your parishioner, or the parents of the boy, should be told of his sex behavior does not seem nearly so important as *how* they are told, if they are told; or *why* they are not told, if, in the interests of the boy's obtaining help, it would seem wiser to by-pass them and obtain psychological guidance for him without their knowledge.

The first step in either case would seem to be to relieve the mother's anxiety, both in regard to the possibility of the ill-effects on her three-year-old daughter, and with respect to the enormity of the boy's "crime." [The fact that, even under this stress which she experiences, she has delayed impulsive action and sought help from her minister, indicates psychological maturity on her part.] If she can be brought to see that the boy's actions reflect a psychological problem, requiring expert help, in the same way that an acute stomach ache would have brought the doctor, or an acute toothache would have indicated a trip to the dentist, some of the heightened emotions which attach themselves so readily to sexual difficulties may subside.

271

Assuming that the mother's anxiety can be relieved, and her attitude somewhat changed, it is still doubtful that she is the person to inform the parents. This could be done much better by the minister, if he is willing to participate as the intermediary who will also seek assistance for the boy at the same time. It is unlikely that the parents can be kept ignorant of the occurrence, nor would it seem wise to let them remain so. This would be necessary only if their attitude was so rigid that they would increase the boy's difficulties by being unable to understand his need for help. If, however, they are told about the incident in a way which does not threaten or censure them, and if constructive ways are indicated through which their son can overcome an emotional difficulty, their cooperation should be easily elicited.

It is also important that some occupation other than baby sitting be devised for the boy. If his parents are unaware of the reasons behind his discontinuing this, he may be forced into lying in an attempt to save face. There seems nothing to be gained, therefore, by having them remain in the dark; but everything to be gained by presenting the occurrence to them in an objective and scientific manner.

As to the important step of getting the boy some understanding guidance, this would somewhat depend on the location. Most large cities have child guidance centers where the names of child therapists would be available. The family doctor, or the local hospital would know of psychiatrists in nearby cities if this vicinity has none of its own.

MOLLY HARROWER, Ph.D.,
Consulting Psychologist,
New York City.

A psychiatrist writes:

The problem of what to do with the boy is clear because the boy is obviously suffering with a behavior disorder. He needs treatment in a child guidance clinic. This type of behavior can usually be treated satisfactorily and a good prognosis would be expected. The treatment, however, should be given by trained personnel, because the steps involved are complex. Unskilled treatment might further his general maladjustment, even though

272

his overt behavior might temporarily be corrected by amateur efforts.

Expediting this procedure, however, is *not* a simple problem. This is the type of situation where the understanding and well-informed pastor can be of tremendous help in getting the right kind of treatment for this boy, and in helping both the mother of the little girl and the parents of the boy see the situation in its proper medical light. It is not an easy assignment for the pastor; he is sure to meet with much prejudice, no matter how skillful and well-informed he is. I believe, however, that he could approach the parents more easily and satisfactorily than almost any other person.

The pastor could tell the mother of the little girl that the boy needs re-education in a special setting and that he will be glad to be the person to approach the parents of this boy. Before he approaches the parents of the boy, however, he should make an investigation as to possible treatment facilities in the area. He should be sure that such a case would be accepted as a patient by a child guidance clinic or its equivalent before such a suggestion is made to the parents. This is important because as soon as the parents know about their boy's behavior they will become anxious and, if they agree to seek treatment for him, they will want to proceed at once.

The parents should be seen confidentially, preferably in the pastor's study. With the proper presentation, the parents can be made to see this as a problem in growth and not as a problem of "evil behavior." They could be told that during early adolescence various types of sexual expression and exploration are not uncommon. The important thing is that this boy be given psychiatric attention, not because he is mentally sick, but because he has certain drives which need re-direction and re-education. They should be cautioned not to "blow up" or blame the boy. They should be reassured that the pastor will help the boy understand what is needed and planned, and that he will be his friend. If the family doctor would understand this therapeutic approach, he also could help this boy understand the need for his cooperation. It is important for the boy's welfare that treatment be ultimately secured.

The possibility of mental trauma to the little girl is not large. However, the mother of the little girl should spend some extra time with her and make a note of any increase in nervous symptoms and reassure her with simple direct statements if she asks questions. If this doesn't comfort her, the pastor should recommend to the mother that she have a talk with a member of the child guidance clinic (the psychiatric social worker, or another member of the clinic team). This would probably not be necessary, but it might help the mother if she were unduly worried.

The pastor has an important role with the boy himself during and after therapy. The pastor can be of great service in helping this boy learn *how* to participate in church group activities, and in giving him understanding in the positive spiritual forces which will strengthen his character. Such a relationship might well develop into a personal relationship that would be of great significance in this boy's gaining ultimate maturity.

C. DOUGLAS DARLING, M.D.,
Student Medical Clinic,
Cornell University.

Another psychologist writes:

This boy should have long-continued chances to learn how to live with his sex feelings in a socially acceptable manner until he is ready in all ways to make the best use of his sexual powers. Someone must teach him all of the facts of sex and help him learn how to turn the extra energy he now has, because he is maturing, in the direction of mastering what he must know—how to earn a living and how to care for a family in order to qualify for a happy and successful adulthood, for example.

That such ends cannot be attained by emotional moralizing and social condemnation for the boy's trial-and-error experimentations, should be clearly apparent to those who are to deal with him. If his parents can sympathize with his problems over becoming a sexually mature person, and know that one lecture or the reading of a book will not be enough, and if they will help their child, rather than become very embarrassed and socially defensive, they certainly should be told. If the parents of the little girl

274

can take an understanding attitude toward this boy, they should be the ones to discuss what has happened with his parents.

Both of the mothers and fathers in this problem need to know, however, that their own lack of suitable training in attitudes and skills for pointing out the need for giving a constructive sex education to a child, need not completely handicap this child's chances to learn. They can put into practice toward the child's sex education the same constructive attitude they would readily apply to his training in other ways.

In other words, if the parents of the little girl are unable to handle this difficulty as they should, or, even if they can handle their part and have serious doubts about the reaction of the boy's parents, they should send an expert in their place. If the boy's parents cannot handle the situation properly, then they should have the expert at hand to help them with it.

Of course, the question then arises as to who this expert will be. The best indication we have from the question is the minister himself. The mother of the little girl went to him before she told her husband. This is a good sign. The minister probably would do well not to describe the incident or to name names. His job would be to call the parents' attention to their son's needs for a more adequate sex education.

Whoever is to talk with the boy's parents should talk with the boy first. Remember not to condemn him. Be helpful and friendly. Tell him what is to be said to the parents. If the minister is to tell them, he should go over the details of the situation with the boy and show him how he intends to be helpful. There should be no chance for the boy to beg off, unless the minister knows he may do more harm than good by bringing the parents into the situation.

GELOLO McHUGH, Ph.D.,
Department of Psychology,
Duke University.

The Minister and the Aged

A minister asks:

What can be done to make life richer and more enjoyable for that ever-growing group who have reached the retirement age—sixty-five? You find many people in this group who have ideas and talent—and time hangs heavy on their hands. It is not enough that one has shelter, food, and clothing. What would you suggest could be done for this group?

A minister replies:

This question opens up for consideration a very large and complex field including about twelve million persons who vary in age from sixty-five to a hundred, and whose capacities and needs are exceedingly diverse. But apparently the writer is concerned primarily with those who have time and talent and he is asking what can be done with them rather than for them or to them.

The answer demands from the minister some creative imagination and some social inventiveness which begins with getting to know his older parishioners and ends by finding a way to "get them into the act." It also involves astuteness enough to find that many older people have talents which have never been discovered or released, and that just because they have never done a thing is no sign that they cannot do it now.

Many older people who have warm and friendly personalities, who like people, and who have sound judgment, can be trained to assist in the program of pastoral care through regular visitation. Other retired workers such as carpenters, plumbers, and painters have talents that can be used for the church. Even professional people often have talents along these lines which they have exercised as a hobby through the years. Older people may serve on host-and-hostess committees at the church service, or operate information desks and serve on telephone committees. Some may teach, particularly in the adult department of the

276

church school. Others may address the parish paper, or keep books, or operate a service which recognizes birthdays and anniversaries of people in the church.

Older people who do not have the physical strength to carry much of the executive load on official committees might still make a contribution on an advisory council or in advisory capacity to official committees.

Another approach to the use of leisure time is to have programs which will occupy that leisure time constructively, such as recreational and social programs. It has been noted that for most retired men, time hangs heaviest on their hands from nine to five when they were formerly at work. If there is some place to which they can go, such as a club or center, and in which they can engage in various kinds of activities, the load is lightened. It is for this reason among others that many clubs and centers for older people meet during this period. The programs carried on in such clubs are not merely diversional but include socially useful projects of many kinds, such as sewing for hospitals; and educational projects, such as courses on government and discussion of current events. Generally it has been found best to open such programs to all the older people of the community rather than restrict them to the members of the church.

Part of the problem is to help older people overcome the notion that they are not capable of doing anything. This may be met in part by letting them know what other older people are doing, and in part by encouraging them to take one step at a time in the direction of participation and creativity. Another part of the problem is to help older people and others see that they do not have to be strenuously and visibly or even remuneratively occupied in order to be accepted or creative. They also serve who only sit and listen well. To love and to pray is to create.

The questioner is referred to *Older People and the Church* by Maves and Cedarleaf. He would also be likely to find some help from the nearest Department of Public Welfare worker, or from case-workers in a family service agency, or from workers in a public health agency.

PAUL B. MAVES,
Associate Professor of Religious Education,
Drew University Theological School.

THE MINISTER'S CONSULTATION CLINIC

Martin Gumpert, the late pioneer in geriatrics, replied as follows:

The majority of people over the age of sixty-five lead an unhappy and frustrated existence today because they are pushed into a corner remote from the stream of life, and are offered charity, pity, and hobbies instead of dignified participation in gainful work. Not only have many people in this group ideas and talent, but they are, often for the first time in their lives, aware of their own human values and how to utilize them, having been taught wisdom by experience.

We cause our society great harm by excluding from our communities the unique assets of old people. Most of us—even many of us who are professionally interested in the problems of aging—concentrate on the miseries and debilities of the aged, on their mental, physical, and economic deterioration. Yet there is ample and convincing evidence that a successful old age leads to creativeness and to a greater understanding of life. We still know next to nothing about the normal, happy, and healthy old persons who grow by aging—because there are now so few of them.

Our prejudices can change only if from childhood on, we change our attitudes toward old age; if we make learning a continuous and life-long task instead of a short-time preparation for adult efficiency; if we look at retirement as the harvest of life instead of the prelude to death.

In practical terms this means an educational effort which must start in the kindergarten and be continued into the most advanced age. We need revision of outmoded, fixed retirement rules, which should be replaced by gradual, progressive retirement together with thoughtful preparation for the period after. We must not try to adjust the growing multitude of old people to the world of yesterday; rather, we must adjust ourselves to their presence and to the world of tomorrow in which old age will have to play its vital part. Successful experiments in this direction, which could be duplicated almost everywhere, are the day-care homes in New York, where thousands of older people discover and develop a new and productive interest in life.

MARTIN GUMPERT, M.D.

Another physician-specialist in geriatrics replies:

"What can be done to make life richer at sixty-five and on-ward?"—an excellent question. Here is my answer from medical experience in guiding, treating, curing, and helping people who are sixty-five years old, more or less. This is the field of geriatrics, which means medical service to prevent the pains and penalties of aging and to bring strength, safety, and power to the later years of life—the years of autumn, the golden years; to make life richer.

There are five points to our life enrichment program. Here they are as I gave them to the Y.W.C.A. for national distribution. You will note that these points are directed at the older person; I trust that a sympathetic reading of them will offer guidance to pastors.

First: *Have fun.* Have a hobby and ride it enthusiastically, and also make up your mind to enjoy everything you do, no matter what it is.

Second: *Give service.* The surest way to be happy is to help others to be happy. Give everything, you have everything. This never fails.

Third: *Do work.* This satisfies our physical and mental makeup. Work is a challenge and a fulfillment.

Fourth: *Be strong.* In body and mind, be well and vigorous. The physician works in all five fields, but this is his specialty.

Fifth: *Praise God.* Get better acquainted with God. Find out what He wants you to do. Do it. It is great; it is thrilling. Everything will be added to you.

Now, for the doctor's special field: be strong; stay well. Get that extra maximum power of the well-trained athlete for the race of life. The medical world is rapidly going forward in this field. You will find the old-fashioned general practitioner scientifically up-to-date. He knows health examinations, the anti-aging service of geriatrics, nutrition, prevention, x-rays, vitamins, endocrines, antibiotics, the latest scientific miracles, and even the old-fashioned things like blackstrap molasses, honey, and buttermilk. The doctor can tell you what you need, what you can do, guide you and protect you against popular fancies, fads, and fallacies over the years.

To get these benefits you start with a thorough examination. This will give you a chance to be relieved of all removable handicaps. This is a clean-up and build-up program. It often has real revitalizing results. There are seven essential factors.

(1) Selective dynamic nutrition
(2) Infection clearance
(3) Stagnation removal
(4) Structural repair and body reconstruction
(5) Vitamin optimum values in addition to daily requirements
(6) Psychological rehabilitation and refreshment
(7) Endocrine support and improvement

Your guidance program throughout the years will cover all these seven points and more.

Now you are on the road to a full lively, serviceable and richly rewarding life. Find your doctor. Trust him and follow him year by year.

This is good sense, good medicine, good geriatrics. It is the wisest and surest way to rich living at sixty-five and thereafter. I hope ministers will communicate its ideas to their older parishioners.

C. WARD CRAMPTON, M.D.,
Chairman, Sub-Committee on Geriatrics
    of the Medical Society of the County of New York.

Unpardonable Sin and the Psychopath

A minister asks:

In some recent attempts at pastoral work with some persons in that group usually known as "psychopathic personalities," a theological question has arisen in my mind. If the psychopath is the ruthlessly aggressive or careless person preoccupied with his own immediate needs, and seemingly incapable of any genuine social relationship or responsibility—does he become, theologically speaking, the classic example of "unpardonable sin"?

I assume that the unpardonable sin has some reference to the sin which makes all other sin possible; that is, in some way it makes impossible any constructive change. It seems to refer, in other words, not to any particular type of act, but instead to a tendency in character which makes one incapable of becoming morally, socially, or religiously sensitive. I would be grateful for comment on this from both the theological and the psychiatric side.

A chaplain replies:

I have little to add to the remarks of your correspondent. The "psychopath," if we may still use that confusing and now discarded term, is indeed a classic example of a person who has accepted defeat and failure and does not want to be helped. That, as I see it, is the one unpardonable sin in interpersonal relationships. I know of no way to pardon those who do not want to be pardoned except as we are able first to elicit some spark of response and aspiration. The attitude of the typical "psychopath" seems irreversible.

Anton T. Boisen,
Chaplain Emeritus, Elgin State Hospital,
Elgin, Illinois.

THE MINISTER'S CONSULTATION CLINIC

A counselor replies:

There is something in common between the "unpardonable sin" of which the Synoptic Gospels speak, and our present conception of the behavior of a psychopathic personality. But I think we do not know enough about the latter to make this connection very clear.

I may not have the latest understanding regarding psychopaths, but psychiatry has found this group, if it is a single group, difficult to classify and describe, and especially difficult to understand. Among the varied characteristics of those who are often included in this classification are some who show a paucity of moral judgment, of sensitivity to the feelings of others, of ability to learn from experience, either through punishment or reward or through unhappy or happy consequences. While psychopaths are most difficult to work with and help, psychiatrists are not hopeless about them. Psychopaths do rationalize frequently and thus, to themselves, minimize and cover their faults. And this is related to the unpardonable sin.

The unpardonable sin seems to me rather to be a far more general experience, as the minister making the inquiry implied. It is evidently the practice of calling black white and white black in ethical judgments; Jesus evil, and His acts the work of Beelzebub. The essence of it is self-deception. The passages in Scripture in the first three Gospels which refer to the unpardonable sin, do not indicate that the act and thought is necessarily a conscious, deliberately chosen one. (Matt. 12:22-32; Mark 3:22-30; Luke 12:10.) Following John Oman's idea (in *Grace and Personality,* I believe) I would think that self-deception is the basis of all sin. We would never do something that violated our own sense of what is right if we saw it clearly. It is when we rationalize it, project it, displace in respect to it, repress it, in the expressive words of St. Augustine, put it behind our backs, "where I had placed myself unwilling to observe myself . . . I had known it, but made as though I saw it not, winked at it, and forgot it," that we deceive ourselves sufficiently to be able to go against our own better conscience. This is not the whole account of sin by any means but it is a vital element. Jesus' statement, "If I had

282

not come and spoken unto them they had not had sin," and
". . . for they know not what they do," referring in both cases
to the Pharisees as well as others, would indicate that He thought
of the unpardonable sin as committed without full understanding
of clear consciousness.

"Initially there is a maximum disequilibrium in the ego, but
minimal distortion," say Irwin Smalheiser and Alan P. Towbin.
"The conditions are reversed in the final response when equilibrium is re-established where the ego is subject to minimum
disequilibrium and in terms of the conditions of the field, maximum distortion."* That is, to apply their thought to this question, when one is faced with a somewhat novel moral problem,
he may well find his customary reaction upset, his equilibrium
disturbed, partly because he sees the situation before him with
little distortion; to him it appears as pain. Therefore, very
quickly, often too quickly for him to realize clearly what he is
doing, he succeeds in distorting the situation by a feat of mental
juggling which serves to restore his previous equilibrium and
maintain the internal status quo. In so doing, however, he has
deceived himself; he can now do what he momentarily felt was
wrong. But that moment gets shorter and vaguer, until finally he
is not at all aware of his self-deception and feels quite comfortable. The emotionally controlled reasoning has become quite
unconscious.

Something like this would seem to be what occurs in what we
call the unpardonable sin. This is neither limited to psychopathic conditions, as the minister realizes, nor is it necessarily
pre-eminent in them. One would guess that psychopathic personalities deceive themselves to an extreme, but whether under
suitable conditions they have the capacity to undeceive themselves is part of the problem of helping them.

However, there is the possibility of reversing the process with
most, perhaps all people. It is not merely that there are indications that Jesus thought it possible—"Father, forgive them," and
the other evidences of His effort to win over, to "save" the very
ones He earlier designated as having committed the unpardonable

* *Complex,* No. 8, Spring, 1952, "The Rorschach Method; A New Con-
ceptualization," p. 18.

sin—but in our present-day psychiatry this is commonplace. The essence of counseling and of psychotherapy is in creating such an atmosphere for an individual who has deceived himself and thus gotten into an unhappy existence, that he shall be able to accept the counselor's or physician's help in reversing that self-deception till he once more can see the psychological situation (indeed spiritual situation) freed of distortion sufficiently to become "unbalanced" and then achieve a new and improved balance. For any growth in character it is necessary to be thrown off one's previous balance and to find a new balance that allows for a fuller integration.

In the three accounts of the unpardonable sin, it is the distortion of truth that is unforgivable. If truth, as Gerald Heard suggests, is "increasing correspondence"—that is, what one thinks and says increasingly corresponds to what actually is (Reality)— the blaspheming of the Holy Ghost would be decreasing correspondence or non-correspondence. This cannot be forgiven for the simple reason that such dealing with truth incapacitates the individual for receiving forgiveness. However much it is offered, he is quite unable to accept it because he sees no need to be forgiven and does not want it. The forgiveness may be there, may be waiting, and there are many passages in the Bible that indicate that; but it is useless.

The therapist is forgiving and non-judgmental to the patient who, for example, is repeatedly quite late for appointments; but the patient believes that he is being judged and reacts accordingly at first. He cannot accept the forgiveness which is offered because he has a mistaken, a non-corresponding conception of the therapist's attitude. He has deceived himself about the relationship between them, basing it falsely on past experiences of censure by others in similar circumstances. Only gradually does he learn his mistake and accepts the forgiveness the therapist has all along been wishing to give him. This way of identifying the physician with former individuals who have strongly affected one's life is not limited to those who are temporarily in the role of patients, but is common to us all. This is the faint picture of the attitude of Jesus toward those who said He was casting out demons by the power of Beelzebub, and were thus committing the

284

unpardonable sin. They never, never could be forgiven as long as they defensively clung to that self-deceiving view of Him and His work. But they might be won to change it, and so He prayed for them on the Cross.

ALECK D. DODD,
Counselor,
Toledo, Ohio.

A minister-teacher answers:

On principle, there is no sin that is not pardonable if the sinner repents. Although the inclusiveness of God's grace is incomprehensible by man, no sin is pardonable without repentance.

Clinically speaking there is a sinful condition in which the sinner cannot afford to repent; hence, he cannot possibly experience a sense of forgiveness—a sense of unbroken fellowship. The sin against the Holy Spirit is the sin against community—the sin of self-isolation.

Experientially it probably works somewhat as follows: Man in his pride of immaturity launches out upon his self-realization. In his brazen and feverish attempt to realize his genius he flies into the face of fellow men, for he flouts the need for community. As he discovers his impasse because fellow men reject him, he rebels against the necessity to be dependent—this negates his very nature. Therefore he is forced to adopt a more vigorous program of self-defense. Depending upon his background, he may express his autonomy in a flagrant defiance of the mores and his conscience, or he may withdraw into his shell. In either case, he is now obviously and helplessly egocentric. And the more he succeeds in this attempt at self-realization, the more he cuts himself off from the supply of oxygen: namely, a sustaining reassurance and inspiration of fellowship. The more he is deprived of this, the more desperately he defends himself. He is now caught in the churning maelstrom of self-defeat. How can he repent?

This poignant cosmic fact is a supreme challenge to the minister. Where the logic of the "irreversibleness" of certain attitudes and behavior cuts across the love of God which woos self-interested man to find his fulfillment in fellowship—there you have the cross—the symbol of the cosmic drama of redemption.

THE MINISTER'S CONSULTATION CLINIC

The psychological category of "psychopathic personality" is for many diagnosticians a convenient sack into which they sort all those who persistently and characteristically behave "abnormally" according to the expectations of the mores. The secular diagnostician often implies that the "patient" is born that way—that there is a constitutional lack of responsiveness to the social demands, that he is not capable of profiting by experience.

In a study of forty-two men selected at random from a prison population of about 1,500, these men differed from the norms established by a standardized personality inventory in that they rated a dramatically high score in a category of the test designated as "psychopathic deviate." The only other score in which they were dramatically different from their "normal" fellow men was that they characteristically had an appreciation for interests and values which our culture considers more feminine than masculine.

In terms of their weekly participation in group psychotherapy for eight months, there emerged the possibility that these were men whose response to refined (if not spiritual) values, was interpreted by the social relationships in which they sought a sense of self-worth as "sissy" and unmanly. As a result of this rejection they became more and more bankrupt of self-acceptance. This in turn drove them to think of themselves as courageous and unmistakably masculine in spite of the prejudices of society. The more they succeeded in this pattern of self-assertion in terms of defensive aggression, the more they had to succeed until fellow men judged them not only as abnormal but as being hopelessly so.

The parallelism between the theological and clinical descriptions above is obvious. They also imply that the unfathomable *agape* concern of God is crucified while the sinner moves with ever-increasing momentum toward the Hell of "unpardonableness." "Take heed then how you hear; for to him who has will more be given, and from him who has not, even what he thinks that he has will be taken away." (Luke 8:18 R.S.V.)

DAVID D. EITZEN,
Professor of Pastoral Counseling,
School of Religion,
Univ. of Southern California.

A Girl Who Will Not Talk

A minister writes:

I have a young lady in my church who is twenty-three years of age and very much of an introvert. She is not exactly shy, for she takes an active part in several activities in our program. However, she is exceedingly quiet, not only with outsiders but even with her own family. She takes part in conversation only to the extent of "yes" and "no" or short factual sentences. She goes out with young men, but not for long. They cannot, as one boy stated, "make her talk on any subject."

I have tried to gain her confidence in many ways and feel I have succeeded in some measure. I feel now that I might be able to help her to get at the reason for her quietness. Before I begin I'd like some suggestions as to procedure.

A minister replies:

It is difficult to tell whether this young woman is a seriously repressed individual or whether she is one of the many socially impoverished people who turn to the church for nourishment. Even properly motivated overtures may cause her to withdraw. It is important not to accentuate her lack of adequate interpersonal skills by trying to do too much for her and by attempting to draw her out.

If she is basically a repressed person, it will be wise to consult a competent psychiatrist or psychologist as to what procedure might be followed which would be acceptable to her. On the other hand, if she is simply lacking in the "know how" of interacting with people, then she should have opportunities to observe others who are naturally skillful in relating to people. Avoid forcing rehearsals; instead provide models.

ROLLIN J. FAIRBANKS,
Professor of Practical Theology,
Episcopal Theological School,
Cambridge, Massachusetts.

287

Another minister writes:

The description given of the young woman who will not talk does not give much indication of the true nature of the problem. Do we have here a lack of verbalizing ability; in other words, is she mentally below par? Is it a refusal to communicate verbally with others, or is it partly an habitual pattern of inarticulateness? Or is it a combination of all three factors? If it is a refusal to talk, is it evidence of rejection or hostility toward others, or is it a sign of fear, perhaps related to feelings of inferiority? If she has nothing to say, is it because her life has been so barren, or because she has been allowed no life of her own, or is it because she has never seen a need for abstractions in the form of words? Rural people are often deeply inarticulate, especially until one has been accepted by them and taken into their confidence. Some rural youths will work like Trojans on a project but close up like clams in a discussion that is on the intellectual level.

One rather infers from the description that we have here a case of conversational blocking due to fears resulting from unfortunate experiences which have followed conversation at some period in her life. Was she laughed at? Was she continually hushed up? Was she ever punished for a confession, or were confidences frequently violated?

But diagnostic speculation, while interesting, does not answer the pastor's query as to procedure. Knowing the source of the difficulty does not in itself cure any disease.

First, the pastor might read Seward Hiltner's article on "Shyness In Counseling" which appeared in the March, 1950, issue of PASTORAL PSYCHOLOGY, for while the inquirer says this is not a case of shyness (since the young lady participates in group activities), it does seem to be shyness to the extent that she does not participate in conversation. Shyness, like the term laziness, is an omnibus word, and may include a number of disparate difficulties. Shyness here takes another form and probably has a different meaning to this young lady than it did to the young woman portrayed in Hiltner's article.

Second, does he have to *do* anything? Is this lack of conversational interest a problem to the girl herself, or only to the people around her, and especially to the pastor? Why should she talk? Garrulousness can be a mask as well as silence. But let us suppose that this shyness is evidence of an inner disturbance. At least it apparently is cutting her off from any permanent attachments to friends, particularly to a possible husband. What can the pastor do to help her before she has come to him asking for help? How can he take what Hiltner calls the "geographical initiative?"

(1) He can respect her right not to talk if she does not feel like it, and he can avoid attempts to draw her out, to coerce her into conversation, or "to make her talk on any subject," a mistake the young men cannot help making. If silence is a defense, one will not batter down that defense without disturbance.

(2) He can continue to be warm and friendly toward her, accepting her as she is, without the necessity of reforming herself before she is accepted. He can greet her with a real welcome when he sees her. He can recognize her presence in a group, not by a direct question but by favorable reference to her, perhaps praising her for her participation in the activities. When in a group conversation he may be able to include her by an occasional friendly smile or wink in her direction, being sensitive to the appropriateness of such a gesture. During a pastoral call he can sit in friendly silence. He will not, of course, allow the silence to get oppressive and ominous. If she is embarrassed or disturbed by such pastoral contacts he may infer that she has more shyness than he now supposes. Always he will be alert to recognize some real interest she has upon which she may want to express herself.

(3) He can continue his attempt to understand her and her reasons for not talking by coming to know her family background and her interpersonal relations outside the family. It may be that no one has ever been really interested enough in her to take the time to express respect toward her and to win her confidence. This may be as true of her own family as of outsiders, and the boy friends may simply be falling into a familial pattern.

(4) He can give her an opportunity to talk by being willing to listen to her, by sitting down and waiting, by not rushing in to fill a conversational void. If her silence is disturbing to the pastor he will try to ask himself why he is disturbed. He will

respond to her communications with understanding, and this includes her non-verbal as well as her verbal communications. The pastor will attempt to learn to read the signs of posture and tension and movement as well as the conventional symbols of sound.

When he has done all this he has probably gone about as far as he can go until she indicates that she is ready to face the blocks and desires to remove them. In the meantime he would probably do well to encourage her participation in activities, particularly activities of a creative or expressive sort such as choir, parties, folk dancing, hobbies, and crafts. If she happens to be less than bright, it may be just as well if she does not talk too much.

And even if she does not begin to talk volubly or come to him for counsel, he should not assume that his friendly interest is without meaning to her or that he has done nothing worthwhile.

For further understanding of counseling procedure itself the pastor may find help in *Pastoral Counseling* by Seward Hiltner, *Counseling and Psychotherapy* by Carl Rogers, *The Art of Counseling* by Rollo May, and section three of *Older People and the Church* by Paul B. Maves and J. Lennart Cedarleaf. An extensive bibliography on counseling can be obtained from the Department of Pastoral Services of the National Council of the Churches of Christ in America, 297 Fourth Avenue, New York 10, N. Y.

PAUL B. MAVES
Drew University,
Madison, New Jersey.

A psychiatrist answers:

Very often it is mental retardedness which makes a person show the behavior described in the query. This, however, does not seem to exist in this case because the minister would have observed it and made mention of it in his description of the girl. Another possibility is that the girl feels intellectually inadequate and tries to hide her imagined inadequacy by the systematic use of the device of inarticulateness.

This kind of self-protection due to the feeling of inadequacy is usually part of a general feeling of inferiority; whether it is connected with a need for self-effacement or the desire to repress a strong neurotic feeling of aggressiveness would require intense psychoanalytic study to discover.

There is still another possibility: persons with a strong fantasy life have the tendency to retire into their daydream world and live in fantasy, which they enjoy much more than real life. Such a withdrawal from reality is often only a tiny step apart from psychotic withdrawal from reality.

The therapeutic approach by the minister has thus far shown some success, and its continuation in the form as done until now should be encouraged. To try to dig much deeper for causes will most likely not lead anywhere, the principle therefore better being: *quieta non movere*. For further information some insight might be gained by consultation of the remarks on Inhibitions in Otto Fenichel's book *The Psychoanalytic Theory of Neurosis* (W. W. Norton & Co.).

PAUL LUSSHEIMER, M.D.,
New York City.

Another psychiatrist writes:

The question asked in this letter may be answered directly and briefly, or certain points may be elaborated. To be brief, it should be noted that the first necessary step toward helping the young lady has already been taken. That is, the pastor has already gained her confidence "in some measure." The salient point in further procedure is not to rush her. She must be allowed to talk as and when she will, to bring up issues that bother her, and to ask for suggestions for help with problems as she sees them. It will be important not to ask too many questions or show much surprise at anything she reveals. Suggestions certainly should not be given before they are asked for, and then should not be too direct and forceful. Instead, she should be led to produce her own answers by setting up alternative possibilities.

There is nothing specific to be read that would give a pattern to follow in this case or, for that matter, in any other. The most difficult lesson in technique for anyone to learn is that of listening carefully, rather than determining the course of a conversation. Accordingly, we recommend that the pastor patiently

291

continue to allow the young lady to express herself. He must, however, be prepared to find at some later time that he is given responsibility for decisions or comments to which he paid little attention at the time.

To go into the letter in more detail, it presents a good example of difficulties often found in an attempt to reach some understanding of what causes a particular person to behave in certain ways. This young lady is inarticulate to an unusual degree; she is called an introvert, but it is noted that she takes an active part in several phases of the church program. While these activities apparently do not call for much speech, they indicate to the pastor that she is not shy. We are told how her confidence was gained, but it is a safe assumption that the pastor did not put pressure on her. How shall he "get at the reason for her quietness?" Actually, the procedure to be followed will depend somewhat upon the reasons, as they unfold themselves. This is no mere play on words, but a serious issue, as we shall attempt to show.

If the young lady is really an introvert and her speech production is so seriously inhibited, there should be blocking of more activities than indicated in the letter. There should also be other symptoms, fairly obvious even to the casual observer, of maladjustment serious enough to indicate the presence of schizophrenia (dementia praecox). It seems clear that this is not the case, so we surmise that she is perhaps not really so introverted as she appears. The interests and energy of the introvert are directed inward, toward inner emotional experiences and the self; satisfactions are found in fantasy rather than in contacts with people and the external world. This process is quite different from that of introspection (the two are often confused), which is a matter of self-examination of thoughts, feelings, motives. The results of this inward-looking may be anything but pleasant or satisfying.

Introverts do not establish free and easy social contacts, but they do form a few very close friendships. They often lack self-confidence and initiative in activity; are commonly serious and sensitive. Continual monosyllabic conversation is not the rule, though introverts are not ordinarily voluble except with especially close friends or in particular situations.

We are not told how long this girl has been so inarticulate—whether this has always been true or whether it is a recent development. Interpretation would differ according to when and how her "quietness" evolved. It seems that she is quiet with everyone, including her parents, young men, and in the church situations where she is active. We wonder if she was also quiet during her school life and, if this is true, what effect it may have had upon her school marks. It is important to learn if she has ever been known to talk freely, and the circumstances under which this may have occurred. We also wonder if she thinks her quietness is in any way unusual, or if she has been embarrassed by it.

Answers to questions such as these would provide the necessary basis for understanding the girl's behavior. If she has always been so inarticulate, yet made a good school record, she must have been able to surmount her reticence under school conditions. This could occur, but it seems more likely that she would have had some trouble with her studies. If there was a time when she spoke freely, only to become inarticulate later on, it seems probable that some particular event or series of events will be found to have played a decisive part in the change.

The most reasonable explanation for her unusual reticence, based on the scant information at hand, would be profound feelings of inadequacy, the cause not being clear at this time. If this turns out to be the correct explanation, then ventilation of the reasons, and reassurance, may be of great assistance to her.

LAWSON G. LOWREY, M.D.,
Psychiatrist,
New York City.

The Problem of Responsibility in Counseling

A minister asks:

Recently I received a letter from a young lady, a junior in college, telling of her involvement with a married man, and asking help from me. My inclination is to write her a cordial letter in which I suggest that she find help from someone close at hand. In other words, I doubt the practicability of letter writing in the counseling process, especially in such a case as this.

Is this reasonable, or am I rationalizing and seeking an "out"?

A minister answers:

A college junior who is involved with a married man is urgently in need of counseling, and in writing you of so intimate a problem she indicates complete trust in you as one who will understand without hasty judgment. To counsel her by mail would be a reckless procedure bound to damage the sound relationship of mutual confidence that has been well-earned by previous attitudes of non-reproach. To offer advice in a letter has the dual danger, first, of making a judgment without knowing the circumstances; and second, of prescribing without opportunity to have adequate diagnosis. Not only is the advice likely to be unsound, but the effort to decide for her is bound to impair the democratic relationship by making her either dependent on your authority or resistant to it. Consequently, she will be less able to decide wisely and you will be less able to counsel her from here on.

This is no time, however, to let her feel that you are giving her the brush-off, or rejecting her in the midst of her distress. If you are the pastor of her home-town church you could well suggest an appointment as soon as she can arrange to come home for the week-end, when you could view the whole situation together. If you know a trustworthy counselor in the vicinity of the college, that alternative might be suggested. But to leave her with no definite opportunity to have counseling would be to cast her off in a storm, whereas, because of her request you have an inescapable responsibility to stand by her.

PAUL E. JOHNSON,
Professor of Psychology of Religion,
School of Theology,
Boston University.

Another minister replies:

The pastor who submits this question demonstrates two significant and relevant insights in the way he asks the question. First, he sees that whatever he might do or say by letter would not be the same as face-to-face counseling. Second, he believes some reply is necessary on his part which is "cordial," by which he seems to mean to reassure the girl that she will not be cut off because she is in this jam. So far very good.

It is true that he does not tell us just what the girl wrote or the extent of her involvement. But one thing can certainly be assumed. If she writes to her pastor about this, she has a sense of guilt about her situation and she associates the minister with the conscience which judges her. What he says, or fails to say, in reply, therefore, is said, so to speak, on behalf of her conscience.

The chances are, especially if she writes the minister, that her relationship with the married man has had a strong compulsive element in it, i.e., she has "tried her best" but found herself slipping into it. In a sense, she wants the pastor to help her whip up her will against it. But if she should try this, he would succeed only in deepening the conflict. She would try harder. But even if she kept away from the man, he would still be the center of her emotional attention. The pastor need not fall into such a trap.

On the other side, he need not let his "cordiality" betray him into telling her that most college girls go through such a phase and not to worry about it. The fact is that many do, but to put it this way would be to deny the individuality and integrity of her problem.

Whatever the pastor can say to help her find someone readily

295

available with whom she may discuss this, is of real importance. If he can suggest someone he knows personally, this is especially good. If that is beyond his knowledge, he may know the kinds of people to look for—a nearby pastor, a college counselor, etc. But he can do more than that. He can suggest and in a measure define to her what talking it over with a counselor (i.e., a competent and understanding person who is not a personal friend) can do to help her. He can define this in such a way as to disabuse her of illusions about getting advice, but show how clarification of what is behind it (within her) can really help her see it straighter and therefore strengthen her capacity for decision. In my view, this should be the main thrust of the letter.

If in her letter there was already the beginning of an attempt to analyze her situation, the pastor might, in his reply, also put in his own words his understanding of what she has said about the issues. Suppose she has written, for example, "Pastor, I don't know what made me get into this in the first place. His wife goes home to her mother's quite often with the children; and when he first asked me to go to dinner one of those times, I suppose I was flattered. I don't have as many dates as most of the girls, and . . ."

The pastor might reply: "If I understand you correctly, your attraction for this man is due partly to circumstances, partly to your feeling flattered, and partly because other dating opportunities have not been as many as you might wish. Such a combination might well lead in the direction you report. But you feel pulled two ways about the situation, which must mean there are forces tugging at you which you do not entirely understand. We could write about this, as we have tried to do here; but in my experience, we can't get down to brass tacks in letters. If my letter helps you a bit toward clarifying the problem, that is good, but it should suggest how much more help you may get from a counselor in person."

In other words—under some circumstances there can be an initial attempt at clarifying already-stated elements in the conflict, however much these may be merely on a symptomatic level. This provides a kind of demonstration of the direction in which counseling can move.

One of my peeves is the otherwise intelligent counselor, pastor or not, who writes: "I do not believe in counseling by letter. See someone nearby." This will appear very cold and rejective to the person who wrote. We can, I believe, guard against letting people believe counseling can be done by mail, without in effect having to appear cold and detached. And we can always say something to help define what counseling means and can achieve. In addition, in some circumstances we can make a demonstrative beginning on how understanding moves in the direction of clarification.

SEWARD HILTNER,
Associate Professor of Pastoral Theology,
Federated Theological Faculty,
University of Chicago.

Non-Directiveness in Marital Counseling

A minister asks:

It would be interesting to me to know how your readers or Advisory Board use non-directive counseling in pre-marital talks with young people for whom they are going to perform the marriage ceremony. So often I find myself "telling" them what they should do. I am wondering if others find this is a problem.

A minister-teacher replies:

If the minister is to open the way with young people who are about to be married so that they will want to engage in lengthy counseling, he may be able to avoid "telling" them what to do and thus move somewhat toward the non-directive method. However, non-directive counseling is not always indicated. What I urge, rather, is that pre-marital talks shall be educational.

With this purpose in view, the minister would do well to:

(1) develop the custom of proceeding slowly, so that his parishioners will soon know that it is well to see him several months before a wedding;

(2) sit back in an expectant, informal manner, so that the couple will want to talk, telling him about themselves and having such a good time with him that it becomes natural and easy to arrange for further talks—perhaps together and separately;

(3) be alert to know when to request that one or both of the young people should go further into some aspect of their lives before he agrees to perform the marriage ceremony;

(4) avoid pushing too hard or too fast lest he give affront to the young people;

(5) facilitate by his unhurried, interested, and inviting manner a desire on the part of the couple to consider the pre-marital talks as their fuller education for marriage and family living.

The clue for the minister to follow is that of motivating the couple *to desire* further exploration of their readiness for marriage, their maturity, knowledge of sex, prospects for job and adequate housing, plans for children, intentions with respect to church life, and more. What the minister must avoid is the danger of unwelcome *probing*. Pre-marital counseling is mainly an educational process. Neither "telling" a couple nor demanding that they probe themselves is educative. Telling people what to do is mere paternalism, and insisting that they enter into extensive non-directive counseling when they reveal no readiness for it, is ministerial presumption.

WESNER FALLAW,
Professor of Religious Education,
Andover Newton Theological School.

A teacher of marriage courses replies:

My work is teaching a course in marriage to college seniors. The counseling is voluntary. It is mostly short contact counseling. A boy comes in saying that he is a hermaphrodite. He says this because he has feminine type breasts. It is explained to him that a true hermaphrodite has the sex organs of each sex. He then discovers that he is not what he thought he was. Another boy says that he has had orchitis in one testis. He wonders whether he will be fertile. I point out to him that many men who have only one testis in the scrotum are fertile. He would like to have a semen examination. I give him the name of a urologist who can do this for him. A girl comes in and says that during puberty she masturbated and that she has recently revived this habit. She is to be married next spring, and wonders whether masturbating will harm her chances of a good marriage adjustment. She says that just before menstruation she has very little control over this habit. The counselor gives her assurance that this will probably not harm her marriage. She has engaged in mutual masturbation with her fiancé. Obviously one cannot tell such persons that they have ruined their marital chances. Our society gives us erotic stimuli all the time and still forbids any expression of sex until marriage. I believe that the church should rethink the ethics of masturbation.

When the contacts are short I do not believe that non-directive

299

techniques are called for. A boy comes in and says that he performed fellatio on a sex pervert when around twelve years of age. He is now twenty-four. He wonders whether this will hurt his marriage adjustment. If he has had no homosexual contacts for twelve years, the likelihood is that he will make a good adjustment. Many of these students are seeking support and reassurance. Many students would be disappointed if non-directive techniques were used in their interviews unless there is to be a whole series of interviews. Of course there are situations in short-contact cases which require that the counselee be left to decide for himself. As in the case of psychotherapy in colitis and stomach ulcers; or whether a boy should have a semen examination; or whether a girl should have a premarital medical examination.

A good deal of short contact counseling involves what might be called individualized instruction, applying general principles to the specific case. Much of this consists of correcting wrong notions which the student has. In counseling students who are already married, some appraisal of the situation is expected. It may be that the husband should take the wife out more, or praise her more, or talk things over with her. It may be that the wife needs an orientation in the sexual aspects of marriage or an interpretation of the rightness of erotic play. Possibly one partner wants a divorce; then there is very little that the counselor can do but to show what divorce means to the partner, to the self, and to the children.

In short contact there is always the danger that the true facts may not be revealed. In longer contacts possibly more facts will emerge. Occasionally other appointments are made but the person does not return. One hazard in short contact counseling is that often the counselor does not know how the case comes out. In all such cases the way should be left open for further interviews if wanted by the client.

HERBERT D. LAMSON, PH.D.,
Professor of Sociology,
Boston University.

A minister-marriage counselor writes:

The non-directive principle does not apply to pre-marital counseling in just the same way as to other counseling. Pre-marital counseling proceeds on the basis of a decision clearly held in mind. In other counseling the purpose is to move toward a decision, or to replace failure with success.

Most pre-marital counselors use some directiveness, yet there is also rich opportunity for non-directive features. Questions about how the couple met and fell in love; about common interests, attitudes of parents, plans for finances, ideas about children and planning the family, religious training, and their plans for a church home—all such can be handled non-directively.

The counselor asks what they have read about marriage, whether they have had or are planning a health check-up. Here is a combination of non-directiveness with some amount of directive purpose. If they have not had a health check-up, the counselor will very likely encourage them to do so. Methods are subsidiary to results.

A valuable non-directive opportunity is in the use of personality inventories and check sheets. In 1950 the Federal Council of Churches put out a booklet developed by James R. Hine of the McKinley Foundation of the University of Illinois, called *Preparing for a Happy Marriage*. This had various checks of maturity, compatibility, and common interests and values. It did not offer a score but it did call attention to major issues which people entering marriage must face. This is being put out again, in revised form, by the National Council of Churches.

It would be helpful if readers would report their experience with non-directive features in pre-marital counseling. We should indeed make it something other than merely "telling them what they should do."

LELAND FOSTER WOOD,
Marriage Counselor,
New York City.

A marriage counselor-teacher writes:

Anything I say in reply to this interesting question must be judged in terms of my background. After seven years of marriage-counseling in my native England, I have been working here only for two years, and am still less familiar than I would like to be with American methods and concepts.

In commenting on the issue which the reader has raised, I would make three points.

First, I am a little concerned about the underlying implication that non-directive counseling is the only method which the pastor may properly employ. I believe that the present emphasis on the non-directive approach in counseling is a corrective which was very badly needed, and which can very greatly improve our counseling techniques. But I do not for one moment believe that the last word has been said upon this subject. And I am disturbed by the attitude which I find not infrequently among ministers that in their counseling they are beginning to do something seriously wrong as soon as they give direction to a person in need. A widespread acceptance of this view could do a good deal of harm to the prestige of the minister in this field.

The second point I want to make is that we need to clarify more precisely the significance of the pre-marital talks which the minister has with the engaged couple. In England we do not use the phrase "pre-marital counseling" to describe these talks, but speak of them as "marriage preparation." I think this is a better term to use. The conferences of the minister with the couple about to be married are not strictly speaking counseling situations at all—although they may of course easily open up into counseling situations. As I understand it, counseling is the relationship which arises between a person who brings the pressure of a definite problem to a skilled person who can help him to resolve that problem. Some young people on the threshold of marriage are certainly aware of problems; but many others are not. If the pastor's approach to the couples who desire him to marry them were a purely counseling approach, then he would talk only with those who expressly asked for a conference with him. But in fact, "pre-marital counseling" is normally an interview, or a series of interviews, initiated at the express invitation of the pastor.

Carroll Wise, in his *Pastoral Counseling*, discerns this clearly, and consequently expresses the opinion that pre-marital counseling is of limited value. In this he is perfectly right, so long as he is speaking of *counseling* as such. But I myself believe, and believe it upon the basis of a very considerable experience in the field, that these pre-marital conferences with the minister are of great value to the couple quite apart from what can be achieved in terms of counseling as such. Essentially these meetings belong to the sphere of education and guidance rather than to that of counseling. We might avoid a good deal of confusion if we were to recognize this plainly, and then proceed accordingly.

The third point I want to make follows upon what I have just said concerning the nature of these pre-marital talks. Once we have accepted the fact that the pre-marital conference is not a counseling situation, but rather one of opportunities which the minister can use for instruction, the difficulty raised by the questioner is at once removed. To initiate a situation, and then to refuse to direct it, would be to risk creating a stalemate; which is exactly what I could imagine happening in the case of a pastor who tried to be strictly non-directive in pre-marital instruction. But to recognize that in initiating pre-marital conferences, one has set oneself a specific task which one must carry through, puts the matter in an entirely different light. This is definitely a directive situation and it is absurd to pretend that it can be otherwise.

As I see it, the pastor's purpose in having pre-marital talks with the engaged couple is to satisfy himself that they have a clear grasp of what marriage means, and particularly what Christian marriage means. He is about to initiate them into an experience which will have far-reaching implications for the whole of their lives, reaching further into the lives of any children who may be born of their union. That is for him, if he views it aright, a solemn responsibility. He wants to satisfy himself that they understand clearly the task which is before them, and that they know how to apply themselves to that task in such a way that they embark upon it with every chance of success.

This being so, I cannot see how the minister can do anything else but "tell the couple what they should do." The whole basis of the conference is that he has something to communicate to them; and if he is reluctant to communicate it, the situation becomes ridiculous.

However, at the practical level there are several different ways of "telling" a person what to do. If it were done in the assertive, aggressive way which some people employ, it could have the worst possible effect. But the wise pastor surely knows how to communi-cate what he believes to be important to men and women in a way which is sweetly reasonable and persuasive. If he doesn't, it may be necessary for him to ask himself whether he is in the right job in being a minister! He will certainly be doing more harm than good to the young couple if he presses his viewpoints and opinions upon them against resistance on their part. But if his approach is to *offer* them the fruits of his own knowledge, experi-ence, and conviction, then it seems to me that he is doing what it is right and proper for every minister to do in preparing people to take part in a ceremony of the Church which involves them in certain clear duties and obligations which they undertake to dis-charge by participating in that ceremony. If this should naturally lead to a counseling situation, well and good; but the counseling situation would be incidental to the purpose of the pre-marital conference.

DAVID R. MACE,
Professor of Human Relations,
Drew Theological Seminary.

A minister-counselor replies:

Before answering the question, let me say that client-centered counseling is not a panacea for the handling of every pastoral relationship. The client-centered approach to counseling has been found helpful in situations in which the person seeking help senses that he is a problem to himself, feels that he can do some-thing about it, and recognizes that it is up to him to take some action in the matter. Initially his minimum of action is that of seeking a counselor for help.

When a person seeks a counselor on this basis, then a client-centered approach can most effectively help him regain his bear-ing without denying the dignity of human self-responsibility. There are numerous pastoral relationships which arise because of a differing set of circumstances, and pre-marital counseling is one of them. We, therefore, should not look for a one-to-one translation of client-centered counseling methods to the pre-marital situation. To expect this sort of direct applicability is to misunderstand the significant contribution of client-centered psy-

ness of one to listen to them and understand the approach they are taking to their marriage. It seems to convey the fact that I am looking upon this as *their* marriage and *their* responsibility.

In addition, it has become a predictable feature of this approach that the couple will sooner or later come to the points which are still in unresolved tension between them. While it is true that no "telling" them will basically help here either, it is at least helpful for them to explore a tension area in a non-tension setting. It is also a great advantage for them to be able to recognize and admit the points which are peculiarly apt to give rough going in the early days of mutual adaptation. It is very likely that if tension does mount to a breaking point later on in the marriage, the couple may associate me with this issue and seek me out so as to continue their mutual exploration of it. But more than the topics discussed, the *manner* in which I have been interested in seeing things their way may mean the difference in whether they will return to me at a point of marital trouble or not.

It may be clear that while a client-centered approach to counseling is not a set of techniques which will serve as a universal crutch in every pastoral relationship, it does have to do with a basic attitude which ought to be more universally present. Where the basic attitude is one of acceptance, understanding and warm personal interest, then the secondary characteristics of the interview may vary all the way from reflecting feelings to asking questions without any appreciable emotional difference in the relationship. The pastor should be ready to recognize the times and places in his pastoral work where the situation, such as the premarital interview, may give a secondary or surface difference in the manner of his counseling. He can accommodate himself to the situation without departing from client-centered principles.

RUSSELL BECKER,
Associate Professor of Psychology,
The College of Wooster,
Wooster, Ohio.

Keeping Records in Counseling Situations

A minister asks:

What sort of records should be kept when one is working under the supervision of psychiatrists with people currently in therapy for specific psychiatric problems? For example, I make a weekly visit to the home of a young woman who went into treatment after having experienced great difficulties in her role as a mother. I find myself unable to keep these "outside visit" records as completely and accurately as I would like. On the other hand, I'm told by the psychiatrists with whom I work that the records which I keep of my office counseling sessions tend to be overly wordy; in fact, I sometimes obscure or "bury" important points. Perhaps there are standard forms which I can use; or perhaps your experts can make other suggestions which will help me.

A minister replies:

A form for counseling data should meet three requirements:

(1) It must contain headings for the systematic recording of such information as family name, address, telephone number, first names of members of the family, birth dates, church membership, and other activities in the church.

(2) There should be plenty of lined space for remarks on personal visits.

(3) It must be small enough to be placed in a vest-pocket-size looseleaf folder.

These requirements are based on the assumption that the minister will do much of his most effective counseling in house-to-house visitation of families. Before leaving his office for the visits he has arranged in advance for that day, he can write out the family name, address, telephone number, and first names of members of the family, including information on their church membership. When he reaches each home in succession, he can pause
308

outside to refresh his memory from the family counseling sheet in his notebook; and after each visit he will immediately jot down the additional facts he has gleaned. (For example, the address of a member of the family in service, the dates of wedding anniversaries, or the prognosis in an illness.) When he reaches home that evening, he can take these sheets out of his notebook, complete his remarks—dating them appropriately, of course—and can then file the data by family name.

The prepared form which most nearly meets these requirements is the four-inch-by-six-inch "family counseling" form sold by Filco Memo-Matic, 4405 29th Street, Mt. Rainier, Maryland. For about five dollars the minister can obtain a plastic, pocket-size, looseleaf folder; several hundred family counseling forms; and additional sheets covering appointments, finances, programs, summaries, and addresses. Unfortunately, the back page of the family counseling sheet is crowded with information too detailed for any busy pastor, and there is an "individual counseling" sheet which is also quite worthless because it too is crowded with detailed information and has practically no space for comments on personal counseling. (Several other companies prepare smaller sheets which are even less valuable since they leave almost no room for follow-up data.)

Because the minister will often obtain a great deal of information in home visits that he wishes to record, and will also wish to make detailed notes of his office counseling, it is well to use cross-references on the pocket-size sheets (i.e., "June 16, 1955: See manila folder"). Complete notes can be written out on typing paper, and placed in a manila folder under the family name. This folder is also the place in which to keep carbon copies of pertinent letters.

If the minister will cultivate the habit of always taking his pocket-size counseling sheets with him, he will be able to keep an accurate record of each visit. Typing sheets will provide all the space he needs for additional information.

One additional advantage of the use of systematic records is the way it helps in analyzing how the pastor spends his time. The Memo-Matic includes a month's summary of church activity. On its sheets the pastor can record each visit that he makes. At the

309

end of the month a moment's glance will tell him how many persons he visited as prospects of the church; how many because they were ill; how many were in the category of "general visitation"; and how many persons come to the office for counsel. Since many laymen are not aware of the amount of time which can be spent in systematic visitation, the pastor will want to present a statistical report of his visitations to his official board each month. No confidences are revealed, but the men are aware that their pastor is fulfilling his ministry to people.

SAMUEL SOUTHARD,
Fort Mitchell Baptist Church,
Covington, Kentucky

A counselor with ministerial experience replies:

Clergymen, whether in a church, university, or institutional setting, have two major record requirements in addition to the "membership roll" used by other officers and the staff. In a large church it becomes a major task simply to keep the membership in mind as persons. A minister needs, first of all, a brief, easily usable and amendable summary of general, pertinent information regarding individuals and families for whom he has responsibility. Second—as in the case of the minister who submitted this question—he needs a confidential record of his interviews, since most clergymen now spend a great deal of time counseling in personal and family problems.

Broad experience in counseling with family members of all ages (and many varying problems) has resulted in the development of an effective method of keeping records. It requires a minimum of work when only brief notations are possible, but becomes a basis for a most complete record system when secretarial assistance is available.

First, it must present a "picture in a nutshell" of the persons and families for whom the minister has responsibility. This part of the record can be simple, yet it should provide space for brief, significant observations made during contacts with parishioners. Some pastors jot such notes in a notebook which becomes crowded, cumbersome, is easily lost and is seldom well-organized. The same disadvantages apply to memoranda made on a copy of the church roll. More elaborate recording systems often become unwieldy, out-of-date and unmanageable.

Meaningful information about every individual in the parish, school, or hospital is easily kept on five-by-eight-inch cards as shown in the illustrations on pages 312 and 313.

The front and a portion of the back of the card request information which most people are glad to give once assured that it is only for confidential use in working with them and their families. The last section of the card can be kept up-to-date as the clergyman makes renewed contacts; incidentally, he may ignore the suggested divisions here if he so wishes, using all of the space for notes.

Those who insist upon making a single-card filing system include their counseling records, too, will find that this form can be used for the total record of any person. It is suitable for marriage counseling as well, since parallel information may be obtained about the spouses. Much more can be recorded on the cards by the counselor who develops his own system of "shorthand" with abbreviations, symbols and brief phrases. If desirable, the names of the persons can be replaced by a code number on this "brief picture card."

Now for the second major record need of the clergyman: A confidential record of counseling interviews is necessary in the intelligent handling of a problem. It will be used as a basis for further counseling in subsequent contacts; as material for clinical study of the counselor's own technique and effectiveness; in research; and for reliable information in referral to and collaboration with other professional persons. Permanent records also facilitate working with and understanding problems of other members of the same family. (Although the subject is highly controversial, it would seem to me to be tragic if such records could not be utilized by pastors who subsequently take over the responsibility of a parish. If some uniformity of record-keeping could be established among ministers, it would provide an invaluable resource for research in the problems handled by the clergy, and

No. _____ Counselor _____ Fee _____ Date _____

Man's Name _____ _____
　　　　　　　Last　　First

Phone Home _____ Business _____

Woman's Name _____ _____
　　　　　　　　Last　　First

Phone Home _____ Business _____

Address _____ _____ _____ _____
　　　　　City　　Zone　State

Referred by _____ _____ _____
　　　　　Name　　Position　Address

Date married _____ Present Marital Status _____

	Man	Woman
Age.............................	_____	_____
Place of birth..................	_____	_____
Reared in country, village, town, city....	_____	_____
Education (grade, degree, school, course)....	_____	_____
Present occupation..............	_____	_____
Previous occupations...........	_____	_____
Income before deductions (weekly or monthly or yearly).....	_____	_____
	Total	_____
Service in armed forces........	_____	_____
If previously married, how ended and date....	_____	_____
Religious (denominational) preference:		
In childhood..................	_____	_____
At present...................	_____	_____
Church attendance now (times per month).....	_____	_____
Distinctive ethnic or nationality background.	_____	_____
Race...........................	_____	_____

Children:

Sex	Birth Date	Where Living	Comments (health, problems, step-child, etc.)

Others in household, and relationship to client:

Dates Seen	Nature of Contact	Presenting Problem	Problems Later Revealed	Outcome

the methods and techniques they employ. Such study, of course, would be contingent upon having a carefully selected research team, operating with the parishioners' permission.)

Two auxiliary needs are basic to an adequate record system: secretarial help and confidential handling of the records. However, secretarial assistance may be inadequate for transcribing interview notes for a variety of reasons. The pastor or parishioners may not trust the regular secretary, or they may feel that it is unfair to burden her with the responsibility of keeping confidences revealed in counseling. The personality of the secretary may in fact preclude her from doing this work. In some instances, therefore, secretarial help is employed from outside the church membership, and on the basis of personality traits and capability. Increasingly, the skilled leadership of churches realizes that an adequate secretarial-receptionist staff is secondary only to the pastor in significance for a counseling program.

Locked filing cabinets are essential, and should be kept in a room which is securely locked when authorized personnel are not in it. Keys must not be available to too many people, and locks must be changed when a key is lost. Each incoming secretary must be instructed thoroughly in the proper record-making and record-keeping procedure. The significance of individual personalities must be emphasized, and the importance of confidences remaining inviolate must be made deeply vivid to her. Better by far to be meticulous and methodical about the record system than to be careless, and then to spend time worrying about how things should have been handled! Records are unlikely to be stolen, although even that has happened. Precautions, then, bring peace of mind to the clergyman responsible for the life confidences of people, and it is equally reassuring to his confidants to know that their affairs are being handled in a professional manner. The entire staff should understand that information about any person, including whether he has been or is being seen, must not be given to anyone, whether a relative or a professional person, without the express permission of the client—*and then only by the pastor or counselor in charge!* The only exceptions would be professional consultants used by the counselor,

314

and a code system eliminates the necessity of giving names to them.

A *code system* is an added guarantee of confidentiality, since it prevents the parishioner's name from appearing in conjunction with any statement about him. A code book or card file containing the names of clients, their code numbers and perhaps the interview dates, should be available only to those actually doing counseling.

Coding methods are limited only by ingenuity, but the simpler they are the better. Records may be numbered chronologically, as persons appear for counseling. One number may serve for all members of the same family, with the letters "M" or "F" added to show the sex of the client. Children who are seen become "MC" or "FC"; if more than one child of the same family and sex are seen, numbers are added in parentheses to discriminate them in the order of birth. For instance, Mrs. Smith is the fiftieth person to request counseling; she becomes "50F." Her husband is interviewed and becomes "50M." They have three girls, but only the daughter born second is seen; she becomes "50FC(2)." Simply by clipping together the notes about each person, the record of the entire family may be kept together.

A number is assigned to the client's record by the counselor at the first interview; or, in a setting which warrants it, by the secretary. The name and number go into the code file; only the number appears with the counseling information itself. Of course, the client does not know his number; he knows only that the records kept are coded for his protection.

With or without adequate secretarial help, a workable record system is essential to modern pastoral counseling. When the minister compiles his own records, they must be brief. As an aid to counseling and as a means of collecting uniform data conducive to research, the author developed the *Individual and Marriage Counseling Inventory*. This is a four-page, printed folder which can be filled out by the individual while he waits for the initial interview. *Part A* provides space for "personal data," which enables the person to portray his own educational, marital, occupational, financial, religious, cultural, and health status, as well

315

as to state the major problems with which he wishes help. *Part B* is devoted to "family data," which gives vital information on the parental family of the person. *Part C* is a guide for the individual to use in discussing the personal relationships in his family, and can be an aid in discovering some of the most dynamic factors involved in the counseling process. The final one-half page of the folder provides essentially the same space for recording interview dates and notes shown on the "record card" reproduced earlier.

The folder is printed upon paper almost as heavy as the manila folders commonly used for filing. Filed with the folded edge down, the code number appears in the upper left-hand corner. Interview notes and other papers may be filed within the folder, eliminating the necessity of purchasing and preparing a "file folder." If it is placed in a standard manila folder, the *Inventory* does not protrude; but because it is nine inches high, it is readily found among standard, eight-and-one-half-by-eleven-inch papers. Page two of the *Inventory* provides space for the name and address of the individual, arranged so that it can be removed with scissors, pasted on a three-by-five-inch card, and filed as the Code Card. This makes it unnecessary to use separate cards for the code file. If cutting the folder is not desirable, this space simply is not used.

Identical file numbers are placed on both the *Inventory* and the code card. These *Inventory* forms are economical in setting up a record system, making it unnecessary to purchase either manila folders or file cards. They are available on a non-profit basis through The Counseling Service, Merrill-Palmer School, 71 East Ferry Avenue, Detroit 2, Michigan. Twenty folders cost $1.00; fifty folders cost $2.00.

Aaron L. Rutledge,
Merrill-Palmer School,
Detroit, Michigan